Ghost Hunter's Guide to Portland and the Oregon Coast

Ghost Hunter's Guide to **Portland** and the **Oregon Coast**

Jeff Dwyer

PELICAN PUBLISHING COMPANY
GRETNA 2015

Copyright © 2015
By Jeff Dwyer
All rights reserved

The word "Pelican" and the depiction of a pelican are trademarks of Pelican Publishing Company, Inc., and are registered in the U.S. Patent and Trademark Office.

ISBN 9781455621163
E-book ISBN 9781455621170

Printed in the United States of America

Published by Pelican Publishing Company, Inc.
1000 Burmaster Street, Gretna, Louisiana 70053

To my sons, Sam and Michael, my stalwart companions during my travels throughout Oregon

Contents

	Acknowledgments	9
	Introduction	11
Chapter 1	How to Hunt Ghosts	43
Chapter 2	Central Portland	67
Chapter 3	East Portland Communities	101
Chapter 4	Vancouver and North Portland	129
Chapter 5	Oregon City and Communities South of Portland	165
Chapter 6	Oregon's Coastal Communities	219
Appendix A	Sighting Report Form	252
Appendix B	Suggested Reading	254
Appendix C	Films, DVDs, and Videos	258
Appendix D	Internet Resources	260
Appendix E	Special Tours and Events	264
Appendix F	History Museums and Historical Societies	267
	Index	269

Acknowledgments

I offer my sincere thanks to my colleagues in the field of paranormal investigation, especially Jackie Ganiy, Loyd Auerbach, Nick Groff, Zak Bagans, and Jeff Bellanger, whose inspiration, support, and encouragement I highly value.

I am also grateful to Doug Carnahan, producer and host of the *Haunted Truth* radio show, who provided me forums to discuss my ideas and experiences with colleagues at Preston Castle and Virginia City; and to my friend Zak Bagans for opportunities to appear with him on the Travel Channel shows *Ghost Adventures* and *Aftershocks*.

Many thanks to my literary agent, Sue Clark, for the support and guidance that has proved to be invaluable on countless occasions and the staff of Pelican Publishing, who, for many years, have patiently guided me through the process of producing and marketing my books.

Introduction

In 1843, Portland was nothing more than a canoe-landing site populated by fur traders who lived in log huts or tents. A drifter from Tennessee, William Overton, and lawyer Asa Lovejoy were among the muddy settlement's residents. Both were anxious to get rich from the region's abundant natural resources, but neither owned land. Forming a partnership with 25 cents provided by Overton, the two men filed a claim on 640 acres and began clearing trees and building a road. Overton apparently grew tired of the work and moved on after selling his share of the claim to Francis Pettygrove. As a township took form, Pettygrove and Lovejoy realized the place needed a name. Each proposed to name the settlement after his hometown. Lovejoy suggested Boston while Pettygrove, who was from Maine, offered Portland. The toss of a penny settled the issue, with Pettygrove winning two of three flips of the coin.

Lovejoy and Pettygrove envisioned Portland as a great city built on the wealth of its natural resources. They also anticipated that quick prosperity would bring civilization to the Pacific Northwest. Instead, Portland went through a period of 30 years as a wild frontier town full of brothels, sailor's boardinghouses, gambling dens, and saloons that were fronts for shanghaiing ship workers. It was not until the close of the 19th century that Portland was able to rid itself of detracting monikers such as the "Forbidden City of the West," the "Forbidden City," the "Unheavenly City," "Mudville," and "Log Town" and become the "Rose City."

The 20th century finally brought the civilization envisioned by Lovejoy and Pettygrove, as prosperity turned Portland into the jewel of the Pacific Northwest. Wealth generated by great lumber mills and the shipping industry built skyscrapers in downtown Portland and fine Victorian homes in several neighborhoods, which stand today as monuments to a vision that took several decades to fulfill. All too often, the history of those decades is composed of tragic stories arising from epidemics, great fires, floods, criminal activity, and shipwrecks.

These tragedies are the basis of Portland's reputation as one of the most haunted cities in the Western U.S.

Epidemics of the mid-19th century and the Spanish flu epidemic of 1918 brought tragedy to many Oregon families, ending lives at a young age and filling many pioneer cemeteries. The first recorded epidemic to hit the indigenous people of the region occurred in 1775. Fur trappers who arrived in ships brought smallpox, which decimated tribes along the Columbia River and north coast villages. Fur traders arriving in 1782 by overland routes brought a second wave of smallpox. This epidemic spread northward and was credited with wiping out half the Spokane Indian population. Smallpox struck again in 1801, leaving many Indians with pockmarked faces described by the explorers Lewis and Clark, when they arrived in 1805. Based on their report, historians believe that smallpox killed more than half the 1800 Indian population of the western Columbia River region. Smallpox further decimated indigenous and immigrant populations in 1824 and 1853. The latter epidemic led to the opening of several pioneer cemeteries that exist today.

In 1830, malaria was imported into the Portland region. An epidemic of this disease started at Fort Vancouver and lasted four years. Accounts by officials at the fort suggest malaria nearly wiped out the entire Indian population along the lower Columbia River. The decimation caused by smallpox and malaria was so complete that after 1835, American and British immigrants to the area found few Indians. Consequently, place names that are in use today reflect the origins of the immigrants—Portland, Astoria, Salem, for example—not traditional names used by indigenous peoples such as those found in Washington state that include Seattle, Yakima, and Tacoma.

The worldwide Spanish flu epidemic of 1918 caused more deaths in Portland than most other U.S. cities. Portland suffered 505 deaths per 100,000 population compared to Indianapolis, which had only 290 deaths per 100,000. Strict quarantine ordinances were enforced and public safety laws enacted, but thousands died, overloading funeral parlors and grave-digging crews at cemeteries. In many fascinating cemeteries, such as Brainard Cemetery, Gresham Pioneer Cemetery, and the old Jones Cemetery, victims are buried in clusters. Some markers indicate that entire families, comprised of young adults and infants, occupy a single grave. Their tragic demise seems to have created spirits who have yet to let go and move on.

As with many pioneer towns, catastrophic fires destroyed some coastal settlements and portions of Portland soon after the city was founded. Fast-moving blazes often destroyed crude wooden shacks and tents, catching many residents off guard and killing them. In 1860, most of Fort Vancouver was consumed in a blaze that started in a kitchen. On August 2, 1873, Portland volunteer firefighters responded to alarms that directed them to both wealthy and poor neighborhoods. Despite their efforts, more than 20 square blocks of the city were consumed, including Chinatown and riverfront warehouses. Historical accounts do not clearly state the death toll, but it is believed that it exceeded 100 persons. Fortunately, the elegant St. Charles Hotel, hailed by the *Oregonian* as "the most magnificent structure on the northwest Pacific coast," was saved.

Large conflagrations are a thing of the past, but small fires occur often in and around Portland, creating fatalities that ultimately lead to paranormal activity. On December 9, 2010, a blaze swept through Lents Village, an apartment complex for senior citizens at 10325 SE Holgate Boulevard, Portland. Eighty residents were evacuated but one fatality occurred. On January 29, 2010, 26-year-old animal rights advocate Daniel Shaull staged a protest against Ungar Furs, a fur retailer, by dowsing himself with gasoline and igniting the vapor as he stood on the sidewalk at 1137 SW Yamhill Street. These tragedies have aroused the interest of ghost hunters, who have reported paranormal activity at the sites.

Devastating fires that resulted in several deaths have also followed airplane crashes in the greater Portland region, cities along the I-5 corridor, and coastal towns, leaving ghosts of victims that wander around towns, cities, and coastal fields. Crashes of small aircraft resulting in numerous fatalities occurred in Sherwood (2009), Hillsboro (2005, 2006), Corvallis (1995, 2000), Astoria (1999), Tillamook (1996, 1997), Oregon City (1991), Seaside (1994), Salem (1990), Eugene (1977), and Portland (1999, 2005). Detailed reports of these incidents, including type of aircraft, fatalities among crew and passengers, fatalities on the ground, and location, can be found through Federal Aviation Administration Web sites or local newspaper accounts. The most tragic, recent airplane crashes occurred in Oregon City and Gearhart. On July 24, 2010, an experimental airplane crashed at Highway 213 and Kirk Road, in Oregon City, killing the pilot. According to witnesses, the plane was engulfed in flames as it plummeted to earth. Having nearly a minute to comprehend his impending fate, the pilot must have experienced a harrowing death. In coastal Gearhart, a horrific crash occurred on August 4, 2008, in which five people were killed. After taking off from nearby Seaside Municipal Airport, a rented single-engine airplane with two persons aboard circled over a residential area, apparently trying to fly under low overcast. Pilot error resulted in the plane crashing into a small house, killing three children who were asleep. Three others in the house were severely burned. Both persons aboard the plane were also killed.

The worst commercial disaster in Portland occurred December 28, 1978, when a United Airlines DC-8 (N8082U) with 181 passengers and crew ran out of fuel and crashed into a residential area between East Burnside Street and NE 160th Avenue. Miraculously, only 10 persons were killed on impact, while 24 were seriously injured. The neighborhood is densely populated but no houses currently stand at the site of the crash. The ground is covered with a stand of trees that surrounds a parking area.

Portland and several nearby communities have endured criminal activity and social injustice that have led to hauntings and legends of ghosts. The misdeeds of several 19th-century outlaws produced many used, abused, confused, and forlorn spirits who stay with us long after their death. The souls of these victims may still seek lost dreams while they remain attached to what little they gained during their difficult lives. Many ghosts who harbor deep resentment, pain, or a desire to complete their unfinished business still roam courthouses, hotels, theatres, modern buildings, cemeteries, and other public places throughout the region.

Like most metropolitan areas in the U.S., Portland has had several crime sprees linked to organized crime and illegal drugs. Deaths of victims, perpetrators, and occasionally police officers have left intense paranormal activity at several locations around the city. In the 19th century, gang-related crime was rampant, starting in 1836 with the murder of two women. Gang activity was so extreme that a police force was created in 1844. Riots in 1863 were linked to the Civil War and, in 1870 and 1874, labor unrest. These riots led to several deaths and improvements in the police force.

The greatest criminal activity of the 19th century was created by the shanghai industry. Starting in 1850, unscrupulous saloon operators discovered they could make a lot of money by kidnapping inebriated men and delivering them to waiting ships, where they were pressed into service by captains desperate for a crew. The industry quickly became sophisticated, with trapdoors in the floors of saloons, underground holding areas, and a complex network of tunnels beneath the city's streets that enabled abductors to deliver their captives to the waterfront. Business was so brisk that Portland was known as one of the most dangerous ports in the world and given the moniker "Forbidden City of the West." Many men who fell through trapdoors died upon impact on the concrete floors below. Others died from beatings or illnesses aggravated by their alcoholism. It is unknown how many men died in Portland's famous underground city, but the tunnels are world-renowned for paranormal activity and exciting tours. In the 1920s and 1930s, the tunnels were expanded, reaching into Chinatown and downtown Portland, and became venues for illegal businesses such as gambling, bootlegging, and prostitution. Tours of the tunnels feature holding cells, a former opium den, cells for breaking the will of young women, trapdoors, and other artifacts.

In the 1980s and early 1990s, Portland's violent-crime rate soared due to a crack cocaine epidemic. Several murders were linked to this illegal trade, while numerous drug users were found dead on city streets or in hotels and apartment houses. By 1993, law enforcement and other measures ended the epidemic and the crime rate dropped sharply. In 2005, the city achieved its lowest crime rate since the late 19th century. Extensive surveillance of high-crime areas led to a reduction in homicides in 2007 and in 2009. This still leaves hundreds of crime scenes that have attracted the attention of paranormal investigators, including the Bethany triple-murder site.

On November 2, 2006, Ricardo Serrano entered a house at 2902 NW Telshire Terrace, in Beaverton, and shot to death three occupants. Two of the victims were children. This horrific crime created intense imprints or residuals that have been detected by sensitive psychics standing in front of the house.

An event that seems to have triggered a tragic series of shootings in public places took place at Clackamas Town Center mall on December 11, 2012. Twenty-two-year-old Jacob Tyler Roberts entered the mall with an AR-15 assault rifle and opened fire on shoppers and employees. After seriously wounding a 15-year-old girl and killing two others, Roberts ended the horrific event by killing himself.

Paranormal investigators who are interested in taking a forensic approach to ghost hunting may want to visit crime scenes listed in reports of serial killers who committed crimes in the Portland region. Detailed information about Randall Woodfield, known as the I-5 killer, and the killing spree perpetrated by Jerry Brudos may be found by searching the Internet. In addition to those tragedies, an unidentified serial killer is suspected of committing brutal murders of young women in remote coastal sites near Newport and Moolack Beach.

Historical records dating from the 19th century indicate several maritime disasters on the Columbia and Willamette rivers and hundreds of shipwrecks along the haunted coast. On April 8, 1854, the steamship *Gazelle* suffered a boiler explosion while approaching the docks near Oregon City. Twenty-four passengers and crew were killed, their body parts scattered all over the waterfront. Among the victims were local businessmen Crawford Dobbins and D. P. Fuller, who were among the first to be interred in the new Lone Fir Cemetery in central Portland.

More recently, in 1976, the charter boat *Pearl C* became disabled near the Columbia River bar. While being towed by the Coast Guard, the vessel foundered and sank, killing eight passengers. Similar tragedies occurred when the charter boat *Taki-Tooo* sank at the entrance to Tillamook Bay in 2003, killing 11, and in 2005 at the Umpqua River sandbar when the *Sydney Mae II* went down with three passengers who were not wearing lifejackets.

Several ships ran aground and were destroyed by the surf near several communities on the Oregon coast. Some of the damaged hulls were incorporated into jetties and sandbars while pieces of wreckage remain scattered along the coast, occasionally found by beachgoers with metal detectors. Some of these tragedies produced bizarre results, such as the *Bawnmore,* which dropped its cargo of cattle into the surf. The cows swam ashore and later filled the woods with a new generation of calves. In some cases, complete mystery surrounded the wreck. A case in point is the steamer *South Coast*, which broke up in the surf at Port Orford. No survivors or victims were found. Artifacts from many wrecks may be found in museums along the coast. Ghost hunters who use psychometry may want to visit these museums and get in touch with psychic remnants of these maritime tragedies.

On October 25, 1896, the four-mast steel sailing vessel *Peter Iredale* tried to enter the fog-shrouded mouth of the Columbia River. Strong winds and a rising tide drove the ship ashore, where it became imbedded in the sand, making salvage impossible. Today, the remains of the ship rise above the beach at Fort Stevens State Park and attract tourists and paranormal investigators. The 324-foot steel steamer *Sujamenco* met a similar fate on March 1, 1929, while trying to find the fog-bound entrance to Coos Bay. The ship's remains can be seen on Horsfall Beach, eight miles north of Coos Bay. A greater disaster occurred at Coos Bay in January of 1910 when the *Czarina*, a 216-foot steamer, entered the harbor only to be slammed into a jetty by a rogue wave. Rescue operations were unsuccessful as all but one crewman dropped into the sea and drowned. The lone survivor died a year later from his injuries. On November 15, 1915, the *Santa Clara* was lost in a similar tragedy that killed 16 crewmen.

Tragic stories and ghostly wreckage may be found near several communities including Brandon at the Coquille River Bar, Cape Blanco, Tillamook, Nehalem, Pacific City, Reedsport, Lincoln City, Newport, Florence, and Depoe Bay.

Situated at the confluence of two great rivers, the Columbia and Willamette, Portland has endured several floods, some of which resulted in many fatalities and the 19th-century nickname "Mudville." The geology of the Pleistocene era reveals that some of the world's greatest known floods occurred in the Portland area. In the early 19th century, numerous floods were recorded by Hudson's Bay Company officials at Fort Vancouver and others who explored the Columbia River gorge. Until recently, floods were commonplace, resulting from heavy rainfall and melting snowfields to the east. In 1890, the Columbia River overflowed its banks, washing away several houseboats, small boats, barges, docks, and other waterfront facilities. The unofficial death toll exceeded 30. In June of 1894, the Willamette River rose more than 30 feet above it banks, flooding the entire business district of Portland, including the infamous shanghai tunnels. Waters receded so slowly that sewage was spread through the city, contaminating wells, cisterns, and other water supplies. After several deaths, the city issued warnings to all citizens advising them to boil drinking water, use disinfectants, and consider spending the summer in the mountains or at the coast.

The greatest flood to hit the city in modern times occurred on May 30, 1948. The Vanport City neighborhood, occupied by more than 20,000 people, mostly African-American shipyard workers, was virtually destroyed when a 200-foot-long dike collapsed. Columbia River waters inundated the enclave, creating a disaster that rivals the flooding of New Orleans after Hurricane Katrina. The official death toll was only 15, but unofficial accounts place the numbers much higher. The worst flood on the Willamette River in the modern era occurred from December 18, 1964, to January 7, 1965. Killing 17 people and causing hundreds of millions of dollars in damage, floodwaters covered 152,789 acres and destroyed countless businesses and homes. As recently as 1996, the Willamette and Columbia rivers continued their winter rampages, inundating several communities but failing to breach the seawall in downtown Portland. Deaths occurred from drowning, electrocution, and infection.

Situated on the Pacific Rim, Portland and Oregon's coastal towns often experienced earthquakes. Lewis and Clark noted Indian reports of great movements of the earth that occurred decades before their arrival in 1805. On November 23, 1873, an earthquake struck that shook buildings as far away as San Francisco. The Richter scale was not in use at that time, but eyewitness accounts mention the collapse of several chimneys and brick buildings that trapped and killed residents. Large earthquakes occurred in 1877, 1896, 1913, and 1915. The great San Francisco earthquake of April 19, 1906, damaged buildings in Portland and most of Oregon's coastal towns. More recently, a series of earthquakes struck Oregon between May 26 and June 11, 1968. In 1993, a 6.0 earthquake caused millions of dollars in damage and killed three people.

All of these tragic events add to the region's ghost legacy and have left powerful emotional imprints created by spirits of the dearly departed who felt a need to stay on. A common factor is the loss of life by a sudden, violent event, often at a young age. Unfortunate crewmembers of the many ships sunk off the treacherous coast, shanghaied sailors, firefighters, passengers in airplanes, and Indians who died of imported diseases or from skirmishes with settlers all passed with great emotional anguish, leaving their souls with an inextinguishable desire to achieve their life's objectives, or with a sense of obligation to offer protection to a particular place or person.

Some ghosts remain on the earthly plane for revenge or to provide guidance for someone still alive. Many of those who came to Oregon for the fur trade, free land, or employment in the logging and shipping industries were caught up in their dreams but met only with frustration and failure before dying alone and in poverty. Their restless spirits still roam Oregon's coastal towns and old neighborhoods of Portland.

ABOUT THIS BOOK

This book focuses on Portland, some of its suburbs and nearby towns, and portions of Oregon's coast that are well known for ghostly activity. This region was selected as the subject of my ninth book on ghost hunting because it is an integral part of the geographic territory throughout which I've conducted paranormal investigations since the 1990s. In many ways, this book completes a West Coast collection. The northernmost entry, *Ghost Hunter's Guide to Seattle and Puget Sound*, includes numerous stories of ghostly activity derived from the region's pioneer and maritime history. A large portion of the Northern California coast, particularly Sonoma and Mendocino counties, was the focal point of *Ghost Hunter's Guide to California's Wine Country*. My first book, *Ghost Hunter's Guide to the San Francisco Bay Area*, includes reports of ghostly activity in three coastal counties that lie between San Francisco Bay and the Pacific Ocean. *Ghost Hunter's Guide to Monterey and California's Central Coast* covers a region nearly 300 miles long, ending in the San Luis Obispo area. *Ghost Hunter's Guide to Los Angeles* takes readers farther south, from Santa Barbara to San Diego.

Chapter 1 of this book will help you, the ghost hunter, to research and organize your own ghost hunt at locations with a well-defined region. Chapters 2 through 6 describe several locations at which ghostly activity has been reported in the greater Portland area, coastal towns, and cities along the I-5, which conveys travelers to and from Portland. Unlike other collections of ghost stories and descriptions of haunted places, this book emphasizes access. Private homes and other buildings not open to visitors are not included. Addresses of each haunted site are provided along with other information to assist you in finding and entering the location. Several appendixes offer organizational material for your ghost hunts, including a Sighting Report Form to document your adventures, lists of suggested reading and videos, and Internet resources.

WHO BELIEVES IN GHOSTS?

People from every religion, culture, and generation believe that ghosts exist. The popularity of ghosts and haunted places in books, television programs, and movies reflects a belief held by many people that other dimensions and spiritual entities do exist.

In 2000, a Gallup poll discovered a significant increase in the number of Americans who believe in ghosts since the question was first asked in 1978. Thirty-one percent of respondents said they believed ghosts existed. In 1978, only 11 percent admitted to believing in ghosts. Less than a year later, in 2001, Gallup found that 42 percent of the public believed a house could be haunted, but only 28 percent believed that we can hear from or mentally communicate with someone who has died. According to a Harris poll conducted in 2003, an astounding 51 percent of Americans believed in ghosts. As with preceding polls, belief in ghosts was greatest among females. More young people accepted the idea of ghosts than older people. Forty-four percent of people aged 18 to 29 admitted a belief in ghosts, compared with 13 percent of those over 65. In 2005, a CBS News poll reported similar findings. Twenty-two percent of the respondents admitted they had personally seen or felt the presence of a ghost. In this same year, Gallup pollsters reported that 75 percent of Americans believed in at least one paranormal phenomenon, including ESP, reincarnation, spirit channeling, ghosts, and clairvoyance.

More recently, in 2007, an Associated Press survey reported that 34 percent of Americans believed in ghosts. A similar finding was released by the HuffPost/YouGov Poll in December of 2012. Thirty-three percent of responders claimed they believed in ghosts because they had had an encounter with a spirit. Another 23.5 percent admitted they believed in the existence of ghosts but had never seen or heard one.

Polls and surveys are interesting, but there is no way of knowing how many people have seen or heard a ghost only to feel too embarrassed, foolish, or frightened to admit it. Many ghost hunters and paranormal investigators believe that a vast majority of people have seen or heard something from the other side, or spirit world, but failed to recognize it.

Today, many visitors to Portland and the Oregon coast choose those destinations because they believe that ghostly phenomena can be experienced there. This is evidenced by the increased popularity of tours of cemeteries; the historic districts of Portland, its suburbs, and quaint coastal towns; and the large number of paranormal investigations staged by local organizations.

Broadcast and cable television channels recognize the phenomenal nationwide interest in paranormal occurrences. The Syfy channel airs a weekly, one-hour, primetime program called *Ghost Hunters*. The popularity of this show has been so great that a spinoff, *Ghost Hunters International*, also airs during primetime. Cast members of these documentary programs have achieved celebrity status. In December of 2007, the Arts and Entertainment Channel premiered a series called *Paranormal State* that followed a group of Pennsylvania State University students as they conducted investigations of ghosts and demons.

The Travel Channel offers two documentary programs that feature ghost investigations. *Dead Files* features physical medium Amy Allan and retired New York Police Department homicide detective Steve DiSchiavi, who conduct independent investigations of a paranormal event and then compare their findings to solve problems for troubled clients. One of the longest-running paranormal shows on TV, *Ghost Adventures*, features Zak Bagans and Nick Groff, who, together with videographer Aaron Goodwin, investigate haunted places all over the U.S. and in Europe.

None of the major networks currently offer paranormal programs, but two popular shows are available for viewing on DVD or reruns on cable networks. For five seasons, NBC produced a weekly primetime drama called *Medium* that followed the true-life experiences of psychic detective Allison DuBois. Working with the Phoenix district attorney's office and other law-enforcement agencies, she used her psychic skills to communicate with ghosts in order to solve crimes. For six years, CBS produced one of the most popular shows in this genre, called *Ghost Whisperer*, which portrayed the experiences of sensitive Mary Ann Winkowski of Ohio.

Internet users will find more than 5 million references to ghosts, ghost hunting, haunted places, and related paranormal phenomena. Search engines such as Google can aid ghost hunters in tracking down reports of ghostly activity in almost any city in America, locating paranormal investigative organizations they can join or consult, and purchasing ghost-hunting equipment or books that deal with the art and science of finding ghosts.

The recent worldwide interest in ghosts is not a spinoff of the New Age movement or the manifestation of some new religious process. Recognition that ghosts exist is simply the reemergence of one of mankind's oldest and most basic beliefs: there is a life after death. Ancient writings from many cultures describe apparitions and a variety of spirit manifestations that include tolling bells, chimes, disembodied crying or moaning, and whispered messages. Legends and ancient books include descriptions of ghosts, dwelling places of spirits, and periods of intense spiritual activity related to seasons or community events such as festivals and crop harvests.

Ancient sites of intense spiritual activity in Arizona, New Mexico, and Central and South America are popular destinations for travelers seeking psychic or spiritual experiences and encounters with the paranormal. More modern, local sites, where a variety of paranormal events have been documented, are also popular destinations for adventurous living souls. Amateur and professional ghost hunters seek the spirits of the dearly departed in historic mansions, old theatres, pioneer-era bars and inns, firehouses, stores, and countless other places, including graveyards and ships. Modern buildings, city parks, restaurants and bars, numerous historic sites such as Portland's famous shanghai tunnels, and seldom-traveled back coastal roads also serve as targets for ghost hunters.

Throughout the past two millennia, the popularity of belief in ghosts has waxed and waned, similar to religious activity. When a rediscovery of ghosts and their role in our lives occurs, skeptics label the notion a fad or an aberration of modern lifestyles. Perhaps people are uncomfortable with the idea that ghosts exist because it involves an examination of our nature and our concepts of life, death, and afterlife. These concepts are most often considered in the context of religion, yet ghost hunters recognize that acceptance of the reality of ghosts, and a life after death, is a personal decision, having nothing to do with religious beliefs or church doctrine. An intellectual approach enables the ghost hunter to explore haunted places without religious bias or fear.

The great frequency of ghost manifestations in Portland and Oregon's coastal towns, as evidenced by documentary reports on TV and other news media, reflects the success of amateur and professional ghost hunters who research and seek paranormal encounters in the region. Ghost hunting has become a popular weekend pastime for many adventurous souls, whether they are serious investigators or only casually interested in the paranormal. Advertisement of haunted inns, restaurants, and historical sites is commonplace. It is always fun, is often very exciting, and may take ghost hunters places they had never dreamed of going.

WHAT IS A GHOST?

A ghost is some aspect of the personality, spirit, consciousness, energy, mind, intelligence, or soul that remains after the body dies. When any these are detected by the living—through sight, sound, odor, tactile sensations, or movement of objects—we may consider the experience to be a paranormal encounter. The encounter may be said to be "ghostly" if there is intelligent interaction with a witness or the environment. This includes interaction by touching, speaking, gestures, facial expressions, movement of objects, and sounds such as tapping in response to questions. It also includes creation of sounds or other electronic analogs on audio recorders and other instrumentation.

The essential criterion for concluding that a ghostly encounter has occurred is intelligent interaction with a living person or the environment. If this strict criterion cannot be met, it is likely that the experience involves something other than a ghost. I've estimated that more than 80 percent of paranormal experiences have nothing to do with a ghost.

The intelligent events that may differentiate ghosts from other paranormal activity include specific interaction with the living, performance of a purposeful activity, or a response to ongoing changes in the environment. Ghosts may speak to the living to warn of an unforeseen accident or disaster, to give advice, or to express their love, anger, remorse, or disappointment. They may also try to complete some project or duty they failed to finish before death.

Occasionally, paranormal activity is bizarre and frightening, or it appears to be dangerous. Witnesses may see objects fly about, hear ominous sounds, or experience accidents. This kind of activity is sometimes attributed to a "poltergeist" or noisy ghost. Most authorities believe that a living person, not the dead, causes these manifestations. Generally, a person under great emotional stress releases psychic energy that creates subtle or spectacular changes in the environment. Noises commonly associated with a poltergeist include tapping on walls or ceilings, heavy footsteps, shattering glass, ringing telephones, and running water. Objects may move about on tables or floors or fly across a room. Furniture may spin or tip over. Dangerous objects, such as knives, hammers, or pens, may hit people. These poltergeist events may last a few days, a year, or more. Discovery and removal of the emotionally unstable, living person often stops the poltergeist.

Always be aware that many other paranormal phenomena can appear to be ghostly manifestations. Reference to the essential criterion can help you determine if you are dealing with an imprint or other paranormal phenomenon. Keep in mind that ghostly activity is real time; the ghost is present. Imprint phenomena represent something from the past. By definition, imprints lack intelligent interaction with the witness or the environment and occur without the consciousness of a dead person.

HOW DOES A GHOST MANIFEST ITSELF?

The process by which a ghost manifests itself is not completely understood, but there are many useful theories that help us understand ghostly behavior.

Ghosts interact with our environment in a variety of ways that may have something to do with the strength of their personality and desire to communicate in the context of confusion resulting from their transformation by death. The talents or skills they possessed in life, their personal objectives, or frustrations arising from the end of life may underlie their efforts in getting our attention. A sudden, traumatic death, strong ties to surviving loved ones or a particular place, unfinished business, strong emotions such as hatred and anger, or a desire for revenge may also trigger ghostly activity.

A ghost may create a change in the environment. Movement of objects such as books, a pipe, eyeglasses, tools, weapons, doorknobs, bedding, etc., that cannot be attributed to normal or natural processes often indicates the presence of a ghost. Some ghosts have been known to rearrange furniture or room decorations to suit their preferences. If new objects are placed in a ghost's favorite room, they may be found moved outside the room, broken, or hidden in another location. Common ghostly activities are movement of a rocking chair, turning of doorknobs, activation of light switches and electronic equipment such as TVs, and disheveling bedding. Ghosts like to knock over stacks of cards or coins, scatter matchsticks, and move your keys. It appears easy for many to manipulate light switches and TV remotes, open and close windows and doors, or push chairs around. Some ghosts have the power to throw objects, pull pictures from walls, or move heavy items. As a rule, ghosts cannot tolerate disturbances within the place they haunt. If you tilt a wall-mounted picture, the ghost will set it straight. Obstacles placed in the ghost's path may be pushed aside.

Some ghosts create odors, particularly those associated with their habits, such as cigar smoke or signature perfumes. Many reports from credible witnesses mention the odors of tobacco, oranges, and hemp as most common.

Ghosts can also create impressions that the physical qualities of an environment have changed when, in fact, no physical transformation has occurred. Ice-cold breezes and unexplained gusts of wind are often the first signs that a ghost is present. Moving or stationary cold spots, with temperatures several degrees below surrounding areas, have been detected. Temperature changes sometimes occur with a feeling that the atmosphere has thickened, as if the room was suddenly filled with unseen people.

In searching for ghosts, some people use devices that detect changes in magnetic, electrical, or radio fields. However, detected changes may be subject to error, interference by other electrical devices, or misinterpretation. Measurements, indicating the presence of a ghost, may be difficult to capture on a permanent record.

Ghosts may create images such as luminous fogs, balls of light called "orbs," streaks of light, or the partial outline of body parts on still cameras (film or digital) and video recorders. In the 19th century, this was called spirit photography. Captured images are sometimes spectacular, but modern digital photographs are easily edited, making it difficult to produce convincing proof of ghostly activity.

The experience of seeing humanoid images is the prized objective of most ghost hunters, but it is rare. When such images are seen, they are often partial, revealing only a head and torso with an arm or two. Feet are seldom seen. Full-body apparitions are extremely rare. Some ghost hunters have seen ethereal, fully translucent forms that are barely discernible. Others report seeing ghosts who appear as solid as a living being.

WHY DO GHOSTS REMAIN AT A PARTICULAR PLACE?

Ghosts remain in a particular place because they are emotionally attached to a room, a building, or special surroundings that profoundly affected them during their lives or to activities or events that played a role in their death. A prime example is the haunted house inhabited by the ghost of a man who hung himself in the master bedroom because his wife left him. It is widely believed that death and sudden transition from the physical world confuses a ghost. He or she remains in familiar or emotionally stabilizing surroundings to ease the strain. A place-bound ghost is most likely to occur when a violent death occurred with great emotional anguish. Ghosts may linger in a house, barn, cemetery, factory, or store waiting for a loved one or anyone familiar who might help them deal with their new level of existence. Some ghosts wander through buildings or forests, on bridges, or alongside particular sections of roads. Some await enemies, seeking revenge. Others await a friend for a chance to resolve their guilt.

There seems to be a close association between aspects of the entity's life and the modalities it uses to manifest itself on our plane of existence. These include places and objects related to sudden, traumatic death; strong ties to surviving loved ones or a particular place; unfinished business; strong emotions such as hatred and anger; or a desire for revenge.

Ghosts manifest themselves on our plane of existence for many reasons. They may want to:

1. protect a cherished possession such as a book collection, art, weapons, jewelry, money, etc.
2. protect a cherished place such as a house, office, lab, workshop, etc.
3. watch over loved ones.
4. enlist the help of a living person to discover something hidden.
5. learn the fate of friends and family members or a particular place or object.
6. offer guidance to family, friends, or business partners.
7. seek revenge.

There may be other reasons, but these motivations explain most spirit activity. Most spirits are place-bound rather than people-bound. That is, they are attached to, or drawn to, a particular place such as a house, office, airplane, boat, movie theatre, etc. This contention is supported by the idea that most ghosts do not travel. For example, a person who feels that his house is haunted rarely reports the same ghostly activity at his workplace, gym, grocery store, etc. This suggests that the ghost has no interest in following the living person to various locations because it is attached to a particular place. The ghost may be interested in living persons, but the primary basis of the haunting is a place.

UNDER WHAT CONDITIONS IS A SIGHTING MOST LIKELY?

Although ghosts may appear at any time, a sighting may occur on special holidays, anniversaries, birthdays, or during historic periods (July 4, December 7, September 11), or calendar periods pertaining to the personal history of the ghost. Halloween is reputed to be a favorite night for many apparitions, while others seem to prefer their own special day or night, on a weekly or monthly cycle.

Night is a traditional time for ghost activity, yet experienced ghost hunters know that sightings may occur at any time. Despite the tradition of overnight investigations presented in many paranormal TV shows, there seems to be no consistent affinity of ghosts for darkness, but they seldom appear when artificial light is bright. Perhaps this is why ghosts shy away from camera crews and their array of lights. Ghosts seem to prefer peace and quiet, although some of them have been reported to make incessant, loud sounds. Even a small group of ghost hunters may make too much noise to facilitate a sighting. For this reason, it is recommended that you limit your group to four persons and oral communication be kept to a minimum.

IS GHOST HUNTING DANGEROUS?

Ghost hunting can be hazardous, but reports of injuries inflicted by ghosts are rare and their veracity suspect. Movies and children's ghost stories have created a widespread notion that ghosts may harm the living or even cause the death of persons they dislike. In 2006, a popular television program showed a fascinating video of a ghost hunter being struck down by his camera equipment. The man's heavy equipment moved suddenly from a position at his waist and struck him on the side of the face. Video of this event was interpreted as evidence of a ghost attack but no apparition or light anomaly was visible. Decades ago, the Abbot of Trondheim ghost was reputed to have attacked some people, but circumstances and precipitating events are unclear.

Many authorities believe that rare attacks by ghosts are a matter of mistaken identity, i.e., the ghost misidentified a living person as a figure the ghost knew during his life. It is possible that encounters that appear to be attacks may be nothing more than clumsy efforts by a ghost to achieve recognition. Witnesses of ghost appearances have found themselves in the middle of gunfights, major military battles, and other violent events yet sustained not the slightest injury.

Persons who claim to have been injured by a ghost have, in most cases, precipitated the injury themselves through their own ignorance or fear. Ghost hunters often carry out investigations in the dark or subdued light and may encounter environmental hazards that lead to injury. Fear may trigger an attempt to race from a haunted site, exposing the ghost hunter to injury by tripping over unseen objects or making contact with broken glass, low-hanging tree limbs, exposed wiring, or weakened floorboards, stairways, or doorways.

You, the ghost hunter, will be safe if you keep a wary eye and a calm attitude and set aside tendencies to fear the ghost or the circumstances of its appearance. Safety may be enhanced if you visit a haunted location while it is well illuminated, during daylight hours for instance. Potential hazards in the environment can be identified and, perhaps, cleared or marked with light-reflecting tape.

Most authorities agree that ghosts do not travel. Ghosts will not follow you home, take up residence in your car, or attempt to occupy your body. They are held in a time and space by deep emotional ties to an event or place. Ghosts have been observed on airplanes, trains, buses, and ships; however, it is unlikely that the destination interests them. Something about the journey, some event such as a plane crash or train wreck, accounts for their appearance as travelers. In some cases, it is the conveyance that ties the ghost to the physical plane. A vintage World War II B-17 bomber may be haunted by the ghost of a man who piloted that type of aircraft in the 1940s. A ship, such as the Queen Mary in Long Beach, California, may be an irresistible attraction for the ghost of a sailor who once worked on passenger liners.

IMPRINTS

The vast majority of paranormal experiences involve imprint

phenomena. Psychics who search for ghosts need to understand this phenomenon, because it can easily be confused with a ghost. If intelligent interaction has not been demonstrated, we must conclude that we are dealing with something that is not ghostly and we may call it an "imprint phenomenon." If the principal feature of this phenomenon is an inanimate object, it is called a "phantom." If it is comprised of a humanoid apparition or vocalization, we may call it an "apparition," being careful to add whenever possible the distinction that it is not ghostly.

Imprints and ghostly manifestations may appear similar. They have common features in terms of what witnesses see, feel, or smell, but an imprint may occur without the presence of a spiritual entity or the consciousness of a dead person. People have reported seeing pale, translucent images of the deceased walking in hallways, climbing stairs, sitting in rocking chairs, or sitting in airplanes, trains, buses, and even restaurants. Some have been observed sleeping in beds, hanging by ropes from trees, or walking through walls. Most commonly, a partial apparition is seen, but witnesses have reported seeing entire armies engaged in battle. Unlike ghosts, hauntings do not display intelligent action with respect to the location—they do not manipulate your computer—and they do not interact with the living.

Imprints may be environmental recordings of something that happened at a location as a result of the repetition of intense emotion. As such, they tend to be associated with a specific place or object, not a particular person. Ghostly figures tend to perform some kind of repetitive task or activity. Sometimes the haunting is so repetitive that witnesses feel as though they are watching a video loop that plays the same brief scene over and over. A good example is the image of a deceased grandmother who makes appearances seated in her favorite rocking chair. She rocks for a few seconds and then disappears, only to reappear later performing the same action.

There is a lot of evidence that people can trigger and experience these environmental recordings by visiting the particular site, touching an object that was a key element of the event, and psychically connecting with the event. Images of hauntings have been picked up on still and video film as well as on digital recordings. The location of strong environmental imprints may also be discovered through devices such as electromagnetic field detectors. Higher magnetic readings have been found at locations where psychics frequently experience hauntings.

TYPES OF IMPRINTS

Imprints may create a variety of experiences in six primary categories:

1. Olfactory (clairsentient): This means the perception of odors or fragrances, which may include perfume, flowers, animal odors, fruit such as oranges, hemp, tobacco, rotting meat, sour milk, or smoke.

2. Auditory (clairaudient): This refers to sounds such as vocalizations, including spoken words, humming, whistling, yawning, sobbing; and non-vocalizations such as musical instruments, footsteps, gunshots, horse's hooves, slamming doors, and breaking glass. These sounds may be heard normally, psychically, or only through recording equipment.

3. Visual (clairvoyant): These may be amorphous shapes, humanoid shadows, partial apparitions, or full-bodied apparitions. They may be seen by one witness but not another, suggesting a psychic process or individual differences in sensitivity.

4. Photographic: This means paranormal images (those lacking a "normal" explanation) not seen with the eyes but found in still pictures or video, film or digital, including orbs, streaks of light, unexplained shadows, or humanoid shapes.

5. Tactile (clairsentient): In some instances, energy emanates from imprints that may create bizarre impressions of a crowded space or the close presence of an unseen being. Other perceptions include thickened air and even cold spots. It is important to note that imprints do not create the kind of tactile experiences ghosts may produce. Ghosts may leave scratch marks, a handprint, and bruises. Imprints don't leave physical evidence of contact and also do not touch, slap, kick, punch, or scratch. When these occur, it is most likely that a ghost is responsible.

6. Emotional (empathic): Pleasant and unpleasant emotions may be imprinted on the environment or an object and perceived by a sensitive person. Emotions may be specific and linked to a particular place or item such as weapons, jewelry, musical instruments, coins and medallions, and doorknobs.

CHARACTERISTICS OF IMPRINTS

It is important to understand that imprints are the result of something that happened in the past. As such, they are the foundation of retrocognition. When we detect an imprint, we experience an odor, emotion, sound, or image that was an element of a past event. This distinction becomes especially important when we investigate crime scenes. Imprints can reveal the movement of a victim and perpetrator, weapons and other objects involved in the crime, and other elements that may not be discovered in a police investigation. A good example of the latter is the familiarity of the victim with the perpetrator.

Imprints can also provide valuable clues that lead to an encounter with a ghost. Called "hot spots" by some psychics, intense imprints can be anchoring points that attach ghosts to a particular place.

Olfactory perceptions may range from the engaging fragrance of expensive perfume to the horrible stench of rotted meat. It is often useful to identify the fragrance, such as magnolia or Chanel No. 5 perfume. Linked with background research, this may indicate that a former female occupant of a house loved magnolias or used Chanel perfume. This link can lead to identification of the person whose emotional experience created the imprint. Offensive odors could be the result of illness that preceded death or the process of decomposition that occurred when a dead body was left undiscovered for a long time.

Auditory imprints comprise the majority of non-ghostly paranormal experiences. Sensitive psychics may mentally "hear" a variety of sounds, such as human vocalizations, musical instruments, gunshots, footsteps, the movement of horse-drawn carriages, slamming doors, etc. Auditory imprints are readily captured on recording devices, too. Thousands of high-quality recordings known as electronic voice phenomena (EVP) and electronic audio phenomena (EAP) may be found on the Internet.

The most exciting imprint phenomenon is the sighting of a humanoid apparition. Apparitions may appear as dark shadows, figures composed of white smoke or fog, translucent partial body parts, translucent whole-body figures, and lifelike bodies. The ability to see imprint apparitions varies greatly among people. The most ardent ghost hunter may never see one, while a casual visitor to a historic site may spot several.

HOT SPOTS FOR GHOSTLY ACTIVITY

Numerous sites of disasters, criminal activity, suicides, devastating fires, and other tragic events abound in Portland and Oregon's coastal towns, providing hundreds of opportunities for ghost hunting. You may visit the locations described in chapters 2-6 to experience ghostly activity discovered by others or discover a hot spot to research and initiate your own original ghost investigation.

Astute ghost hunters often search historical maps, drawings, and other documents to find the sites of military conflicts, buildings that no longer exist, or sites of tragic events now occupied by modern structures. For example, maps and drawings found online or displayed in museums, such as Fort Vancouver, the Oregon Maritime Museum, the Oregon History Museum, and the Pearson Air Museum in nearby Vancouver, Washington, or at historic locations such as the Pittock Mansion, may be a good place to start.

People who died in natural or maritime disasters or train or stagecoach robberies, of epidemics, or from infections that ensued after minor injuries, and those displaced by other tragic events such as fires, may remain with us as active ghosts. In Portland and many of Oregon's coastal communities, ghosts haunt the site of their unmarked graves, favorite bars or restaurants, workplaces, mysterious tunnels, ship wrecks, or cherished homes.

Historic homes of pioneers and early residents are often the focal point for successful ghost investigations. These places typically offer a well-researched history, authentic artifacts, personal belongings of former occupants, and easy accessibility. Among the most famous historic homes in the Portland region, now open as restaurants, inns, or museums, are the 1911-vintage White House, former home of lumber baron Robert Lytle; the Pittock Mansion (1909), center of a political scandal involving one of its owners, Will H. Daly; the Ermantinger House (1845), built by Francis Ermantinger and site of the famous coin toss in 1845 that gave Portland its name; the Ulysses S. Grant House (1846), used by the general before the Civil War; and the Stevens-Crawford House (1907), home of Mary E. Crawford and Harley Stevens.

Fascinating histories and ghostly atmospheres may also be found in historic commercial buildings and homes that are now modern businesses, such as the legendary White Eagle Saloon, the Crow Bar, Old Town Pizza, Commodore Grocery, the White House restaurant, Yellow Brick Road Antiques store, and the Bagdad Theater.

Portland, nearby cities, and many coastal Oregon communities have established historic districts and other venues that have attracted the attention of professional and amateur ghost hunters. These include the preserved and restored structures of downtown Portland, the former warehouse and industrial area now known as the Pearl District, Old Town Chinatown, the trendy subcultural-oriented Hawthorne District, and Alameda Ridge, which contains some of the oldest homes in the region. Gresham offers tree-lined streets with many historical buildings that now house quaint stores and restaurants.

On the coast, Fort Stevens in Hammond, Newport's Nye Beach district, the old fishing village of Charleston at Coos Bay, and 11 fascinating lighthouses provide ghost hunters with opportunities to get in touch with local history before searching for spirits.

Travelers on I-5 may want to visit Eugene's South University Historic District and the Blair Historic District anchored by Sam Bond's Garage. In Salem, horse-drawn carriages and streetcars preserve the historic atmosphere of the 19th century.

Fort Vancouver offers ghost hunters opportunities to visit some of the most historic structures in the Portland region. Founded in 1824, the rustic fort was nearly destroyed in 1866 by a major fire. It was quickly rebuilt with a Victorian architectural motif modified to serve military needs. Among the buildings targeted for paranormal investigation by local ghosts hunters are the houses of Officer's Row, including the Grant House (now a restaurant), the McLoughlin House (1846, home of fort administrator Dr. John McLoughlin), the Barclay House (1850, home of fort physician Forbes Barclay), the George C.

Marshall House (1889, home of the famous general and Nobel Peace Prize winner), and the General O. O. Howard House; the former post hospital; and the 1919-vintage Red Cross building.

Many churches established in the 19th and early 20th centuries exist throughout the Portland area, some standing next to graveyards that contain pioneers and notable historic figures. The cornerstone of the Victorian-style Calvary Presbyterian Church, known as "the Old Church," was laid on September 11, 1882. Thought to be "too far out in the country" by its earliest members, it is located in what is downtown Portland today. The Old Church, cited as one of the most beautiful buildings in the Pacific Northwest, no longer serves a congregation. It is currently used as a social venue for weddings, lectures, concerts, plays, and meetings. The historic character and spooky atmosphere of the Old Church are accented by its amazing architectural features.

Built in a Gothic Revival style, the Zion Lutheran Church was opened in 1890. A newer church now occupies the site, but architectural remnants remain. The newer church was dedicated in 1950, and several emotional events have occurred in the sanctuary and narthex that have created residual paranormal imprints. The Venetian Gothic-style First Congregational Church on Park Avenue in Portland opened in 1895. Massive stone arches, huge stained-glass windows, brick construction, and the off-center tower give the place a beautiful, eerie appearance. In the Portland suburb of Milwaukie, the Oaks Pioneer Church has been serving its congregation since 1865. The old church has been moved three times, once on a river barge, and underwent major renovations in 1869, 1883, and 1928.

These regionally important churches are accessible to the general public, and ghost hunters, as places of historical interest while most continue to offer worship services.

Ghost hunters who have an interest in old churches should visit nearby Salem, where 14 historic churches may be found. Of particular interest are St. Joseph Catholic Church (1853), First Baptist Church (1859), and First United Methodist Church (1878). Farther south, along the I-5 corridor, the First Christian Church of Eugene (1911) has a massive dome and huge stained-glass windows that create a sacred ambience, but spirits are also attached to the place.

Across the boulevard from Fort Vancouver, the stately French-Carpenter Gothic-style Providence Academy building was opened in 1874 as a young ladies' school. The chapel was dedicated as a religious center in 1883. Once considered the official chapel of Fort Vancouver, the place served as a venue for funerals and memorial services.

Several historic cemeteries in the Portland region provide plenty of opportunities to discover fascinating histories of early residents and experience a paranormal encounter. Many of them date from the mid-19th century and include interesting architecture, intriguing epitaphs, and overgrown foliage that create a spooky atmosphere. These cities of the dead include unusual tombs, peculiar statuary, and unmarked mass graves. Here you will find Portland's pioneers, politicians, prostitutes, civic leaders, cultural icons, and a few criminals.

Established during the homesteading period of 1850 to 1870, many of the metropolitan region's 14 pioneer graveyards are well known by local ghost hunters as good places to experience paranormal phenomena. The oldest graveyards are Powell Grove Cemetery, containing headstones with death dates from 1837, and Lone Fir Cemetery, which was opened in 1846. The Columbian Cemetery contains graves of veterans of the Civil War and every subsequent war including those in Iraq and Afghanistan. Ghost hunters fascinated by military history should visit the Grand Army of the Republic Cemetery in Southwest Portland. Douglass Cemetery contains the grave of its founder, John Douglass, who fought in the War of 1812, traveled west on the Oregon Trail, and subsequently became a prominent Portland shipbuilder.

A few miles from downtown Portland, Gresham Pioneer Cemetery began burials in 1859, offering a final resting place to loggers and train operators who died in the many disasters that occurred in the region's forests. It also contains the remains of locals who served as Union soldiers, sailors, and marines in the Civil War.

Asylums, prisons, and farms for the indigent almost always opened burial grounds for residents who died while detained or incarcerated. Often, these burial grounds contain unmarked or desecrated graves, which retain spirits at the site. The Multnomah County Poor Farm Cemetery is one of those burial sites that have been the target of ghost hunters who seek the spirits of people who were condemned to misery and hopelessness in life only to suffer the indignity of a disturbed or ignominious grave after death. Located southeast of Mount Calvary Cemetery, the poor-farm graves include a colony of lepers and countless others who were sick, poor, or mentally ill.

Despite its location across the Columbia River in the state of Washington, the city of Vancouver has close geographic, historic, and cultural ties with Portland. The Old City Cemetery in Vancouver contains the remains of some of Portland's pioneers and offers the region's ghost hunters fascinating histories of colorful figures and a few ghosts. The earliest burials were made within the present limits of Vancouver Barracks. In the 1860s, another cemetery was opened near the west boundary of the Post, across Reserve Street from the Academy. As Fort Vancouver and the surrounding community grew, many graves from these early sites were moved. In 1867, the city purchased 10 acres of John Maney's Land Claim and began relocating graves from earlier sites. Despite care, many headstones were misplaced and some were set over the wrong graves. This often leads to ghostly activity. In March of 2011, paranormal activity increased after vandals pushed over 44 monuments along the southwest corner of the cemetery.

Founded in 1882, River View Cemetery contains some peculiar monuments that may have enticed spirits to stay behind in our physical world. Simon Benson, Portland's wealthiest lumberman in 1907, is buried in Section 8. His grave marker is a simple granite block, but monuments to Benson's civic pride remain all over downtown Portland in the form of drinking fountains known as Benson Bubblers. Minnie Merchant Smith's grave is topped with a marble angel that casts fascinating shadows around the burial site. One of the most visited graves in the cemetery is that of frontier gunfighter and lawman Virgil Earp. Brother of famed lawman Wyatt Earp, Virgil died in 1905 in Nevada, but his body was brought to Portland by his daughter, Janie Law.

The most fascinating and spiritually active graveyard in the Portland region may be Lone Fir Cemetery. Founded in 1846 as a burial ground for the Stephens family, the place became a community cemetery in 1854 to accommodate victims of a tragic steamboat explosion on the Willamette River. It covers 30 acres with more than 25,000 graves. Lone Fir Cemetery staff members conduct monthly tours, which reveal fascinating histories and clues to paranormal activity that occurs there. Visitors have experienced paranormal activity at several sites, including Dr. Hawthorne's plot, which contains the remains of 132 patients from his insane asylum, and Block 14, which contains an unknown number of bodies in unmarked graves.

Most county Web sites list pioneer cemeteries and offer links to local organizations that care for the graves and grounds. The best way to see the cemeteries of the haunted coast, and learn fascinating histories of those entombed, is to tour them with a knowledgeable guide. (See Appendix E: Special Tours and Events.) Some of these places are too spooky and possibly unsafe after dark unless you are accompanied by people who can ensure a pleasant visit.

LOCAL GHOST HUNTERS

Several local organizations conduct investigations of ghostly activity and other paranormal phenomena in greater Portland and several locations on the Oregon coast. They can help you locate haunted sites, provide information about previous ghost investigations they have conducted, or sharpen your skills as a paranormal investigator. These organizations include the Pacific Paranormal Research Society, Believers of Oregon Spirit Society, Oregon Ghost Hunters, PSI of Oregon, Northwest Paranormal Investigations, Salem Spirit Trackers, Oregon Paranormal Investigations, Oregon Coast Paranormal Investigators, Oregon Paranormal, Oregon State Paranormal, Oregon Ghost Hunters, Bridgetown Paranormal Research, and West Coast Spectre Society. The activities of these organizations have been reported on their respective Web sites and featured in a variety of news media. Some of these groups host special events and offer classes and training seminars. See Appendix D (Internet Resources) for contact information. Tours of haunted places are available in the greater Portland area, cities on the I-5 corridor, and in coastal towns (see Appendix E). If you inquire at a local bookshop or historical society, you may meet a history buff or ghost hunter who can take you to sites not mentioned in published media.

THREE SIMPLE RULES

Three simple rules apply for successful ghost hunting. The first is to be patient. Ghosts are everywhere, but contact may require a considerable investment of time. Second, respect the boundaries of private property and the rights of property owners to restrict or deny access to places you may wish to investigate. The third rule is to have fun. Ghost hunting can be a fascinating and exciting experience. You may report your ghost-hunting experiences or suggest hot spots for ghost hunting to the author via e-mail at ghosthunter@jeffdwyer.com. Visit the author's Web site at www.jeffdwyer.com.

Ghost Hunter's Guide to **Portland** and the **Oregon Coast**

CHAPTER 1

How to Hunt Ghosts

You may want to visit recognized haunted sites, listed in chapters 2 through 6, using some of the ghost-hunting techniques described in this chapter, or search for a new haunted site. If you are looking for a haunted place that has not yet been discovered, start with an old house in your neighborhood or a favorite historic bed-and-breakfast inn. You may get a lead from fascinating stories about ancestors that have been passed down through your family, rumors circulating among your friends and neighbors, or reports posted on the Internet.

Your search for a ghost, or exploration of a haunted place, starts with research. Summaries of obscure and esoteric material about possible haunted sites are available from museums, local historical societies, and bookstores. Brochures and booklets, sold at historical sites under the Oregon State Parks system, can be good resources too.

Guided tours of historical sites such as the famous Shanghai Tunnels in old Portland; old neighborhoods in Eugene, Salem, Oregon City, and Troutdale; the historic grounds of Fort Vancouver; or old churches and pioneer graveyards, are good places to begin your research. Tours can help you develop a feel for places within a building where ghosts might be sighted or an appreciation of relevant history. Ghost, cemetery, and history tours of fascinating towns on the Oregon coast and the I-5 corridor are popular and offer a good way to learn a lot about local paranormal activity in a short time.

By touring haunted buildings, you will have opportunities to speak with guides and docents who may be able to provide you with clues about the dearly departed or tell you ghost stories you can't find in published material. Docents may know people—old-timers in the area or amateur historians—who can give you additional information about a site, its former owners or residents, and its potential for ghostly activity.

Almost every city has a local historical society (see Appendix F). These are good places to find information that may not be published in mainstream print media. This could be histories of local families and buildings; information about tragedies, disasters, criminal activity, or legends; and myths about places that may be haunted. You will want to take notes about secret scandals or other ghost-producing happenings that occurred at locations now occupied by modern buildings, roads, or parks. In these cases, someone occupying a new house or other structure could hear strange sounds, feel cold spots, or see ghosts or spirit remnants.

Newspapers are an excellent source of historical information as well. You can search for articles about ghosts, haunted places, or paranormal activity by accessing the newspaper's archives via the Internet and entering key words, dates, or names. Newspaper articles about suicides, murders, train wrecks, plane crashes, and suspected or documented paranormal phenomena can provide essential information for your ghost hunt. Stories about authentic haunted sites are common around Halloween.

Bookstores and libraries usually have special-interest sections with books on local and regional history by local writers. A few inquiries may connect you with these local writers, who may be able to help you focus your research.

If these living souls cannot help, try the dead. A visit to a local graveyard is often useful in identifying possible ghosts. Often you can find headstones that indicate the person entombed died of suicide, criminal activity, local disaster, or such. Some epitaphs may indicate that the deceased was survived by a spouse and children or died far from home. Grave markers that have been desecrated or damaged by weather, vegetation, erosion, or earthquakes are good places to look for paranormal phenomena.

Perhaps the best place to start a search for a ghost is within your own family. Oral histories can spark your interest in a particular ancestor, scandal, building, or site relevant to your family. Old photographs, death certificates, letters and wills, anniversary lists in family Bibles, and keepsakes can be great clues. Then you can visit gravesites or homes of your ancestors to check out the vibes as you mentally and emotionally empathize with specific aspects of your family's history.

Almost every family has a departed member who died at an early age, suffered hardships or emotional anguish, or passed away suddenly due to an accident or natural disaster. Once you have focused your research on a deceased person, you need to determine if that person remains on this earthly plane as a ghost. Evaluate the individual's personal history to see if he had a reason to remain attached to a specific place.

Was his death violent or under tragic circumstances?

Did he die at a young age with unfinished business?

Did the deceased leave behind loved ones who needed his support and protection?

Was this person attached to a specific site or building?

Would the individual be inclined to seek revenge against those responsible for his death?

Would his devotion and sense of loyalty lead him to offer eternal companionship to loved ones?

Revenge, anger, refusal to recognize the reality of transformation by death, and other negative factors prompt many spirits to haunt places and people. However, most ghosts are motivated by positive factors. Spirits may remain at a site to offer protection to a loved one or a particular place.

Also, remember that apparitions can appear as animals. Apparitions of ships, buildings, covered wagons, bridges, and roads by the strictest definitions are phantoms. A phantom is the essence of a structure that no longer exists on the physical plane. Many people have seen houses, cottages, castles, villages, and large ships that were destroyed or sunk years before.

BASIC PREPARATION FOR GHOST HUNTING

If you decide to ghost hunt at night or on a special anniversary, make a trip to the site a few days ahead of time. During daylight hours, familiarize yourself with the place and its surroundings. Many historical sites are closed after sunset or crowded at certain times by organized tours.

TWO BASIC METHODS FOR FINDING GHOSTS

Based partly on the kind of paranormal activity reported at a site, the ghost hunter must decide which method or approach will be used.

Some will feel competent with a collection of cameras, electromagnetic field detectors, digital thermometers, computers, data recorders, and other high-tech gadgets. These ghost hunters prefer to use the Technical Method. Others may discover they have an emotional affinity for a particular historic site, a surprising fascination with an event associated with a haunting, or empathy for a deceased person. These ghost hunters may have success with the Psychic Method. Another consideration is the ghost hunter's goal. Some desire scientific evidence of ghostly presence while others simply want to experience paranormal activity.

THE TECHNICAL METHOD

Ghost hunters who favor the Technical Method often use an array of detection and recording devices that cover a wide range of the electromagnetic spectrum. Technical methods of ghost hunting can be complicated and expensive and require skilled people to operate the devices. Ghost hunters who want to use the Technical Method yet keep their investigations simple and inexpensive may get satisfying results with common audio and video recording devices and other low-tech approaches.

Equipment Preparation

A few days before your ghost hunt, clear audio and image media of previous recordings. Test your batteries and bring new backup batteries and freshly charged power packs to the investigation site. You should have two types of flashlights: a broad-beam light for moving around a site and a penlight-type flashlight for narrow-field illumination while you make notes or adjust equipment. A red lens will help you avoid disruption of your night-adapted vision. A candle may be a good way to light the site in a way that is least offensive to a ghost.

Still-Photography Techniques

Many photographic techniques that work well under normal conditions are inadequate for ghost hunts. That's because ghost hunting is usually conducted under conditions of low ambient light.

This requires the use of long exposures. Some investigators use a strobe or flash device but these can make the photos look unauthentic or create artifacts.

If you use film-based photography, practice taking photos with films of various light sensitivities before you go on your ghost hunt. Standard photographic films of high light sensitivity should be used—ASA of 800 or higher is recommended. At a dark or nearly dark location, mount the camera on a tripod. Try several exposure settings, from one to 30 seconds, and aperture settings under various low-light conditions. Your equipment should include a stable, lightweight tripod. Handheld cameras may produce poorly focused photographs when the exposure duration is greater than 1/60 second.

Make notes about the camera settings that work best under various light conditions. Avoid aiming the camera at a scene where there is a bright light such as a streetlamp or exit sign over a doorway. These light sources may "overflow" throughout your photograph.

Some professional and advanced amateur ghost hunters use infrared film. You should consult a professional photo-lab technician about this type of film and its associated photographic techniques. Infrared photography can yield some amazing pictures of spirits not detected by other means. Infrared film has become scarce and expensive since 2007, when manufacturers such as Kodak encountered a significant decline in the demand for the product.

Because digital cameras are inherently sensitive to infrared light, minor adjustments allow users to take pictures that may reveal entities that would not be seen with conventional photographic techniques. It has been theorized that spiritual entities exist at frequencies of the visual spectrum that lie below those of humans. If you use a camera filter that blocks out visible light while admitting infrared light, images of ghosts may be obtained. In some digital cameras, these adjustments are quite easy, requiring nothing more than selecting a "night vision" mode.

If you use digital photographic methods, practice taking pictures under conditions of low ambient light, with and without artificial lighting. Most digital cameras have default automatic settings that might not work well during a ghost investigation. These settings may not be easily changed as ambient conditions change at the haunted site unless you have practiced the procedures. Many cameras have features that enable automatic exposures at specific intervals, e.g., once every minute. This allows a hands-off remote photograph record to be made. Repetitive automatic exposures also allow a site to be investigated without the presence of the investigator.

While every ghost hunter armed with a camera wishes to capture the full-bodied image of a ghost, most have to settle for light anomalies. These may be amorphous, luminescent clouds or narrow streaks of light resembling a shooting star. The light anomaly most frequently captured on film and in digital images is the orb. An orb is a symmetrical, white disk that appears most often in photographs and digital images made under low-light conditions. It may appear hovering near a ceiling, over a bed, or inside a car. A photograph may contain a single orb or show so many, of varying size, that they cannot be counted. Impressive pictures of light anomalies may be viewed at several Web sites.

Many ghost hunters claim that orbs are spirit manifestations without explaining why the spirit of a human would appear as a disk of light. Some of these have a humanoid shape but fail to convince critics and skeptics that the image is that of a ghost because the image is so perfectly illuminated it appears fake. Software for processing digital images has reduced the power of proof that was once attributed to photographs. Critics and skeptics point out that orbs may be the result of bugs, dust particles, or water droplets suspended in the air close to the lens or inside the camera. Excited ghost hunters have displayed pictures of light anomalies that turn out to be the result of wisps of hair, a camera strap, a finger, cigarette smoke, light reflected from jewelry, or smudges on the lens.

It is interesting to note that orbs were virtually unheard of in the field of paranormal investigation until digital cameras became available. Consequently, many people suspect that orbs may be the result of the camera's operating characteristics. Under conditions of low light, digital pixels may not fill in completely. This has been called under-pixelation. As a result, no image information or electronic signal is generated. The lack of a signal is detected by the camera's software, which then fills in the missing spot in the picture's signal array with white light. The result is an orb.

Is it possible that a spirit will manifest as an orb? Yes, although many experts suggest that as many as 99 percent of orb pictures do not represent anything paranormal. I've seen some very impressive orbs, however. Ghost hunter Jackie Ganiy, president of Sonoma SPIRIT, captured a picture of an orb hovering over the flight deck of the aircraft carrier USS *Hornet* in Alameda, California. This orb was symmetrically rounded but a skull was visible within it. Books by Melvyn Willin and Troy Taylor present fascinating collections of the best pictures of ghosts and other paranormal light anomalies, including orbs.

Generally, light anomalies should not be readily accepted as evidence of spirit presence unless there is corroborating evidence derived from other technical devices. This includes audio phenomena, changes in electromagnetic field, isolated changes in air temperature, or other still or video images. Corroborating evidence might also be found in psychic impressions experienced at the time and place that the light anomaly was captured. For example, psychic impressions of intense emotions, sobbing, cries for help, or screaming might be obtained while standing in an old hospital room as a photographer captures a picture of an orb hovering over the bed.

Audio Recording Techniques

Digital or tape recorders provide an inexpensive way to obtain audio evidence of ghostly activity. The popular term for this is "electronic voice phenomena" or EVP. The American Association of EVP defines it as any intelligible voice detected on recording media that has no known explanation. Most ghost hunters accept a wider definition that includes the sound of moving objects, such as doors, windows, or glass objects; whistling; sobbing; laughter; screams; humming; gunshots; footsteps; explosions; musical notes; or tapping and knocking. Given this wide variety of sounds, I have proposed that the term EVP be replaced by EAP, electronic audio phenomena, and defined as any audio recording that cannot be attributed to normal phenomena.

EAP are obtained as a ghost hunter investigates an allegedly haunted place. The ghost hunter may record EAP while remaining stationary at a site, such as next to a grave, or while walking around a location. This is called an EAP or EVP sweep. Generally, questions are asked to which spirits may respond. These questions should be simple and follow an invitation for any spirits present to communicate. Typical questions include:

"What is your name?"
"Did you die here?"
"How old are you?"
"Do you want me to leave?"
"Why are you here?"

Your research may indicate specific questions you can use in your EAP investigations. If you seek a ghost of a farm worker who committed suicide by hanging himself in a barn, you may ask, "Did you die in this barn?" and "Did you hang yourself?" The ghost hunter may also ethically provoke a spirit through verbal challenge.

In most cases, spirit responses cannot be heard by the ghost hunter when they occur but they may be discovered on the audio recording during playback. Typically, responses are brief, rarely lasting more than a few seconds. Vocalizations sometimes have amazing clarity but most often they are unintelligible and, as with other sounds, rarely repeated in subsequent recordings. If the spirit's response comprises a clear and reasonable answer to the question, the recording may be called a "specific EAP." Other responses, whether they are vocalizations or other sounds, must be labeled "random EAP" and scrutinized as the result of processes that may not be paranormal. For example, the sound of a conversation between two living people may be carried a long distant across a body of water. A ghost hunter who is unaware of others in the area may ask, "What is your name?" The response discovered during playback may be "I am cold." This is a random EAP and likely a non-paranormal recording of words spoken by a living person. Random EAP may be created by natural or normal processes, such as the wind against a window or drafts in an old house, and there is high likelihood that they do not reflect a spirit's intelligent interaction with the investigator. Specific EAP has greater value as evidence of ghostly presence because clear and reasonable responses to specific questions are not likely to be created by living people nearby or natural processes.

Often, EAP consists of nonvocal sounds. Musical instruments, slamming doors, gunshots, footsteps, and tapping sounds may be evoked by the ghost hunter's questions. Ghosts that are unable to generate vocalizations may resort to these sounds as the only means of communication. These may be random EAP but still comprise good evidence of a ghostly presence. You may ask, "Why are you here?" On playback, the recording may reveal the sound of footsteps moving away from the microphone. In this instance, the ghost may have been troubled by the question and decided to leave.

Before you begin your EAP sweep, test your recorder under conditions you expect to find at the investigation site in order to reduce audio artifact and ensure optimal performance of the device. Does your recorder pick up excessive background noise? This may obscure ghostly sounds. If so, consider upgrading the tape quality or select a high-quality digital audio recorder. Also, consider using a wind guard on the microphone.

Consider using two or more recorders at different locations within the site. This allows you to verify sounds such as wind against a window and reduce the possibility of ambiguous recordings or misinterpretation of an EAP.

Allow time, at least 15 to 60 seconds, for a response. EAP can be heard only during playback, so ghost hunters should review recordings every 5-10 minutes during the investigation, rather than waiting until the investigation is completed. This will enable the identification of hot spots for spirit activity that may be investigated more thoroughly.

You can use sound-activated recorders at a site overnight. They will automatically switch on whenever a sound occurs above a minimum threshold. Be aware that tape recorders may yield recordings that start with an annoying artifact, the result of a slow tape speed at the beginning of each recorded segment. The slow tape speed could obscure the sounds made by a ghost.

Remote microphones and monitor earphones allow you to remain some distance from the site and activate the recorder when ghostly sounds are heard. If this equipment is not available, turn the recorder on and let it run throughout your investigation, whether you remain stationary or walk about the site.

Wear a lapel microphone connected to a small audio recorder carried in your pocket. Operated in the sound-activation mode, this device will also provide you with a means of making audio notes rather than written notes. A headset with a microphone is especially useful with this technique.

Ghost hunters must carefully analyze their audio recordings, and the environment in which they are obtained, to be certain they are not inadvertent recordings of natural or normal sounds. Sound may carry great distances, particularly over bodies of water and when there is fog or low cloud cover. If a tape recorder is used, a new tape may reduce the chances of artifact. I recommend computer software such as Adobe Audition for editing your EAP recording. With a little practice, you will be able to subdue or eliminate extraneous sounds while enhancing spirit communications.

The American Association of EVP maintains a Web site for general information and advice: www.aaevp.com. Several Web sites may be accessed to hear examples of EVP. Use the keyword "EVP" to locate them.

Video Recording

Video recorders offer a wide variety of recording features from time-lapse to auto-start/stop and autofocus. These features enable you to make surveillance-type recordings over many hours while you are off-site. Consult your user's manual for low-light recording guidelines and always use a tripod and long-duration battery packs.

If you plan to attempt video recording, consider using two recorders, at equal distance from a specific object such as a chair. Arrange the recorders at different angles, preferably 90 degrees from each other.

Another approach you might try is to use a wide-angle setting on the first camera for a broad view of a room, porch, or courtyard. On the second camera, use a closeup setting to capture ghostly apparitions at a door, chair, or window.

You may have more success with sequential, manual, or timer-actuated recordings than a continuous-run technique. If you try this technique, use recording runs of one to five minutes. Practice using the method that interrupts the automatic setting should you need to manually control the recording process. Always use a tripod that can be moved to a new location in a hurry.

High-Tech Equipment

You can purchase high-tech devices such as electromagnetic field detectors, infrared thermometers, barometers, and motion detectors at your local electronics store or over the Internet. Good sources for high-tech ghost-hunting equipment are the Society for Paranormal

Investigation, the Ghost Hunter Store, and the EMF Safety Superstore.

Inexpensive, battery-operated motion detectors can be placed at several locations within an investigation site. Some of these allow users to select an audio signal or a silent flashing light signal and connect the output to a central monitor. These devices work by measuring optical or acoustical changes in the environment. Therefore, they are most reliable when remote surveillance is performed and investigators are certain that no living beings have entered the site.

Infrared thermometers have been used to search for cold spots that may signal the presence of a ghost. While these devices are widely utilized, and sometimes displayed on paranormal TV shows, they are often used incorrectly. They cannot assess changes in the temperature of clear air because of its very low density and minimal emission of infrared energy. However, infrared thermometers can detect the surface temperature of solid objects, liquids, dense gases, and clouds. With a laser to assist aiming, the device can be used to measure the temperature of objects that cannot be reached due to obstructions such as fences, hazards such bodies of water that cannot be crossed, unsafe structures, or animals.

Night vision goggles can be useful in low-light situations. These devices enhance the intensity of light within the visual spectrum and augment the resulting image with nonvisual sources of electromagnetic radiation such as near-infrared or ultraviolet light. Night vision devices enable you to see doors and other objects move that you might not otherwise see. The resulting scene appears monochromatic but preserves fine details.

The most advanced and expensive piece of equipment used by ghost hunters is the FLIR imaging device. This acronym stands for forward-looking infrared. FLIRs detect thermal energy in the infrared range. The FLIR lens focuses the scene on a vast array of sensors that produce thousands of simultaneous measurements of thermal energy. Software then assembles the thermal measurements into a mosaic or picture that is displayed on a handheld video screen. In the picture, elements of the scene are colored according to the temperature or level of infrared radiation. The result resembles a coloring-book image in which some elements are blue, indicating colder temperatures, while others are yellow, orange, or red, indicating warmer temperatures.

FLIR systems can see through atmospheric obscurants such as smoke or fog and in total darkness. Ghost hunters use them to detect spirits that do not generate an image within the human visual spectrum. Theoretically, when spirits appear on our plane they draw energy from the environment, creating a cold spot. A FLIR will detect subtle changes in temperature and depict the shape of the cold spot on the video screen. When the shape of the cold spot is humanoid, ghost hunters claim they have evidence that a ghost is present.

Despite the technical sophistication and expense of FLIRs, the images they produce may be misinterpreted. FLIRs may detect sources of heat or cold created by normal processes not noticed by the user. A living being who occupied the scene moments before a FLIR-equipped ghost hunter arrived may leave residual heat in a chair or on a doorknob. Finding the scene unoccupied by any living being, the ghost hunter might mistakenly cite the detected thermal anomaly as evidence of a ghostly presence.

Electromagnetic field (EMF) detectors are used by paranormal investigators to detect the presence of ghosts in spite of the lack of scientific evidence that EMF and spirit presence are linked. Ghost hunters who use EMF detectors claim that spikes in a local electromagnetic field are created when a ghost transitions onto our plane of existence. These devices, however, often pick up EMF generated by unseen electrical appliances, faulty wiring in an old house, cell phones, walkie-talkies, video recorders, and numerous other sources including solar flares and geomagnetic storms. EMF detectors may be useful if proper controls are established and all possible sources of natural EMF are identified.

Electronic gadgets can be useful and fun, but unless you have a means of creating a record of the instrument's output or storing images or data in a computer, your reports of light anomalies, apparent paranormal motion of objects, changes in the physical characteristics of the environment, or apparitions will not constitute the kind of hard evidence you need to satisfy skeptics. Keep in mind that even expensive instruments may produce erroneous data or signals if they are incorrectly calibrated, misused, or improperly maintained. Also, data can be easily misinterpreted if the user does not understand the technical or operating limitations of the device. Using expensive high-tech gadgets does not guarantee accurate results, nor do they validate a ghost hunt as a scientific investigation.

Very Low Tech Devices

I have had great success in detecting spirit activity with common household items. Ghosts often become active when they are irritated by changes in their favored environment. If you tilt a picture hanging on the wall, leave an object in the ghost's rocking chair, or leave a book open, a ghost may straighten the picture, remove the object from his chair, or close the book.

Spirits may be attracted to objects they can manipulate easily. Leave four aces at the top of a deck of cards. A ghost may shuffle them throughout the deck. Ghosts are often attracted to water. A glass left full may later be found empty and the contents wetting the floor. A paper and pencil may be used by a ghost to leave bizarre marks or a legible message. Leave two stacks of coins—10 pennies in each stack—on a stable surface and leave the room for an extended period of time. When you return, the coins may be scattered. If both stacks are scattered, a gust of wind or vibration of the building may account for the change. If one stack remains untouched while the other is scattered, that may be the work of a ghost. I used this technique at the Myrtles Plantation in St. Francisville, Louisiana. I found 10 pennies rearranged in a circle around the other stack of coins, which remained standing.

Other Equipment

Various authorities in the field of ghost hunting suggest the following items to help you mark sites, detect paranormal phenomena, and collect evidence of ghostly activity.

- White and colored chalk
- Compass
- Stop watch
- Steel tape measure
- Magnifying glass
- First-aid kit
- Thermometer
- Metal detector
- Graph paper for diagrams
- Small mirror
- Small bell
- Plastic bags for collecting evidence
- Light-reflecting tape
- Matches
- Tape for sealing doors
- String
- Cross
- Bible
- Cell phone

THE PSYCHIC METHOD

The Psychic Method relies upon your intuition, inner vision, or emotional connection with a deceased person, object, place, or point of time in history. You don't have to be a trained psychic to use this approach. All of us have some capacity to tap into unseen dimensions and use some of the psychic tools described in my book *Psychic: Use Your Psychic Powers to Experience Ghosts*, the parapsychology literature, and popular books by psychics such as Sylvia Browne and Jane Roberts. Your ability to use psychic tools for successful ghost hunting depends upon three factors: your innate ability, receptivity, and sensitivity.

You may have an ability to successfully use psychic tools in a ghost hunt if you are one of those people who can readily identify isolated places within a room that elicit a chilling feeling that there is something bizarre or paranormal about the spot. The ability to identify these places must include a capacity to sort out your impressions, clear your mind of extraneous thoughts and distractions, and focus your attention on the particular point from which a paranormal impression emanates.

You may have sufficient receptivity to effectively use psychic tools if you feel more intensely connected to a place or past era than others or often feel mentally transported to another era. Do you often get that curious feeling that some unseen person is standing behind you, watching you, or touching you? When you touch an artifact, such as a weapon, do you get the impression that you have become aware of information about the object or its user? If so, you are receptive to unseen dimensions and likely to have success hunting ghosts with psychic tools. Highly receptive people often visit a place for the first time yet feel they have been there before. This is called ESP, or extrasensory perception, and reflects a high degree of receptivity.

Your receptivity can provide considerable focus to your ghost hunt if you first obtain information about the key elements and historical context of the entity's death. This includes architectural elements of a home, theatre, airplane, or ship and objects such as furniture, clothing, weapons, or any implement or artifact of the specific time period of the entity's death. Touching or handling pertinent artifacts, sitting in the deceased person's chair, or standing within the historic site will enable you to get in touch with the historical moment that is most pertinent to the ghost.

You may have exceptional sensitivity if you get vivid impressions of emotions in specific locations within allegedly haunted places. Do you walk into a historic building and get that eerie feeling that something or someone from the past still lingers there? Do you get a sense of "vibes" of fear, anger, pain, or suffering when you visit historic places or places known to be haunted? If so, you may be sensitive to residual energies from past events, emotions that played out in a particular place, or the actions of people who have been gone from the scene for decades. Sensitive people often detect a distant time or a voice, sound, touch, or texture of another dimension often described as a change in atmosphere.

Your sensitivity will pay off in a ghost hunt if your investigation is aimed at strong paranormal imprints or attachments of spirits. Strong imprints and attachments are indicated by the frequency, duration, and consistency of the detected paranormal activity that reportedly occurs at a particular place. The strongest imprints are created by intense emotions such as fear, rage, jealousy, revenge, or loss, especially if they were repetitive over long periods prior to death. Strong attachments are created by love for a person, a place, or an object or a sense of obligation to provide guidance and protection. Biographical research may reveal this kind of information, particularly if personal letters or diaries are examined. Old newspaper articles, suicide notes, and photographs are useful too.

You may enhance your sensitivity by developing and expressing empathy for the ghost's lingering presence at a haunted site. Empathy can be based on your research, which may reveal information about the entity's personal history and probable emotions, motivations, problems, or unfinished business at the time of death. You may also learn that a ghost may be trapped, confused, or has chosen to remain at a site to protect someone or guard something precious. Historical sources such as newspaper articles and obituaries, old photographs, or biographies can provide this kind of information.

Your sensitivity to ghostly environmental imprints and spirit manifestations may also be increased by meditation, the relaxing of one's physical body to eliminate distracting thoughts and tensions and achieve emotional focus. Meditation allows you to concentrate your spiritual awareness on a single subject—a place, entity, or historic moment in time. Markers of time or season, artifacts or implements, furniture and doorways are a few suggestions of things to focus on. As the subject comes into focus, you can add information obtained from your research, information that relates specifically to the spirit under investigation such as the type of device used for a suicide or murder, favored book, musical instrument, etc. Through this process, you will become aware of unseen dimensions of the world around you, creating a feeling that you have moved through time to a distant era. Meditation gets you in touch with the place, date, and time pertinent to a ghost's imprint or death. It also enables you to disregard personal concerns and distracting thoughts that may interfere with your concentration on the ghost you seek.

Keep in mind that it is possible to be in a meditative state while appearing quite normal. The process is simple and easy to learn. When you arrive at the site of your ghost hunt, find a place a short distance away to meditate. Three essentials for any effective meditation are comfort, quiet, and concentration.

Comfort: Sit or stand in a relaxed position. Take free and even breaths at a slow rate. Do not alter your breathing pattern so much that you feel short of breath, winded, or lightheaded. Close your eyes if that enhances your comfort, or focus on a candle, tree, or flower. Do not fall asleep. Proper meditation creates relaxation without decreasing alertness.

Quiet: Meditate in a place away from noises generated by traffic, passersby, radios, slammed doors, and the like. If you are with a group, give each other sufficient personal space. Some people use mantras, repetitive words or phrases, or speak only in their mind in order to facilitate inner calmness. Mantras are useful to induce a focused state of relaxation, but they may disrupt the meditation of a companion if spoken aloud. A majority of ghost hunters do not believe that mantras are necessary in this instance. They point out that ghost hunting is not like a séance as depicted in old movies.

Concentration: First, clear your mind of everyday thoughts, worries, and concerns. This is the most difficult part of the process. Many of us don't want to let go of our stressful thoughts. To help release those worries, let the thought turn off its light and fade into darkness. After you clear your mind, some thoughts may reappear. Repeat the process. Slowly turn off the light of each thought until you can rest with a completely cleared mind. This might take some practice. Don't wait until you are on the scene of a ghost hunt before you practice this exercise.

Once your mind is clear, focus on your breathing and imagine your entire being as a single point of energy driving the breathing process. Then, open yourself. Think only of the entity you seek. Starting with the ghost's identity (if known), slowly expand your focus to include its personal history, the historical era of the ghost's death or creation of the emotional imprint, the reported nature and appearance of the haunting, and any specific ghostly activity.

Acknowledge each thought as you continue relaxed breathing. Find a thought that is most attractive to you, and then expand your mind to include your present surroundings. Return slowly to your current place and time. Remain quiet for a minute or two before you resume communication with your companions, then move ahead with the ghost hunt.

Psychic Tools

Clairaudience: The perception of sounds generated by paranormal sources is called clairaudience. The term is derived from the French, meaning "clear hearing." People with this ability may hear the voices of spirits who are trying to communicate or the sounds of events that occurred years or decades earlier. The latter are most often environmental imprints created by intense repetitive emotions or events that had a strong emotional component.

Clairsentience: Some ghosts manifest by creating impressions of physical sensations in receptive people that may include a feeling of being touched. Others are accompanied by fragrances or odors. The ability to perceive or detect these physical sensations and smells that do not truly exist on this plane is called clairsentience. Signature perfumes or the fragrance of favorite flowers can help you identify a ghost. At the world-renowned haunted Myrtles Plantation in Louisiana, the ghost of Sarah Woodrooff creates the fragrance of her favorite flower, the magnolia. Odors such as cigars, oranges, and hemp are common ghostly manifestations. Sometimes, ghost hunters encounter the noxious odors of rotting meat or burning flesh.

Clairvoyance: Information or impressions may be received from objects or spirits without the use of "normal" senses. The process is called clairvoyance and usually refers to visual impressions. People who see ghosts, whether the image is lifelike or merely a human-shaped fragment of a shadow, are clairvoyant. Visual information or impressions may include orbs, amorphous clouds, or objects. Since clairvoyance is limited to "real time" events, any visual experience suggests a ghost is present at the moment.

Retrocognition: Perception of visual or audio impressions of events from the past is a form of clairvoyance or clairaudience called retrocognition. Psychic Derek Acorah dramatically portrayed his retrocognition ability during ghost investigations in the popular TV show *Most Haunted*. If you watched my TV shows *Ghosts of the Queen Mary* and *Legends of Alcatraz*, you've seen me perform retrocognition.

The most famous case of retrocognition was reported by two teachers, Charlotte Moberly and Eleanor Jourdain, after they visited the Petit Trianon at the Palace of Versailles in France in 1901. In what has become known as the Moberly-Jourdain incident, the women reportedly witnessed people dressed in 18th-century clothing and saw structures that no longer existed. Their detailed descriptions of the experience, published in their 1911 book, *An Adventure,* match obscure historical records, suggesting the retrocognitive experience was genuine. Detailed accounts of the Moberly-Jourdain incident can be found online.

Psychometry: Information about an object or one of its users may be obtained by psychically gifted or skilled people through psychometry. First described in 1842 by Joseph R. Buchanan, the process has been used in séances, ghost hunts, and crime scene investigations. After a few minutes of handling an object, practitioners of psychometry get visual impressions or become aware of information that cannot be the result of logical inference (piecing things together from clues you might have). Ghost hunters can use psychometry to gain information about a spirit's affinity for a chair or a book or why it moves a particular glass or key. Any object that has reportedly been moved by a ghost should be examined by psychometry. Investigators may get clues about the identity of the ghost or reasons for its haunting activity.

Retrieval of information by psychometry may be possible because of changes in an object's electromagnetic field (EMF) created by repetitive handling. Its owner's use may have altered its EMF and left durable traces of the user's energy, much like a fingerprint, especially if intense emotions were associated with frequent use. A good example is my Civil War cavalry saber, which was used in several battles. Psychometrists who handle the saber become aware of fear, rage, and remorse and perceive the image of a middle-aged Union Army officer.

GROUP ORGANIZATION AND PREPARATION

It is not necessary to believe in spirits or paranormal phenomena in order to see a ghost or experience haunting activities. Indeed, most reports of ghost activities are made by unsuspecting people who never gave the matter much thought. But you should not include people in your group who openly express negative attitudes about these things. If you include skeptics, be sure they agree to maintain an open mind and participate in a positive group attitude.

Keep your group small, limited to four members if possible. Ghosts have been seen by large groups of people but small groups are more easily managed and likely to be of one mind in terms of objectives and methods.

Meet an hour or more prior to starting the ghost hunt at a location away from the site. Review the history of the ghost you seek and the previous reports of spirit activity there. Discuss the group's expectations based on known or suspected ghostly activity or specific research goals. Review any available reports of audio phenomena, still or video images, and visual apparitions and decide what methods would be optimal for recording these phenomena during your investigation.

Most importantly, agree to a plan of action if a sighting is made by any member of the group. The first priority for a ghost hunter is to maintain visual or auditory contact without a flurry of activity, such as making notes. Without breaking contact, do the following: activate recording devices; redirect audio, video, or photographic equipment to focus on the ghost; move yourself to the most advantageous position for listening or viewing the ghostly activity; attract the attention of group members with a code word, hand signal (for example, touch the top of your head), or any action that signals other hunters so they can pick up your focus of attention.

Should you attempt to interact with the ghost? Do so only if the ghost invites you to speak or move. Often, a ghost hunter's movement or noise frightens the ghost or interferes with the perception of the apparition.

SEARCHING FOR GHOSTS

There are no strict rules or guidelines for successful ghost hunting except be patient! Professional ghost hunters sometimes wait several days, weeks, even months before achieving contact with a ghost. Others have observed full-body apparitions when they least expected it, while concentrating fully on some other activity. Regardless of the depth of your research or preparation, you need to be patient. The serious ghost hunter will anticipate that several trips to a haunted site may be required before some sign of ghostly activity is observed.

If you are ghost hunting with others, it may be advantageous to station members of your group at various places in the ghost's haunting grounds and use a reliable system to alert others to spirit activity. In the event that one member sights a ghost or experiences some evidence of ghostly activity, confirmation by a second person is important in establishing validity and credibility. In the previous section, a hand signal (hand to the top of the head) was recommended as a means of informing others that they should direct their eyes and ears to a site indicated by the person in contact with a ghost. Because of this, ghost hunters will need to keep their companions within visual range at all times and be aware of hand signals.

An audio signal can often reduce the need for monitoring other ghost hunters for hand signals. A distinct audio signal may prove invaluable for alerting other hunters who may be some distance away, as when each member patrols a different portion of the site. Tugging on a length of string can be an incredibly simple yet effective signal. So can beeping devices, mechanical "crickets," and flashing penlight signals, i.e., one flash for a cold spot and two flashes for an apparition.

Handheld radios, or walkie-talkies, can also be effective. Some models can send an audio signal or activate flashing lights. Cell phones can be used but the electromagnetic activity may be uninviting to your ghost.

Remaining stationary within a room, gravesite, courtyard, or other confirmed location is often productive. If a ghost is known to have a favorite chair, bed, or other place within a room, he will manifest. If your ghost is not known to appear at a specific place within a room or an outdoors area, position yourself to gain the broadest view of the site. A corner of a room is optimal because it allows the ghost unobstructed motion while avoiding the impression of a trap set by uninvited people who occupy his favorite space. If you are outdoors at a gravesite, for instance, position yourself at the base of a tree or in the shadows of a monument to conceal your presence while affording a view of your ghost's grave. If your ghost is a mobile spirit, moving throughout a house, over a bridge, or about a courtyard or graveyard, you may have no choice but to move around the area. Search for a place where you feel a change in the thickness of the air or a cold spot or detect a peculiar odor.

Once you are on site, the above-described meditation may help you focus and maintain empathy for your ghost. Investigate sounds, even common sounds, as the ghost attempts to communicate with you. Make mental notes of the room temperature, air movement, and atmospheric sensations as you move about the site. Changes in these factors may indicate the presence of a ghost. Pay attention to your own sensations or perceptions, such as the odd feeling that someone is watching you, standing close by, or touching you. Your ghost may be hunting you!

WHAT TO DO WITH A GHOST

On occasion, professional ghost hunters make contact with a ghost by entering a trance and establishing two-way communications. The ghost hunter's companions hear him or her speak but the ghost's voice can only be heard by the trance communicator. In her book *Adventures of a Psychic*, Sylvia Browne describes several trance communication sessions. Most ghost encounters are brief with little opportunity to engage the entity in conversation. But the ghost may make gestures or acknowledge your presence through eye contact, a touch on the shoulder, sound, or a movement of an object. The ghost hunter must decide whether or not to follow the gestures or direction of a ghost.

Visitors to historic buildings in Salem and Oregon City, the historic neighborhoods of Portland, and the towns of the Oregon coast often feel the touch or tug of a ghost on their arm or shoulder. In the famous Shanghai Tunnels of historic Portland, ghosts of sailors, prostitutes, gamblers, opium-den patrons, gangsters, victims of kidnapping, or Chinese diggers often give unwary tourists the scare of a lifetime by screaming, touching, slapping, or kicking. Patrons of the legendary White Eagle Saloon may be caught up in the ghostly mayhem of a double murder and suicide.

On the highway near Cannon Beach, the Bandage Man appears alongside the road and in rearview mirrors, causing some drivers to lose control of their cars. Some witnesses report that he has attacked hitchhikers. Near Tillamook, a flannel-clad man named Lazlo is often seen by travelers. He stands in a roadside creek, fishing. Close to Lincoln City, a highway known as the Van Duzer Corridor is haunted by several apparitions. Drivers have reported a scary feeling that control of their car was taken over by an unseen being. This area is also known for strange lights that appear on the road and hover over nearby hilltops.

Lighthouses at Yaquina Head, Newport, Heceta Head, and Cape Blanco are haunted with spirits who often try to get the attention of visitors to help them find something or merely clean up their former home. While roaming coastal haunted sites, ghost hunters may also glimpse phantom ships at sea, which may be on fire or sinking, and hear the cries of doomed crew. The ghost ships of Siletz Bay and Coos Bay sometimes surprise unsuspecting visitors with a replay of horrific maritime disasters.

The idea of a close experience with a ghost is frightening to most of us. More often, the ghost's activities are directed at getting the intruder to leave a room, house, or gravesite. If you sense your ghost wants you to leave, most hunters believe it is best not to push your luck. When you have established the nature of the ghost activity, ascertained that your companions have experienced the activity, taken a few photographs and run a few minutes of audio tape, it may be time to leave. An experience with an unfriendly ghost can be disturbing.

Residents of haunted houses and employees of haunted business establishments often accept a ghost's telekinetic or audio activities without concern. It is part of the charm of a place and may add some fun to working in a spooky building.

AFTER THE GHOST HUNT

Turn off all recorders and remove them to a safe place. Some ghost hunters suspect that ghosts can erase recording media. Label your media with the date, time, and location of the ghost hunt. Use a code number for each recording. Keep a separate account of where the recording was made, date, time, and contents. Place media in a waterproof bag with your name, address, telephone number, and a note that guarantees postage in case it is misplaced. If you use photographic film, have it developed at a professional color laboratory. Pros at the lab may help you with special processing and image enhancement. Have copies made of the negatives that contain ghostly images.

All members of the group should meet right after the hunt, away from the site, for debriefing. Each hunter who witnessed a ghostly activity or apparition should make a written or audio statement describing the experience. The form presented in Appendix A should be completed by the group leader. Video and audio recordings made at the site should be reviewed and reconciled with witness statements. Then, plans should be made for a follow-up visit in the near future to the site to confirm the apparition, its nature and form, and the impressions of the initial ghost hunt.

Data about the ghost's location within a site may indicate the optimal conditions for future contact. Things to be aware of include the time of day or night, phase of the moon, season, and degree and size of cold spots, as well as form and density of the apparition. Patience and detailed records can help you to achieve the greatest reward for a ghost hunter, unmistakable proof of ghostly activity.

CHAPTER 2

Central Portland

Known as the Rose City since 1905, Portland has had several less flattering nicknames. Before Francis Pettygrove won the coin toss in 1845 that gave him the right to name the tiny settlement on the Willamette River "Portland," this place was known as "Stumptown" due to the many tree stumps that remained after timber had been harvested to build the first homes and piers. Unimpressed visitors also called it "the Clearing" and "Mudtown." Later in the 19th century, the infamous underground industry of kidnapping gave rise to the moniker "Shanghai City." Early in the 20th century that nefarious business was eradicated and the city became known for its culture, economic power, educational institutions, and architecture. Nine bridges spanning the Willamette River have inspired the unavoidable nickname "Bridge City," while other features encouraged "Rip City," "Little Beirut," "Cloud City," "Forbidden City," and "Portlandia." Some ghost hunters have offered "Spook City" in recognition of the many haunted places that attract visitors from all over the U.S.

While many of Portland's most famous ghosts transitioned into the spirit world in the 19th century, there are plenty of modern ghosts to be found in fancy hotels, unique bars and restaurants, and sites where tragic accidents and criminal activity occurred. The well-known Shanghai Tunnels are a good place to start your Portland adventure because docents will begin with an overview of the city's dark history, which includes many downtown buildings. After visiting haunted locations in central Portland, take a short drive to Pittock Mansion for a spectacular vista of the Rose City. Then drive north through the thriving Northwest District, also known as "Snob Hill" and "Trendy Third," to the site of the horrific Vanport Flood and Portland's northwest industrial area, marked by the St. Johns Bridge, where the ghost of a young murder victim keeps local legends alive and ghost hunters busy. If you plan to spend a night or two in downtown Portland, consider one of the city's haunted hotels if you truly want to have a cozy experience with some fascinating ghosts.

GHOSTS OF SHANGHAI VICTIMS

Shanghai Tunnels Tours
Meet at: Hobo's Restaurant
120 NW Third Avenue
Portland 97209
503-622-4798
www.shanghaitunnels.info

Many of the cities I've investigated sit upon an underground maze of tunnels that once housed gambling and opium dens, rooms for storing contraband such as sex slaves and liquor, cells for keeping kidnapped persons, and lockers for weapons and explosives. Early residents of Seattle, San Francisco, Sacramento, Boston, Savannah, Chicago, and Baltimore built these underground cities to keep their nefarious businesses away from the eyes of citizens, who usually had no idea what horrific enterprises were conducted a few feet below a fancy hotel or restaurant where they enjoyed high social status and the finest accommodations and cuisine these booming cities could offer. With the collusion of police and other city officials, who were often paid to ignore kidnappings, prostitution, rape, murder, gambling, and trafficking in drugs and humans, these businesses thrived for many years before cave-ins, intrusion of city projects such as new sewers, fires, floods, and disease put an end to them. Today, these underground cities attract curious tourists and ghost hunters, but most of them have been sealed or nearly destroyed, leaving only fragments of passageways and dusty rooms where many people died of disease or assault, miles from home, in the company of ruthless people who gave them no thought as their lives ended. The infamous Shanghai Tunnels system of Portland is probably the best surviving example in the U.S. of the extent of underground illegal activity and the astounding network of rooms and tunnels that made it possible. These tunnels may also be the most haunted place in the Pacific Northwest.

The Shanghai Tunnels that run beneath the streets of modern Portland started in 1850 as modest passageways between basements, usually connecting businesses owned by the same person. The subterranean link was developed to enable the movement and storage of goods and passage of workers without having to cross busy, muddy streets. Within a few years, several tunnels became connected, creating an expansive maze of tunnels lined with brick and shored up with heavy beams. It is believed that the tunnel system became so extensive that it linked many waterfront warehouses and docks with buildings as far west as NW 19th near NW Davis Street. Historical research has revealed major tunnels that stretched from the current intersection of West Burnside Street and NW 19th Street to Bunco Docks, Wooden Nickel Docks, Turk's Hotel for Sailors, Bosh Wharf, and Greenhorn Dock. These tunnels also joined a subterranean thoroughfare that ran parallel to the shore of the Willamette River, connecting warehouses, flophouses, and bars. The seclusion of these tunnels and the rooms they linked, and the ease by which entry was regulated, fostered their rapid transition from convenient passageways to networks of crime and depravity. By 1855, the underground had become a veritable city, with kitchens, storage rooms, bunkrooms, gambling dens, rooms for numerous stables of prostitutes, and cells in which kidnapped persons were kept.

Portland's Shanghai Tunnels get their name from the business of abducting drunk or drugged men and selling them to the captains of waiting ships who were desperate for crewmen. Men called "crimps" would circulate through the bars and hotels searching for potential victims. Initially, the crimps would befriend the lonely sailor and offer to buy drinks. With the collusion of the bartender, the drink was laced with a barbiturate that quickly rendered the victim nearly unconscious. The unfortunate man was then positioned over a trapdoor, called a "dead fall," and dropped into a basement, where others employed in the business would take the man's shoes and toss him in a cell until he could be transported though the tunnels to a waiting ship. It is said that many men died in the damp, dark cells of exposure, starvation, drug overdose, or injuries before they could be moved to the docks.

At the docks, a quick deal with unscrupulous captains usually netted $50 per man. Hours or days after the ship had sailed, the men would awake from their drugged or drunken stupor only to find themselves hpressed into service as sailors. Apparently, the practice was rampant in the Far East and was given the moniker "shanghai" for the city in which it started. It is said that Portland's shanghai business

The Shanghai Tunnels system, which runs under several blocks in downtown Portland, is a maze of stone walls and blocked passages that still harbor ghosts.

continued until 1941, when World War II created tens of thousands of legal jobs on merchant ships and naval vessels. Some historians believe that as many as 1,500 men were shanghaied each year from 1855 to 1941.

The tunnels were also used to house women kidnapped from the streets. Crimps posing as missionaries or police would spot women newly arrived in town and recommend a particular boardinghouse or hotel. Once checked in, the women would be drugged and transported to underground cells, where they underwent days or weeks of deprivation and psychological attacks. In many cases, they were told that they must work in the sex industry or their family would be informed that they had taken up a depraved life in Portland. Seeking to avoid an unbearable reputation, they became easily managed and locked into a sordid life that often ended with a very early death.

Historians surmise that none of these horrific enterprises could have continued without the collusion of the police department and other public officials. Word did circulate around the city, however, that waterfront bars and hotels were dangerous places even for able-bodied seamen, lumberjacks, and ranchers who had landed in town with a lot of money, eager for a good time. Some stories surfaced that were horrifying, but others were somewhat humorous. One crimp was so eager to make a few bucks that he wrapped a blanket around a wooden statue of a Native American—known as a "cigar-store Indian"—and sold the "sailor" to the captain of a ship about to set sail. Hours later, when the deceit was discovered, it so angered the captain that he threw the stature overboard. It is said that a dredge brought it to the surface 60 years later. Crimps often transported "unconscious" captives aboard a ship knowing that the unresponsive person was actually dead. It has been said that many captains were far at sea before they learned that half their crew were deceased.

Nearly 90 years of misery, fear, anger, hopelessness, hatred, and unspeakable cruelty left some indelible imprints in the tunnels that are easy to detect. Some of these are intense, leaving unsuspecting tourists dazed and frightened by the emotions that suddenly sweep through them while they snap a few pictures or chat with friends. The dusty, still air is often filled with soft moaning, sobbing, screams, gasps for air, and pleas for help. Disembodied footsteps, the squeaking hinges of cell doors, heavy breathing, grunting, and the crack of a whip are common audio experiences.

Ghosts fill these spaces, rising up from dusty cells, stacks of wooden bunk beds, the floor beneath the dead fall, or the dark passages not open to tourists. The most frequently sighted ghosts in these tunnels are those of crimps who may be condemned to remain in the dark, damp spaces where they ruined the lives of thousands of men and women. Psychics and others with sufficient sensitivity and receptivity describe the crimps as large shadowy figures, very dark, with red eyes. When they appear, even the least sensitive person gets a very uneasy feeling, as the atmosphere becomes dense and cold. Often, while listening intently to docents, tourists sense a large presence behind them as a crimp hovers over their shoulder.

A large group of ghosts, thought to be the crew of the ill-fated ship *Jennifer Jo*, shows up occasionally in various parts of the tunnels. They skulk about, searching for the crimps who pressed them into service. Legend says that a large number of men, all beaten, starved,

Remnants of bunk beds, jail cells, and kitchens stand as dusty, dark reminders of the misery of life in Portland's Shanghai Tunnels.

This ghost hunter seeks EVP from the ghosts of sailors who were drugged and jailed here until they could be smuggled aboard a ship.

and drugged, were hauled unconscious aboard the *Jennifer Jo*, a ship desperate for a crew. Not willing to wait for the shanghaied men to awaken, the captain set sail from Bunco's Dock in the middle of the night, only to sink somewhere in the Columbia River. All hands went down with the ship, including the shanghaied crew who were still locked below decks. Angry and seething with pain, these men manifest in the tunnels by laying a wet hand on the shoulder of tourists.

Not all the ghosts in these tunnels are angry or in pain. The ghost of a young boy, said to be about nine years old, has been spotted by many witnesses as he moves from a bunk-bed cell to a hallway and then vanishes. Some ghost hunters report that he carries a bucket or chamber pot. It is likely that this boy was an orphan who found a job in the tunnels emptying the large volume of waste produced by all the men and women help captive there.

With rare exceptions, access to the Shanghai Tunnels is possible only by joining a scheduled tour. Knowledgeable docents provide plenty of anecdotes and history, and a few ghost stories, while allowing tourists time to snap pictures and perform EVP sweeps. Despite the

Ghost hunters meet at Hobo's Restaurant before descending below Portland's streets to the Shanghai Tunnels.

large number of people in a tour, ghostly manifestations are common. Spirits come forward and speak up as if they wish to get the attention of anyone who might free them of their miserable existence. Be patient and be ready.

GHOST OF THE MURDERED PROSTITUTE

Old Town Pizza
226 NW Davis Street
Portland 97209
503-222-9999
www.oldtownpizza.com

For more than 100 years, the ghost of Nina (pronounced Nigh-na) has wandered through the old Merchant Hotel building, but no one has determined why she remains near the site of her murder. At times, her presence is indicated only by the faint fragrance of her signature perfume, the swishing sound of her long skirt, or a sweet voice whispering a word or two. When she has sufficient energy, and potential witnesses have the necessary level of sensitivity, Nina appears in a black dress with her long dark hair pulled back in a tight bun. She apparently likes what she sees in the renovated building, because she walks through Old Town Pizza without an expression of distress and sometimes smiles at astonished patrons. Ghost hunters have captured several light anomalies in digital images and a few fascinating EVP that may be Nina's manifestations. Staff members of the restaurant report that they have left out a bowl containing Scrabble tiles overnight only to find that a ghostly hand has arranged particular letters in curious but intelligible messages. Nina is often sought in a small booth that was once the elevator shaft of the Merchant Hotel. Her name, allegedly inscribed by her ghostly hand, can be seen on one of the bricks in a wall of the booth, although there is no unequivocal historical record that a woman named Nina ever lived or worked in the building. Local psychics, however, report frequent interactions with this ghost that affirm her name is, indeed, Nina and her life was tragically cut short by murder.

In 1881, the Merchant Hotel was conceived as a state-of-the-art hotel that was so advanced in its architecture, plumbing, gas lighting, and other conveniences that construction spanned four years. Built by lumber barons Adolph, Louis, and Theodore Nicolai, the place opened in 1885 and immediately attracted clientele from the city's high society who sought the best drinks and food and most luxurious rooms for private liaisons. It is unlikely that Nina lived or worked in the fine rooms and suites of the Merchant Hotel, however. Her life was that of a prostitute, possibly kidnapped as a teenager and kept in the dark rooms of the hotel's basement that connected with Portland's infamous underground city.

Legend says that Nina was contacted by local missionaries who promised her a safe escape from pimps and guards if she would reveal the identities of the men who operated the wretched prostitution, gambling, and shanghai business in the underground caverns that stretched from the basement of the Merchant Hotel to numerous other buildings and, ultimately, the waterfront. Feeling assured that

Old Town Pizza occupies the once-glorious Merchant Hotel, where Portland's elite partied and died.

she would be safely delivered from her miserable life, Nina agreed to give up the information. This risky plan was discovered, however, by someone associated with her captors, so she was summoned to the third floor of the hotel under the pretext that she was to entertain a special guest. Upon arriving at the meeting, Nina was accosted and thrown down the elevator shaft to her death.

I could find no historical record of the murder, but local ghost hunters and purveyors of urban legends insist it is true. The killer, of course, was never captured or identified. Many years later, the hydraulic elevator was removed, leaving the shaft where Nina died as an air vent. Today, a popular booth in Old Town Pizza occupies the spot, and patrons often linger there for hours hoping to have an encounter with Nina.

I found her there on one occasion. After I sat alone for nearly an hour, the space around me was suddenly filled with the fragrance of a perfume and the sound of a swishing skirt. Instantly, the small space felt crowded, as a faint voice said in a lilting, melodic tone, "I'm here." During other visits to Old Town Pizza, my companion and I have heard the tapping sound of a woman's boot on the floor at a time when

It is said that the ghost of Nina, murdered at this spot, scratched her name on this brick.

no one close by was moving about. Again, the fragrance of a pungent perfume filled the space around us before suddenly vanishing.

SUICIDE GHOST

The Heathman Hotel
1001 SW Broadway
Portland 97205

The number three seems to be linked to a haunting at the Heathman Hotel. For many years, rooms that end with the number have been the site of intense paranormal activity that experts have attributed to a suicide that took place in room 1003. In 1999, a celebrity psychic known to me visited the Heathman and perceived the presence of a woman about 30 years old who jumped to her death from a window. Some speculate that the woman cursed the hotel as she fell to the ground, passing rooms with numbers that ended with a three. Her reason for cursing the hotel and haunting these rooms is unknown. My research failed to uncover an official record of a person committing suicide at this hotel. The place opened in 1927, however, and old records are difficult to locate. Also, powerful businessmen often had great success burying a story that might harm the reputation of a successful enterprise.

In room 803, an apparition manifests that is most often vague and transparent. On some occasions, the manifestation reveals more details and resembles a woman with shoulder-length, brown, curly hair and a sharp chin. Details sometimes include a facial expression of deep anguish or fear. The paranormal activity in this room has been described as poltergeist manifestations, but it seems clear that this is incorrect terminology. Experts attribute poltergeist activity to a living person who is emotionally or mentally disturbed. When that person, termed the "agent," is removed from the scene, all paranormal activity ceases. In the case of room 803, there is no single, identifiable, living person consistently at the scene when bizarre events occur. These events include intense cold spots, sounds that include sobbing and moaning, and the movement of personal objects to strange locations.

In addition, guests have reported returning to the room after an absence of a few hours only to find that furniture has been moved, towels used, and glasses of water placed at various locations. Similar but less intense activity has been reported in room 703.

In every one of the "3" rooms, guests have called the front desk to report an eerie presence. Sometimes a face stares at them from out of the darkness. When the log for the electronic lock is checked, there is no indication of inappropriate entry.

The Heathman Hotel should not be confused with its predecessor of the same name. The original Heathman was completed in 1926 at the corner of SW Park and SW Salmon. Designed to cater to wealthy timber barons and politicians, it was so successful that construction of the New Heathman Hotel was begun early in 1927. Standing 10 stories tall and faced with brick, it was even more luxurious than its namesake. It opened on December 17, 1927, with the expectation that it would attract the growing population of wheeler-dealers in Portland. The party staged to celebrate the hotel's opening was a grand event. All 1,200 workmen who built the place were invited, in addition to the members of wealthy society who were expected to make the business a success. By some accounts, this party was a wild affair with guests visiting many of the rooms and, perhaps, conducting several private parties behind closed doors. Liquor flowed generously despite Prohibition, which may have caused the happy event to lead to an accident, suicide, or something sinister. It isn't too much of a stretch to wonder if a private party turned into something quite negative and, in a drunken stupor, a man tossed an uncooperative woman out a window.

GHOSTS OF FANCY GUESTS

Benson Hotel
309 SW Broadway
Portland 97205
866-599-6674

The Benson Hotel is one of a handful of historical hotels that include the Heathman (built 1927), Commodore (built 1925), Imperial (built 1894), and Governor (built 1909). Constructed in 1912 by Simon Benson (1852-1942), and opened on March 5, 1913, the hotel fulfilled his wish to create a world-class hotel in Portland. A philanthropist but always a wise businessman, Benson also saw the opportunity to cash in on Portland's population boom, which occurred between the 1905 Lewis and Clark Centennial Exposition and the Great Depression. Today, the 287-room hotel is distinguished by its French Second Empire style, spectacular décor, elegant staircase that conveys guests into a large lobby complete with a huge fireplace, and ornate ceilings from which French chandeliers hang.

Simon Benson occupies a prominent place in Portland history for many reasons. His philanthropy included a gift of $100,000 to the Portland School District to help fund the construction of a polytechnic school. During World War I, the school was used to train soldiers, but in 1919 it officially opened as Benson Polytechnic High School. In 1921, he deeded nine acres of land overlooking the Willamette River that ultimately became Madrona Park. These and many other generous acts were the result of Benson's philosophy expressed in this quote: "No one has the right to die and not leave something to the public and for the public good."

Simon Benson may be remembered most for a gift of $10,000 to the city of Portland used to install 20 bronze public drinking fountains. Being opposed to the consumption of alcohol, even after Prohibition, he was often incensed by drunks who wandered the streets. Since many of these men claimed they drank beer or liquor because they were thirsty, Benson believed that the installation of water fountains might quench their thirst and reduce their visits to Portland's many bars. Many of those fountains, dubbed Benson Bubblers, are still in use today.

The ghostly image of a well-dressed gentleman has been seen descending the Benson Hotel's staircase to the lobby before moving into the lounge, where guests often enjoy a drink or two. He is said to cast a disapproving look at people before disappearing. Moments later, guests discover that their drinks have been toppled. This kind of behavior recalls Benson's aversion to alcohol. Ghost hunters might trigger the manifestation of this ghost by taking a seat in the lounge and ordering a tall drink.

Opened in 1913, the Benson Hotel retains the beauty and atmosphere of the period while offering guests modern amenities and chance encounters with ghosts.

Ghosts dressed in early-20th-century clothing have been spotted descending this elegant staircase to the lobby of the Benson Hotel.

A stylishly dressed female ghost wanders the hallway on several floors. Witnesses have reported that she wears a turquoise dress and walks with a graceful gait. She often appears lifelike, but when astonished guests turn to watch her, she vanishes. This ghost is most often sighted on the seventh and 12th floors and in the lobby.

Several guests at the Benson have posted reports of their experiences with the ghost of a little boy. Appearing to be three years old, he shows up at the bedside, looking at guests who are about to drift off to sleep. One woman reported that she touched the kid and he felt warm and solid. Apparently, he likes to play, because he makes faces described as "scary" and pulls blankets from the bed.

In researching hotels and inns for paranormal activity, most ghost hunters look for a history of untimely natural death, suicide, or murder. At the Benson, there is only one official demise, that of Mitch Mitchell (1947-2008). He was the drummer for rhythm-and-blues and rock performer Jimi Hendrix (1942-70). Many years after Hendrix's death, Mitchell was featured in the 2008 Experience

Hendrix Tour. After four weeks on the road with performances in 18 cities, he was showing signs of slowing down and an unsteady gait attributed to many years of alcohol-related illness. On the night of November 12, Mitchell retired to his room at the Benson, only to be found dead at three o'clock in the morning by a hotel employee. The Multnomah County medical examiner ruled that the death was due to natural causes.

Some writers believe that Mitchell haunted the Benson Hotel, manifesting as a child because he was a child actor in England and that was the happiest period of his life. I don't believe that this assertion is valid, however. Mitchell achieved stardom as a teenager on a TV show in the UK called *Jennings and Derbyshire* and landed a leading role in the 1960 British film *Bottoms Up*. If he haunts the hotel as an earlier version of himself, it would likely be as a teenager. Witnesses claim that the child ghost of the Benson Hotel is about three years old.

GHOSTS OF THE OLD HOTEL

Meier and Frank Building
The Nines Hotel
525 SW Morrison Street
Portland 97204
877-229-9995
www.thenines.com

The ghosts that haunt this luxury hotel are linked to the former Meier and Frank department store. Constructed in 1913 with major additions in 1915 and 1932, the building seems to have ghosts on several floors connected to the early history of the store. Meier and Frank, founded in Portland in 1857, was the flagship store and headquarters of what as to become the largest retailer west of the Mississippi. Acquired by May Department Stores in 1966, the enterprise ultimately ended up in the hands of Macy's. Since 2008, the Nines Hotel has occupied the top nine floors, while the lower floors are retail space for Macy's.

The 17-story, glazed terra-cotta building, located in downtown

Portland, replaced an earlier structure built in 1898. Conceived by Sigmund Frank (1850-1910), the current building featured an astounding 11 acres of retail space. Since Sigmund died before its completion, there is speculation that he roams the floors to this day, admiring the huge building he envisioned. Aaron Meier (1831-89) may wander about the place, too. At the age of 26, he founded the retail business in a 35-by-50-foot mercantile store at 137 Front Street at a time when Portland had a population of only 1,300. In 1878, the Great Portland Fire destroyed the store together with 20 downtown blocks. A partnership with Emil Frank, Sigmund's brother, enabled him to rebuild at the same site. In 1888, Emil left the business, and Sigmund headed the organization after Meier died in 1889.

Long after Sigmund's death, Meier and Frank executives hired a 21-year-old man named Clark Gable (1901-60) to work as a necktie salesman. Clark stayed on the job only a few years while he gained experience in local theater.

Among the credible accounts of ghostly activity in the building is that of former Meier and Frank executive Kay Hale. Working late one night, Kay decided to sleep on a sofa in her office rather than drive to her home. Much of the floor where her office was located was filled with old merchandise awaiting shipment to other stores or to the manufacturer. Sometime during the night, she was awakened by loud noises, as if a crew of men were moving heavy boxes around. Occasionally, the sound of the freight elevator gate moving up and down echoed across the floor and through the thin walls of Kay's office. Several times, she heard the elevator move as if it were descending to lower floors. During all of this commotion, Kay heard several voices speaking sharply in hushed tones and sometimes laughing. Too frightened to open her door to see if a night crew had arrived to move merchandise, Kay locked her door and waited until the noise had abated. In the morning, she inquired if a crew had, indeed, worked through the night on her floor. She became nervous as fellow executives denied any knowledge of a work order that might account for Kay's experience. To make this episode even more chilling, Kay found that none of the boxes on her floor had been moved, yet she had heard men working for hours. No one in the building could offer information that might explain the ghostly sounds that Kay had heard. When she approached a security guard for his opinion, he said, "It must have been the ghosts."

The Macy's shoe department on the second floor has been the site of some interesting paranormal activity. For a period of several weeks, when store staff members arrived in the morning, they found that several pairs of shoes had been mixed in the most bizarre way. It was assumed this was a practical joke until surveillance video revealed shoes flying off a shelf and socks tossed into the air.

The most disturbing account comes from members of a cleaning crew who worked in the kitchen of the eighth-floor Georgian Room Restaurant one night. They all witnessed bizarre paranormal activity that included utensils flying across the room, objects sliding off the counters, drawers opening and slamming shut, and supplies such as flour and salt blasting into the air. Some of the workers reported that they perceived an evil presence that wanted them to leave the floor. When asked to describe this entity, one man said it was "too terrible to describe." This experience was so frightening that the entire cleaning crew quit the job.

The Georgian Room is beautifully furnished and the food is great. In April of 2014, I spoke to a person who had worked there for three years. She denied having a paranormal experience in the kitchen or any other place within the restaurant. She did, however, tell me about the experiences of her co-workers. Apparently, they never encountered anything malevolent, but there does seem to be a spirit in the kitchen that likes things put back in their proper place.

The library is a spectacular room decorated in an Old World style with leather furniture and built-in walnut bookcases. I experienced a benevolent presence there. This spirit was that of an elderly man who seemed quite pleased with the energy of the place. I suspect this ghost is Sigmund Frank.

THE LOTUS CARDROOM AND CAFE

932 SW Third Avenue
Portland 97204
503-227-6185
www.lotuscardroomandcafe.com

Regulars and workers at several bars in central Portland can tell some fascinating ghost stories that will give you a chill. Joe's Cellar (1332 NW 21st Avenue), the Silverado (318 SW Third Avenue), Hobo's (120 NW Third Avenue), Kells Irish Restaurant and Pub (112 SW Second Avenue), Scooter McQuade's (1321 SW Washington Street), and Ash Street Saloon (225 SW Ash Street) all have a reputation for paranormal activity. The Lotus Cardroom and Café, however, may be haunted by a powerful spirit that shows up frequently and leaves witnesses shaking.

The three-story brick building was opened in 1909 as the Albion Hotel. With a large basement that was once connected to Portland's notorious Shanghai Tunnels, the busy bar had a number of customers who had a few drinks and then disappeared. It is likely that some dropped into the cellar and were shanghaied onto waiting vessels at the nearby waterfront.

In 1924, the Albion Hotel became the Lotus Hotel, featuring a cardroom, bar, and café. A mural that stretches across the entire back wall of the building depicts elements of this history. It does not indicate the bar's notoriety as a speakeasy drinking establishment during Prohibition, however. That is left to the dark history of downtown Portland, but it is likely that a brisk bar business continued through the 1920s and into the 1930s, because local police were inclined to ignore liquor traffickers and other nefarious enterprise.

Whatever went on in the basement of the Lotus Hotel has left something there that has been described as male, evil, and frightening. It has been reported that, for many years, several employees could not muster the courage to go into the cellar alone. Even fully illuminated, the place is said to have a darkness and musty atmosphere that is disturbing. The spirit that occupies this space hasn't hurt anyone, but he is clearly angry about something that likely led this death. Perhaps this fellow was drugged and dropped into the basement only to die before he was carted off to a ship awaiting a shanghaied crew.

In the bar, stunned witnesses have watched as glasses move and barstools shake. Bursts of sound have been experienced here that include a honkytonk piano, a lady singing, and several men speaking simultaneously.

The rooms on the second and third floors of this building have a bizarre atmosphere that has been described in terms that suggest

Blocked tunnels don't stop ghosts from running through the Shanghai Tunnels under the Lotus Cardroom and Café.

paranormal activity occurs here. People who have spent a lot of time on these floors have reported unexplained footsteps in several rooms and hallways, the sound of creaking doors without movement of the doors, indistinct visual impressions, and that creepy feeling that unseen being is standing close.

GHOSTS OF THE MURDERED MOB

Scooter McQuade's Restaurant and Bar
1321 SW Washington Street
Portland 97205
503-248-4060

In the latter part of the 19th century, the building that houses Scooter McQuade's Restaurant and Bar was an integral part of the shanghai industry. Drunk or drugged men were dropped through a dead fall to the basement below and kept until they could be transported through the tunnels to the waterfront. Throughout Prohibition (1920-33), the shanghai business was much less active, but the dark spaces underneath downtown bars and the tunnels that connected them were filled with bootleggers who stored contraband whiskey and beer. With so much booze, parties in the tunnels were quite frequent, despite the dark and dingy atmosphere. Urban legend tells us that one night in the 1920s, a large group of revelers was attacked by a rival gang wearing stolen police uniforms. As the assailants fired tommy guns and swung axes, the panicked crowd ran through a progressively narrowing tunnel until they created a human plug that would deny anyone safe egress. It is said that the attackers killed everyone and then smashed barrels of whiskey, leaving a telltale odor in the basement for decades.

Nearly a century later, paranormal investigators and unsuspecting patrons of this popular bar often encounter a frightened mob of spirits as they emerge from the cellar and dash to the door before vanishing. Witnesses describe these ghosts as angry or scared, glowing humanoid shapes. Some of them are quite lifelike and glare at astonished patrons as they knock over drinks and cause chairs to scoot across the floor. Psychics who try to communicate with these ghosts report that many of these spirits are in a "snarky mood."

A group of ghost hunters staged a formal investigation of the basement and experienced some amazing audio phenomena. Pressing their ears to the bricks that now seal the tunnel, these investigators reported hearing moans, terrified cries, and loud taps that may have been gunshots. The sounds were so clear that ghost hunters had the very strong impression that they started some distance down the tunnel and then grew louder as the ghostly mob approached the brick wall.

GHOSTS OF THE JITTERBUG DANCERS

Crystal Ballroom
1332 West Burnside Street
Portland 97209
503-225-0047

Ghostly dancers may still gyrate across the floor of the Crystal Ballroom, oblivious to the passage of time and numerous changes in the style of music and entertainment offered at this iconic venue. Built in 1914 and opened as the Cotillion Hall, the place has staged grand balls, dance recitals, beat poetry readings, and concerts with music ranging from folk to blues to rock. In the 1920s, Portland's citizens paid a nickel to spend the evening square dancing on the third floor. The only refreshment available was apple cider, due to Prohibition. That didn't stop dancers from creating so much revelry that the ballroom became an official venue of the "Roaring Twenties," complete with police raids.

Early in the 1930s, owner Dad Watson died, leaving the place in the hands of Ralph Farrier, who renamed it the Crystal Ballroom. Farrier continued weekly square dances until the mid-1950s, but he is credited with expanding the ballroom offerings to a wide variety of entertainment. In the 1960s, famous acts such as Marvin Gaye, Ike and Tina Turner, and James Brown performed. Later, Gregg Allman and the Grateful Dead appeared there, but from the 1970s to the mid-1990s, the place was essentially closed. Eventually, space was rented to artists and private parties were staged, but squatters and vandals almost ruined the venue. Fortunately, in 1997 the McMenamin brothers bought the place and made extensive renovations that included a bar and restaurant on the first floor, a dance floor on the second floor, and a huge ballroom on the third floor. The décor is beautiful with flamboyant wall sconces and light fixtures, peculiar paintings, and huge windows that offer a view of West Burnside Street. People who come there for music and dance seem to easily pick up on the energy created by a century of music and joy. Social scientists call this phenomenon "the power of place."

People who work in this building have spotted apparitions of men and women in clothing typical of the 1920s and '30s. Some of these ghostly images move about in a style of dance called the Jitterbug. The term is early-20th-century slang for the tremors sometimes seen in alcoholics (delirium tremens). Bodily motions are somewhat chaotic and often don't conform to the rhythm of accompanying music. The term "Jitterbug" is often applied to swing dancers or those dancing the "Jive." One dancer described it as "cutting loose and going crazy." The

Ghosts of Jitterbug dancers and other spirits still roam the hallways of the Crystal Ballroom in downtown Portland.

Jitterbug is a high-energy dance that is fun and thrilling, sometimes giving people the greatest joy of their young lives. So it's no wonder that ghosts have returned to the Crystal Ballroom to relive those precious times.

Staff members also hear crowds of people talking and laughing, both men and women. Unexplained sounds often include footsteps and the sliding of shoe leather across the dance floor. Sensitives, including myself, perceive intense energy emanating from the brick walls of the building. It is likely that the minerals of the bricks have "recorded" sounds and images of musicians and dancers that play back at times. The energy of the ballroom may enable ghosts to manifest as well.

GHOST OF THE DIMINUTIVE WOMAN

Commodore Grocery

621 SW 16th Avenue
Portland 97205
503-224-0661

Commodore Grocery is a tiny convenience store tucked into one of the basement floors of the stately Commodore Building. Built in 1925, the art deco features of the structure have elements that seem more gothic, making the place seem a little spooky. Several gold-painted bird effigies, mounted on a ledge above the first floor, appear to be cormorants decorated with Inca headgear and contribute to the impression that there is something weird about the place. The main entrance to the building faces SW Morrison, but the grocery is entered from SW 16th Avenue. The place is easy to miss, but ghost hunters will find this little store quite interesting because it is haunted by the ghost of a young woman.

People who have worked in the store and regular customers agree that the ghost of Commodore Grocery is a small woman or girl, standing less than five feet tall. She always appears disheveled, wearing a dirty white jacket or hoodie, with her dark hair gathered in a ponytail. Those who have seen her clearest manifestations report that her face looks wrinkled. At times she has given witnesses the impression that she is Native American or Eskimo. This ghost usually appears in the rear of the store and remains motionless for several seconds before vanishing. On some occasions, she has been seen dashing back and forth across the central aisle. This ghost never speaks or makes hand gestures to astonished witnesses. She does, however, project intense emotions that sensitive people detect. These emotions include fear and anxiety, which, in turn, evoke sadness in witnesses, leaving them quite unsettled. Some customers who have watched as this ghost vanished have been frightened by the experience, but there was no impression of malevolence.

There is no record of a robbery involving a shooting or other horrific event in Commodore Grocery that might explain the presence of this ghost. She may have been a homeless person who died nearby and found comfort amid the grocery's humming cooler cases and dim lighting.

Despite its current elegant façade, the Commodore Building was once a flophouse for sailors and other transients. During the 1940s,

This quaint neighborhood grocery may be a meeting place for ghosts dating from the days when the Commodore Building was a flophouse for sailors.

stories circulated about a ghostly "woman in white" that wandered the halls, creating a trail of cold air while emitting a bizarre laugh. A pharmacy once existed in the space occupied by the grocery, prompting some writers to speculate that this ghost may have had something to do with that business.

GHOST OF THE MATRON

Pittock Mansion
3229 NW Pittock Drive
Portland 97210
503-823-3623
www.pittockmansion.org

At first, Georgiana Pittock didn't like the idea of moving from downtown Portland to a house perched on the crest of West Hills.

She was certain she would feel isolated in this spot that was a half-mile beyond the city limits and accessed only by a very steep, winding road. But the 23-room, Tenino Sandstone mansion surrounded by 46 acres of manicured gardens overlooking Portland convinced her that, at the age of 68, she could make the move and be quite happy in the grand house.

Within days of her arrival, Georgiana set the gardeners to work planting her favorite roses and added personal touches to the interior décor. Her husband, Oregon publisher and industrialist Henry Pittock, had spared no expense creating the spectacular mansion. He even called in a few political favors to ensure that the place was completed before the end of 1914. A spectacular marble staircase, great windows with panoramic views, chandeliers, a music room, and several bathrooms comprised a home that would be a dream house for anyone on the planet. Modern conveniences included an elevator traveling between the three floors, indirect lighting, intercoms, a walk-in refrigerator, central heating, a dumbwaiter, and a central vacuuming unit.

With a family of children and grandchildren, and frequent social events attended by the finest people in the city, the place was always filled with happiness. Georgiana loved the grand mansion, but her time there was short. In 1918, only four years after settling into the place, she died at the age of 72. Many believe she is still there, unwilling to give up the house on a hill, the things that gave her comfort in her final years, and her beloved gardens.

Henry Pittock (1835-1919) died a year after Georgiana, leaving a legacy of accomplishment that, to many, epitomizes the pioneer spirit. Arriving in Portland in 1853, penniless and only 18 years old, Henry struggled to find work in the printing trade. Over a period of six years, he worked his way up to manager and editor of the weekly *Oregonian* newspaper. By 1861, he owned the newspaper, and over the next four years he made a fortune by publishing news of Civil War battles and Lincoln's assassination ahead of his competitors. After a long career that included political scandal and feuds, he died in his grand mansion on January 28, 1919, at the age of 83, leaving an estate worth nearly $8 million.

Henry may haunt the manse, but many paranormal experts believe that Georgiana is the most active ghost in the place. In 1958, the last Pittock family member moved out and the house stood vacant until 1964, when the city of Portland purchased it to save it from further

This magnificent mansion stands as a monument to Henry Pittock, who arrived in Portland penniless but became one of the city's wealthiest residents.

deterioration. After 15 months of restoration, the Pittock Mansion opened to the public in 1965. About 80,000 people visited the site in 2013.

Since 1965, staff members and visitors have recorded numerous strange events that many attribute to the ghost of Georgiana. A boyhood picture of Henry Pittock was placed on a mantel in one of the bedrooms, but unseen hands move it from time to time, setting it in locations that were Georgiana's spots. The fragrance of roses often fills a room when fresh flowers are nowhere to be found in the house. Voices of two elderly people, a man and a woman, have often been heard. Typically these are brief bursts of sound in which each voice speaks only two or three words. Slow-moving footsteps have been heard passing over the threshold of several rooms. A few feet beyond the threshold, the sound is no longer heard.

A few fortunate visitors have spotted Georgiana's apparition in the basement, music room, and her bedroom. Occasionally, her image is seen reflected in a mirror, glass covering the paintings, and the windows. Georgiana has been known to create that creepy feeling that some unseen being is standing close behind.

The Pittock family lived and died in this mansion, leaving behind imprints and a few ghosts.

The ghost of Georgiana Pittock is sometimes seen in her charming sitting room, serving tea to a guest.

Henry manifests infrequently, but his presence is unmistakable. Standing behind people who criticize the opulence of the house or its period furnishings, he creates a strong impression of a man bearing down on the person who dared disparage his great accomplishment. Henry is pleased, however, when people marvel at the beauty of the mansion. He walks about with them as if he is hosting a special tour.

A variety of other paranormal phenomena occurs in the house and gardens. Staff members have turned off the lights for the night only to witness all of them turn on without explanation. Heavy footsteps have been noted leaving the house through a door on the lower floor. These footsteps have been detected in the garden, heading toward a side door of the mansion. On the second floor of the house, window latches have been known to lock and unlock when the weather changes abruptly.

Listen for slow, shuffling footsteps that might be made by an elderly person, and sniff the air for the fragrance of roses. If you detect these phenomena, Georgiana and Henry may be near.

GHOSTS OF THE SPIES

Wilcox Mansion
931 SW King Avenue
Portland 97205

This spectacular 13,000-square-foot mansion was built in 1893 as a home for industrialist Theodore Burney Wilcox (1856-1918) and his family. Many believe that Theodore's ghost, or that of his son, Theodore, Jr., haunt this place, but my experiences there, and the reports of others, suggest that the paranormal activity may be attributed to the manse's somewhat dark history.

The mansion consists of a basement, two floors constructed of sandstone, and two upper floors of wood. The interior mahogany woodwork is considered some of the finest in the Pacific Northwest. In fact, a lady I spoke to at the house told me that it is superior to that found in the Pittock Mansion. The place has nine fireplaces, a lot of hand-carved decorative trim, and a spectacular staircase. When I last visited, it had undergone renovation into offices and meeting rooms. The radio station KWJJ, which operated in the house since the 1950s, moved a few years earlier, and access is now restricted to those having legitimate business there. That hasn't stopped the circulation of stories about this mansion, however.

Almost 20 years after the death of Theodore, Sr., the manse was leased by a Soviet agency whose staff traveled the Pacific Northwest purchasing farming equipment to ship to the Soviet Union. By 1939, the agents operating out of the house focused on military supplies. Following Germany's invasion of the Soviet Union in 1941, the staff that occupied the Wilcox Mansion was augmented by Soviet spies whose job it was to capture German spies operating on America's West Coast. It has been suggested that many Germans were brought to the house from Portland's docks, as well as San Francisco and Seattle, and then incarcerated in the basement while they were interrogated. This imprisonment may have included the torture and even death of German spies.

Former staff members of the radio station, who worked in cubicles

The Wilcox Mansion has a fascinating history that includes use by Soviet agents during World War II.

in the basement, reported that it had the disturbing atmosphere of a dungeon, often causing them to take a break upstairs. Frequently, the apparition of a short, stocky figure would be seen floating across the room. Invariably, this figure would move to the entrance of a tunnel that led to the carriage house. Nothing sinister was ever experienced in the basement, but a woman hired to clean the place was truly frightened when she went there one night. Moving about the darkened space looking for cleaning supplies, she heard loud, heavy breathing. She raced upstairs and immediately quit.

Employees reported that when the atmosphere in the basement became thick and oppressive, people on the main floor would notice that a huge chandelier would start swinging.

A piano located on the main floor would sound as if an invisible ghost were playing it. Two DJs had numerous sightings of a man walking around the piano. Dressed in a white suit and hat, this fellow gazed upon the piano as if it were a cherished object. This ghost was never menacing, but the DJs reported they were so spooked by his appearance that they locked themselves in their sound booth while working late at night.

The ghost of a female servant has been spotted walking the hallways on the second floor. She wears a black uniform and a white hat and gives witnesses the impression that she is from the 1920s. The apparition of an older man, perhaps 70, has also been spotted moving about the place. This has led to speculation that Theodore Wilcox, Sr., haunts his beloved mansion.

Other places to hunt ghosts:

LOST GRAVES

Across the street from Venue 126
SW Second Avenue at SW Pine Street
Portland 97204

Astute ghost hunters don't limit themselves to historical buildings or places where horrendous crimes took place. Often, spirits are found where you least expect them. An innocuous-looking parking lot might be the site of intense paranormal activity. For instance, across the street from a Portland nightspot called Venue 126 is a parking lot that accommodates about 50 cars. So many strange things have happened in this space that many locals believe it is haunted. EMF detectors, dowsing rods, psychics, and EVP experts have obtained enough evidence to confirm suspicions. But why would this parking lot be haunted?

Some have speculated that it covers a burial ground for Indians who died from diseases imported by Yankee and British pioneers. My research suggests that a building once stood at this site that was connected to the nearby waterfront by a tunnel. Similar to the Shanghai Tunnels, this passageway was used to smuggle prostitutes and men who had been drugged and kidnapped. A fire in 1908 destroyed the building and killed several people who had been trapped in the basement and tunnel.

KELLER AUDITORIUM

222 SW Clay Street
Portland 97201
503-274-6560

The Spanish flu epidemic hit Portland in two waves, one in 1918 and another in 1923. In the first one, about 1,000 people died in a 10-week period. As fear gripped the city, Mayor George Baker banned all public meetings, including school events, church services, and sporting activities. Hospitals, funeral homes, and morgues became so filled that the Civic Auditorium was quickly adapted to care for those who might make a recovery and to process bodies for burial.

It is now known as Keller Auditorium, and hundreds of people were brought here for medical treatment, only to be moved to the makeshift morgue. Many of them have left imprints here of the intense emotional experience of fighting for one's life amid an epidemic that killed so many. Residual energy in the form of unexplained cold spots and places where sensitive people feel misery, fear, and strong anxiety may be found in several locations.

GHOST OF THE FEMALE COMIC

Comedy Sportz
1963 NW Kearney Street
Portland 97209
503-236-8888

This unassuming building sits in a residential neighborhood a few blocks from busy NW 21st Street, where visitors find some fantastic bars and restaurants. The Comedy Sportz Club may be a little off the track of all of those poplar eating and drinking establishments, but it has a huge following in Portland. Known for showcasing up-and-coming comics, the place offers open-mic night for improv as well as some hilarious comedy by professionals. Despite all the laughter, staff members and patrons sometimes notice the ghost of a female comic that haunts the place. In the rooms behind the stage, people often hear disembodied laughter interspersed with a woman speaking in a loud but usually incoherent voice. Those who have heard this voice get the impression that a female comic is delivering a barrage of one-liners. This ghost also creates light anomalies in various parts of the building, plays with light switches, and causes chairs to vibrate.

GHOSTS OF THE OLD STUFF

Hoodoo Antiques
122 NW Couch Street
Portland 97209
503-360-3409
www.hoodooantiques.com

Opened in 1994, this small but incredibly fascinating antique store harbors some spirits that ghost hunters will find eager to communicate with the living. In my experience there, communication is usually not through spoken words but emotions and beneficent influences. For that reason, empaths will have a great time in this store.

The store's Web site makes the point that "hoodoo" is colloquial English for "Voodoo," a word originating in the West African

Places such as Hoodoo Antiques are depositories for all kinds of arcane objects that may have ghosts attached.

language Fon. To many people, Voodoo means magic, witchcraft, occult religion, and the invocation of arcane spirits that may affect living persons in good or bad ways. Hoodoo, on the other hand, has evolved to mean something rare and priceless linked to supernatural forces or beings. Evoked by a practitioner, hoodoo helps people attain power or good luck, usually in a quest for money, health, or love. I don't know if positive things come to those who shop in this store, but when I visit this place, I always get the feeling that they will.

Certainly, all the old stuff here has a lot of spirit attached. That is true of virtually every antique store. The old brick walls and vast array of metal and stone objects seem to have created the right conditions to sustain spirits that can't let go of cherished items from their lives.

CHAPTER 3

East Portland Communities

In the latter part of the 19th century, the Willamette River separated Portland's business center and more affluent neighborhoods from the industrial east shore. The social dichotomy resulted in the eastern half of the city becoming a micro-region where lawlessness was common, social justice was a rare commodity, and misery was the standard. All of this created vast numbers of tortured souls who, despite the passage of many decades, haunt places that are prime venues for ghost hunters.

Today, the river is spanned by nine bridges, virtually eliminating these social, economic, and transportation barriers. The unification of Eastside and Westside urban centers was further cemented by the location of the Portland International Airport, the Moda Center (home of the Portland Trail Blazers basketball team), and several other cultural attractions on the east side of the Willamette River. Despite the tremendous growth of the city since the 1960s, many unique neighborhoods remain on the east side of Portland where ghost hunters will find old coffeehouses, theatres, bars and restaurants, beautiful parks, and fascinating historic sites. These places with a strong local character provide visitors with different experiences than may be encountered in downtown Portland. Several haunted locations highlight local history, social development, and tragic events that created some very active ghosts. And while you roam the east side of Portland, don't forget to stop by the famous Voodoo Doughnut store at 1501 NE Davis Street.

GHOST OF THE LONELY MAN

North Portland Library
512 North Killingsworth Street
Portland 97217
503-988-5394
www.multcolib.org/library-location/north-portland

There is no historical record of a death occurring inside the North Portland Library but there is substantial evidence that the place is haunted. The second-floor meeting room, a space that is always kept locked unless a lecture or other gathering is staged, is often visited by a male ghost whose image was first noted on a security monitor. This fellow appears seated in a chair, motionless, as if he were listening to a lecture or waiting for someone. Library staff members spotted him on the monitor and, initially suspecting an intruder, raced upstairs to the meeting room only to find it locked and empty. Often appearing lifelike, the man has been described as thin with gray receding hair, about 50 years old, and wearing a white T-shirt and tan pants. No one on the staff recognizes the man as a regular user of the library or someone often seen roaming the neighborhood.

It is possible this ghost was one of the workers who built this stately library. In 1912, a Carnegie grant provided funds for construction of this building that included fancy exterior brick designs and vaulted ceilings with massive curved beams anchored by corbels carved with the faces of literary characters or local flora. In addition, some of the ceilings are coffered with huge plaster medallions from which chandeliers hang. After a century of use, this place still looks spectacular and totally different from the bland architecture of libraries constructed since the 1960s. Preservation of its unique style was a prime objective of a major renovation that closed the building for a year. Since it reopened on March 21, 2000, ghostly activity on the second floor and on Commercial Street increased significantly.

It has been suggested that the ghost of the North Portland Library may be a visitor from the mortuary that once operated across the street. Reliable sources have reported mysterious footsteps on NE Commercial Street that seem to approach witnesses and pass directly through them. At times, the footfalls are heavy, suggesting that the unseen being is wearing boots. When the pavement is wet, footsteps have been heard crossing Commercial Street, heading toward the library.

It seems likely that at least one spirit whose body was prepared for burial at the Little Chapel of the Chimes may have decided that the library is a more interesting place to linger on the physical plane than a mortuary. After visiting the library, you can investigate the mortuary, since it has been converted to McMenamins Chapel Pub.

The old North Portland Library may harbor spirits who crossed the street from the former mortuary.

GHOST OF THE PIANO MAN

Kaiser Central Clinic
3600 North Interstate Avenue
Portland 97223
503-813-2000

    Hospitals are among the most haunted places on the planet. The Central Building at Kaiser's Interstate Campus is no exception. This building houses the oncology library and lab, but I suspect that the ghost that haunts this place is linked to the rehabilitation services on the second floor, which include physical and occupational therapy, and the disability assessment clinic. A security guard has reported that many employees at the clinic know of a ghost named Frank who wanders the hallways but moves quickly to the piano in the dining area outside the cafeteria whenever anyone strikes a few keys. Frank does not play the piano, but he is so strongly attracted to it that many suspect he used to play but is now unable to do so because of a stroke or other debilitating illness or injury.

The ghostly image of Frank has been viewed on security cameras. He has been observed walking between the East Building and the Central Building and standing near the piano. Security-staff members suspect that Frank unlocks doors after they are locked. I asked an employee if Frank has demonstrated an affinity for a particular kind of music. She has witnessed his partial apparition several times, regardless of the style of music visitors chose to play. There have been many occasions when Frank shows up simply because the keys have been struck indiscriminately by a visitor who cannot actually play a tune. Frank seems to lose patience with these people and vanishes if children pound on the keys, making a sound that would be irritating to a skilled musician.

GHOST OF PRIVATE PAUL

The Crow Bar
3954 North Mississippi
Portland 97227
503-280-7099

In 1919, thousands of young men returned from World War I to their homes in Portland still deeply affected by the horrors they had endured while fighting in France. Some had no physical wounds but suffered severely from shellshock, now referred to as post-traumatic stress disorder. Others came home with lungs that were scarred by mustard gas, a new chemical weapon used by the Germans. These soldiers had frequent episodes of airway spasms, similar to asthma, that drained them of energy. In order to help them continue a healing process that was often never completed, several small clinics or rehabilitation facilities were set up in the Portland region. One of those facilities was located on North Mississippi Avenue above a row of storefronts. The apartments were broken up into tiny rooms, each containing two or three beds. A small central kitchen and treatment rooms were located on the first floor. While most soldiers treated at this place recovered sufficiently to return to their families or find a place of their own, it seems likely that some of them died there. That suspicion seems to be confirmed by the ghostly manifestations of a man dressed as a World War I soldier that occurs in the building.

In the modern apartments on the second floor, residents have witnessed the apparition of a soldier sitting in a rocking chair. Dubbed Private Paul, he appears with considerable detail, including high-top leather boots, an empty gun holster on a belt, and a wide-brimmed hat. The ghost rocks in the chair as he gazes out the window. Witnesses get the distinct impression that his breathing is labored. At times, they hear wheezing and gasping before he vanishes. Private Paul sometimes manifests only by creating a strong gust of air or an intense cold spot.

On the ground floor, the Crow Bar was closed when I last visited (it has now reopened). For many years, patrons reported seeing candles and glasses slide across the bar and wispy apparitions from the corners of their eyes. Women have reported that creepy feeling that a tall person is standing close behind, breathing heavily or wheezing.

People who worked in the Crow Bar had frequent encounters with Private Paul. Some witnessed bottles falling off the shelves, as if unseen hands were pushing them. In the basement, a chair scooted over the floor, often blocking the path of workers who were moving bar supplies around. Once the Crow Bar closed, this ghost seemed to manifest at the Miss Delta restaurant at 3950 North Mississippi.

Psychics, including myself, who have visited the building confirm that the spirit of a soldier does, indeed, haunt it, moving between the basement and second-floor apartments. Clearly, he suffers from a severe breathing disorder but hopes to make a full recovery. He is probably waiting at the rehabilitation facility for the day when he is able to return home.

GHOST OF THE OLDEST PROFESSION

White Eagle Saloon and Rock 'n' Roll Hotel
836 North Russell Street
Portland 97227
503-282-6810
www.mcmenamins.com/whiteeagle

The White Eagle Saloon is an iconic watering hole on the east side of the Willamette River that has stood for more than a century.

Any paranormal expert would probably name the White Eagle as the most haunted place in the Portland area. Constructed in 1899, the two-story, brick building was originally intended to be a respectable café and boardinghouse for the people who labored in the warehouses and factories and on the docks of the industrial side of the Willamette River. For a while, St. Stanislaus, the West Coast's first Polish Catholic church, held their organizational meetings in the building.

By 1905, it had become known as a place that was not safe for polite society. Its owners, Bronislaw Soboleski and William Hryszko, renamed it the White Eagle Saloon and catered to Polish workers who lived and worked in the neighborhood. As industrialization along the riverfront proceeded, bringing with it more bars, brothels, and flophouses, respectable families moved out. They were replaced by a growing number of workers and sailors who stopped at the White Eagle for food, strong drinks, and the services of prostitutes. These services were segregated. On the second floor, 11 small rooms provided space for a busy industry that featured white women. In the basement, black and Asians girls were offered. Supervised by a hulking bouncer, this despicable business went on for years and led to much of the paranormal activity experienced by staff members and astonished patrons of the famous White Eagle Saloon and Rock 'n' Roll Hotel.

Music buffs, connoisseurs of good food and drink, and ghost hunters come together at the famous White Eagle.

The place is a veritable time capsule for those who take the time to examine numerous architectural features of the first and second floors retained since 1905 and the historical photographs mounted on the wall near the entrance. The basement is generally off-limits to patrons, but access may be granted under special circumstances.

The ghost of a bouncer stalks the main floor late at night, usually 30 minutes before closing, looking for unruly customers he intends to throw out onto the sidewalk. Tall and wide, with huge rounded shoulders and a scowl on his face, this tough guy should be taken seriously. He walks from the rear of the bar, near the restrooms, to the front door, pushing aside anyone in his path. Late at night, tired patrons who may have had a long evening don't notice the ethereal hands shoving them out of the narrow aisle, but two people have reported to me that they later discovered palm and finger prints on the skin of their backs.

The bouncer shows up in other locations. Condiments, utensils, and other supplies have flown from the shelves, traveling horizontally for some distance before falling to the floor. Toilet paper in the lady's restroom flies about, toilets flush, and doors swing open before slamming shut. A staff member reported being pushed by large, strong hands as she descended the stairs to the basement. She sustained only minor injuries, but the event was truly frightening. There is no doubt that the bouncer was tough on customers at the White Eagle. One day he failed to show up for work. Days later, rumors began to circulate that he had been drugged and shanghaied, or killed. Perhaps this is the reason he has resumed his duty at the place where his authority was supreme.

The basement of the White Eagle now contains refrigerators, freezers, shelves for storing nonperishables, and an office. Decades ago, flimsy walls divided the space into cells occupied by black and Asian prostitutes. It is believed the girls were kidnapped and kept as sex slaves for paying customers. Some hapless patrons were drugged and shanghaied through a tunnel to the docks. It's no wonder that psychics who enter the space detect sadness and pain. Some sensitives also perceive violence perpetrated on the girls or unruly customers. It seems certain that more than one girl died in the basement, from illness or suicide, and a few patrons also lost their lives to drug and alcohol excess or a beating delivered by the pimps or bouncer. The result is an angry spirit that haunts the place. This ghost opens and closes the freezer doors, causes coins to fall from the ceiling, and touches living persons. It may be responsible for pushing the employee as she descended the stairs.

Another spirit in the White Eagle is believed to be that of Sam Warrick. It has been reported that he was born in one of the second-floor rooms and spent his entire life in the place. As a child, Sam was the gofer and kitchen helper. Later, he tended bar and cleaned up the place. After that, Sam did odd jobs around the saloon to cover his room and board. Sometime in the 1940s, Sam died in one of the hotel rooms. Some of his personal items have been placed in several of the rooms, prompting him to manifest. Passersby on the street have spotted him gazing out the windows. Hotel guests who have wandered down the hall in the middle of the night to the central restroom have become wide awake when they realized they could see through the haggard old man who stood facing them. Ghost hunters should take a look at historic photos hanging on the walls of the main floor. In some of them, you can see Sam Warrick.

Sam's name has been attached to the legendary ghost story of the White Eagle, but historians are certain he was not the character described as the dapper piano player who fell in love with a second-floor prostitute. The story of Sam and Rose may be little more that urban legend, but given the decades of bar fights, clashes of rivals who wanted the same woman, and lives wasted in the place, it does not seem like too much of a stretch. It has been said that Sam desperately wanted to leave the seedy enterprise and miserable neighborhood and take Rose with him. After several months of planning and saving his money, he visited Rose in her room late one December night after her customers had gone home. Hoping to convince her to run away with him that very night, he showed her his wallet packed with money and two train tickets to Seattle. Then he proposed that she leave with him and become his wife.

The legend says that Rose laughed at poor Sam and the ridicule caused him to fly into a rage, smashing her furniture, breaking her mirror, and screaming at her. The bouncer heard the terrible racket and burst into the room just as Sam pulled a pistol from his coat pocket. The two men fought and, although the bouncer was the larger

This antique photograph, taken about 1919, may include the bartender implicated in a double murder that produced some of the saloon's most famous ghosts.

man, Sam broke free of his grasp and shot him. Still in a rage, he shot Rose and then turned the gun on himself.

Many people believe that this murder-suicide created spirits that are responsible for most of the paranormal activity on the second floor. Overnight guests often hear sound bursts of a piano, a woman crying, mirrors shattering, furniture breaking, and the groaning of two men caught in an eternal fight caused by unrequited love.

GHOSTS OF THE PIONEERS

Lone Fir Cemetery
2115 SE Morrison Street
Portland 97214
503-797-1709
www.oregonmetro.gov/cemeteries

In 1846, when James Stephens buried his father, Emmor, on land owned by Seldon Murray, he had no idea the memorial would eventually be surrounded by the graves of more than 25,000 of Portland's citizens. James and his wife, Elizabeth, ran a ferry service across the Willamette River and never gave any thought to getting into the cemetery business. Even as a few more graves were added to the shady spot now bordered by SE 20th Avenue and SE Stark Street, the place was not formally known as a cemetery. The explosion of the steamship *Gazelle* on the Willamette River in 1854 changed that forever.

On April 8, 1854, at 6:30 A.M., while the ship was tied to a dock, the engineer allowed its steam pressure to rise to dangerous levels. Sensing the imminent disaster, he jumped onto the dock and started running. Ten minutes later, the ship's boilers exploded, killing 21 people instantly. Four others later died of their wounds, while 40 were seriously injured. The large collection of body parts so disturbed local citizens that a decision was made to bury the dead as quickly as possible. Thus 25 graves were opened near that of Emmor Stephens, and locals began to think of the place as a cemetery.

Less than a year later, sensing a good business opportunity, sexton and gravedigger Colburn Barrell purchased 10 acres surrounding the early burial sites and officially established the cemetery. In 1866, Barrell added 20 acres to the enterprise and tried to sell the cemetery to the city of Portland. The offer was declined because the graveyard, sitting east of the Willamette River and reached only by an unreliable ferry and muddy roads, was considered too remote. Noting the compelling name, Lone Fir Cemetery, deriving from the solitary tree standing near the original graves, investors Levi Anderson, Robert Pittock, and Byron Cardwell stepped forward and purchased the grounds.

Today, Lone Fir Cemetery is a veritable storehouse of Portland history, containing the remains of 25,000 of the city's famous and infamous citizens in addition to an estimated 10,000 unmarked graves. Among them are the graves of the couple considered to be the Lone Fir's founders: James and Elizabeth Stephens. Their monument is an effigy of the couple, standing side by side and facing the tree that inspired the cemetery's name. On the back of their monument is a touching epitaph: *Here we lie by consent, after 57 years 2 months and 2 days sojourning through life awaiting nature's immutable laws to return us back to the elements of the universe, of which we were first composed.*

Lone Fir Cemetery staff members and volunteers offer monthly tours that provide visitors with fascinating histories and explanations of some of the bizarre monuments. They also offer information about paranormal activity known to occur in this beautiful place. In October, the Friends of Lone Fir Cemetery stage a Halloween tour called "Untimely Departures," which highlights the graveyard's paranormal legacy.

Most people who stroll through this cemetery feel something odd. Sometimes it is simply the play of shadows and wind, but others have reported passing through the gate and immediately becoming aware of an inexplicable change in atmosphere. On warm days, it is common for visitors to step into a column of air that is so cold that they start to shiver and pull a jacket over their shoulders. At several graves, visitors get a feeling that they should not stand close to the headstone or monument. Some have reported feeling pushed away or

The tomb of Dr. James C. Hawthorne is the tallest monument in Lone Fir Cemetery and a gathering place for ghost hunters and ghosts.

hitting an invisible wall. At times, voices fill the heads of astonished and frightened visitors.

One portion of the cemetery in particular creates eerie sensations. In 1858, Dr. James C. Hawthorne (1818-91) established a private insane asylum supported by Multnomah County. Over the years, hundreds of patients died while under his supervision. Often, the deceased had no immediate family willing to take charge of the remains, so Dr. Hawthorne buried them in unmarked graves in a section of Lone Fir Cemetery now known as Hawthorne's Plot. The remains of 132 patients have been discovered through excavation, but it is likely that many more lie hidden beneath the green sod. Upon his death, Dr. Hawthorne was buried near his patients in the southeast portion of the cemetery. His monument stands tall and marks the spot where exciting ghost hunts begin.

Block 14 is also a site of intense and frequent paranormal activity, attributed to an unknown number of Chinese who were buried there. In 1956, the county exhumed several bodies and relocated them, with the assumption that all of the unfortunate deceased persons had been accounted for. In 2000, excavation for a new building turned up more remains, bringing construction to a halt. At this site, sensitive visitors feel as though they are being pulled downward by unseen hands. Sound bursts in Cantonese are frequent, and ghost hunters often feel as though they are pushed aside.

More than 250 Civil War veterans are buried here, in addition to several notables from Portland's past:

Colburn Barrell: He descended from *Mayflower* pilgrims and sailed with Captain Gray on a trade voyage that discovered the Columbia River. Barrell owned the steamship *Gazelle* which exploded, sending 25 souls to this cemetery. Block 1/Lot 1/Grave 2N.

Cornelius Beal: He was a divorce attorney from the early days. Block 18/Lot 5A/Grave 3S.

William Beck: He was a pioneer gun merchant and advocate for the first bridge over Willamette River (Morrison). Block 1/Lot 47/Grave 3S.

Angeline Berry: She founded the Humane Society, Good Samaritan Hospital, and YWCA and donated land for Grace Episcopal Church. Block 8/Lot 46/Grave 2N.

Crawford Dobbins: He died in the *Gazelle* explosion. His burial led to the formal declaration that this was a cemetery. Block 1/Lot 1/Grave 2S.

Dr. James C. Hawthorne: He ran the Oregon Asylum for the Insane/Moral Treatment at the end of the Oregon Trail. He buried 132 inmates at Lone Fir. Block 8M/Lot 44/Grave 1N.

Asa Lovejoy: He founded Portland but lost the coin toss that named it. He established Oregon's first telegraph company, Oregon City Woolen Mills, and Portland's first Masonic Lodge. Block 8M/Lot 50/Grave 2N.

Esther Lovejoy: This "Doctor to the World" was a suffragette, the first female director of the city's Health Department, and the first director of the Medical Women's International Association. Block 34.

Donald MacLeay: This Scottish businessman worked in banking; raising wheat, lumber, and salmon; and shipping. He invested his profits in Portland's growth, and his family donated MacLeay Park to the city. Block 17/Lot 3/Mausoleum.

Martha MacLeay: She was married to Donald for seven years and had four children. She was known as a progressive philanthropist. Block 17/Lot 3/Mausoleum.

Robert Pittock: This brother of Henry Pittock was a grocer. Block 1/Lot 37/Grave 2S.

Earl Riley: He was a colorful but corrupt mayor. His father built the original Canyon Road. Block 8/Lot 47/Grave 2S.

Dr. William Royal: This Civil War doctor was infamous as a captain who allegedly shanghaied his own son. Block 13/Lot 12/Grave 3N.

William Warren: He is one of over 250 Civil War burials in Lone Fir Cemetery. Block 1/Lot 52/Grave 1N.

Capt. Daniel Wright: He went to California for the Gold Rush and used some of his money to purchase a beautiful spot in the cemetery. Block 4/Lot 70/Grave 3N.

THEATRICAL GHOSTS

Bagdad Theater
3702 SE Hawthorne Boulevard

Portland 97214
503-236-9234
www.mcmenamins.com/219-bagdad-theater-pub-home

There are good reasons why old theatres are ranked in the top five places to experience paranormal phenomena. Theaters that have stood for many decades have invariably soaked up intense emotions and energy from members of the audience, dancers, singers, musicians, actors, comediennes, directors, producers, and even stagehands and retained them in the walls, chandeliers, stage, seats, and dressing rooms. These residuals or imprints of emotions and energy often "play," creating sound bursts of past performances that may include a voice speaking lines or singing, the applause of an audience, or cues shouted by a director. Residuals may also include the sound of musical instruments, flashes of light, and apparitions of performers, members of an audience, and stagehands who may have fallen from a catwalk only to die onstage. People who work in these old theatres and patrons who attend screenings of modern movies, rock concerts, or comedy performances are often astonished when they encounter the apparition of an actor, musician, or member of an audience dressed in clothing from a long-bygone era. This is no surprise to ghost hunters, however, because nearly all old theatres are haunted. After death, performers, directors, conductors, and stagehands often chose to stay at the site of their greatest accomplishments, awaiting the applause of an adoring audience. Often, ghostly members of an audience remain as well, hoping to see an actor or actress with whom they have fallen in love.

The old Bagdad Theater has all the elements to make it a haunted venue despite renovation into a modern movie house, pub, and private party rooms. First-run films, a huge screen, 20,000-watt Surround Sound, a digital projector, "rocker" seating, and first-rate food and drink concessions haven't diminished the imprints and ghostly activity that may be experienced at this fascinating theatre.

The Bagdad opened in 1927, on the very cusp of the commercialization of talking pictures. The $100,000 construction budget was huge for the day, allowing architects and builders to create a spectacular entertainment venue that included a Middle Eastern motif, a grand fountain, a colonnade hundreds of feet long, red-tile hoods above the windows, decorative molding, rafters, arched doorways, and wrought-iron balconets and lighting features. Carrying the Middle Eastern theme to the extreme, usherettes wore uniforms described as "Arabian style."

Declared by Mayor George Baker at the time to be a "triumph of artistry and craftsmanship," the place was spectacular and immediately became known as the foremost entertainment venue on the east side of Portland. Talking movies and vaudeville attracted the first patrons, but the Bagdad's popularity continued through the 1950s with first-run movies and live stage performances by renowned entertainers such as Sammy Davis, Jr. In the 1970s, the Bagdad hosted the premiere of *One Flew Over the Cuckoo's Nest*. Upon joining the McMenamins restaurant and entertainment group, the theatre underwent extensive renovation, with great care taken to preserve its original character.

Is this fascinating theatre haunted? Yes, it remains a literal hotbed of paranormal activity, but none of it is frightening or threatening to those who are fortunate enough to encounter a ghost or experience the replay of an imprint from the 1930s.

The old Bagdad Theater offers patrons modern amenities, but it retains its 1920s character as well as several ghosts from that era.

For many years, the apparition of a male figure has been spotted walking about the upstairs lobby. At times, this apparition is so lifelike that witnesses have been able to see the wide lapels of his jacket, his shiny bowtie, and his slicked-back hair. This ghost moves around as if he is on duty and charged with making sure theatre guests are having a good time. He shows up most often when a patron spills a drink, bumps into a chair, or collides with another guest.

A female ghost manifests in various seats of the last two rows. It seems clear that this woman was an ardent fan of a man who was a regular performer at the Bagdad Theater. She may have fallen in love with his singing voice or dramatic delivery, or simply watched one movie after another for many years, silently wishing she had become an actress. This ghost appears to be wearing a small hat that was stylish in the 1940s and a fur draped over her shoulders.

Patrons who are not fortunate enough to witness these ghosts may encounter unexplained gusts of wind, cold spots, and the dimming of lights. In the restrooms, doors to the stalls often vibrate as if a ghost desperately needs to gain entry but cannot generate the energy to open the door fully. In addition, balls of light often flash in front of the screen before a movie starts and then move up and down the aisles.

MYSTERIOUS LADIES OF THE LAKE

Laurelhurst Park
SE Cesar E. Chavez Boulevard at Stark Street
Portland 97255
503-823-2525

In most of the cities where I've conducted paranormal investigations, I've encountered stories of a female ghost that appears in or near an urban lake or pond where she allegedly drowned by accident, suicide, or murder. With very few exceptions, no historical record or other documentation could be found to support the legend. In a few cases, witness reports of a ghostly image are so frequent and similar that paranormal investigators concede there may be some truth to the supposition that a woman did, indeed, die in the lake and that she haunts the location of her death. It is quite unusual, however, that we have a name, date, and other evidence that verifies the death while pointing to suspicious circumstances that may serve as a basis of the haunting.

Ten-year-old Donald West played at Laurelhurst Park so often that he knew every spot at the edge of the lake that would allow him to get close to the ducks or drop a fishing line in the cloudy water. Close to noon on October 9, 1936, while making his usual stroll around the lake searching for dead fish and ducks, Donald spotted something unusual. He found a woman's shoe and coat resting on the mud of a tiny inlet. Donald immediately notified park watchman E. J. Dahl. Dahl's initial notion was that someone went swimming in the lake and, dripping wet and cold, raced to a nearby car, leaving some clothing behind. In the pocket of the coat, however, he found some cash and $300 in traveler's checks. He also found material indicating the coat belonged to Alla Warineth, aged 45, of Spokane, Washington. Pondering the significance of this discovery, Dahl looked out over the cloudy surface of the lake only to see Alla floating face down. Later, police and firefighters recovered her body, and the coroner concluded that the death was a suicide. A search of the entire park failed to turn up other articles of clothing, an abandoned car, or other evidence that might explain how or why Alla had traveled from Spokane to this idyllic park in Portland.

Alla Warineth might have been forgotten if it weren't for another unusual discovery that occurred many years later. While jogging the perimeter of the lake one morning, a man spotted a woman standing at the edge of water, hands clasped and head bowed as if in prayer. Moments after passing her, he heard a splash that seemed to echo through the cold, damp air. Retracing his steps, the man saw her about 20 yards from shore, floating face down. He jumped into the lake and attempted to reach her. Stroking through the algae-choked water, he found that as he came within a few feet of the floating, motionless body, it seemed to move farther away. As his rescue efforts continued, he became chilled and extremely frustrated that he could not reach the woman. Finally, with cramping muscles and gasping breaths, he made one last attempt, only to watch the body disappear before his eyes. The man was certain she did not slip beneath the surface but clearly vanished as if she were never there.

Soon after this story circulated around the neighborhood, others came forward to report a woman suddenly appearing, either floating on the lake or standing at the water's edge, then vanishing. So far, no one has reported intelligent interaction with this woman, so we cannot conclude that witnesses have actually seen the ghost of Alla Warineth. The images seen by many people may be residuals or imprints of the tragic event that were triggered to "play" by specific environmental conditions or the sensitivities of witnesses.

It is possible that the ghostly image of a woman floating on the lake is not that of Alla Warineth. On February 25, 2008, the body of another woman, 37-year-old Heidi Anderson, was found in the lake at Laurelhurst Park, after she had been missing since February 8. A hiker had discovered Heidi's hat, coat, cellphone, and wallet under a shrub. The wallet, which contained money, the presence of the cellphone, and the neatly folded clothing suggested to police that the tragedy was not the result of a robbery. In fact, nothing at the scene raised suspicions of an assault, and the autopsy found no evidence of a crime.

The calm waters of the lake and peaceful atmosphere of Laurelhurst Park enable psychics to experience the presence of two women who committed suicide there.

Family, friends, and co-workers reported to police that Heidi had had no problems with drugs, alcohol, or mental health. On February 8, the last day she was seen alive, however, she reportedly got out of a friend's car after the sudden onset of paranoia. She then boarded a bus but got off after traveling for only one minute. Within hours, a missing person's report was filed and a search initiated at the corner of 90th Street and Sandy Boulevard, the last place Heidi was seen alive. More than two weeks later, the search ended with the discovery of her body in Laurelhurst Park.

Paranormal investigators who visit Laurelhurst Park should conduct EVP sweeps in an attempt to capture a female voice that may respond when the names Alla and Heidi are spoken. Also, imaging devices should be used to obtain characteristics of the ghostly woman seen here. Pictures of Alla cannot be found online, but several photos of Heidi are available.

PARANORMAL CSI

Fatalities in Tragic Car Collision
SE Gladstone Street at SE 28th Place
Portland 97202

At this scene of a horrific two-car accident in 2013, offerings are often found attached to a utility pole, assuring the deceased that they are not forgotten. Friends and neighbors pin notes or crosses, leave flowers, or light a candle to honor the memory and mourn the loss of Paul Lawrence Knepper, aged 55, and his 90-year-old mother, Hazel Agnes Knepper. These mementoes may have something to do with the paranormal remnants of this event that sensitives perceive as they walk the path of the Kneppers' car after it was crushed by a speeding SUV and thrown against the utility pole, killing Paul and Hazel.

Daniel Troy Johnson, aged 29, spent much of the afternoon of March 9, 2013, drinking with friends. A few minutes before five o'clock, he jumped behind the wheel his Cadillac Escalade, with three pals and a dog taking the remaining seats. Fully inebriated and joking with his friends, Johnson sped north on 28th Place. According to witnesses and the police investigation, he was traveling far in excess of the posted speed limit. At the intersection with SE Gladstone Street, Johnson ran the stop sign, slamming into the passenger side of a Toyota Corolla driven by Paul Knepper. Hazel, sitting in the front passenger seat, was probably killed instantly by the impact. It threw the Toyota across the intersection into a utility pole on the northeast corner, severely injuring but not killing Paul. Moments later, as shocked residents tried to render aid to Paul, he died.

This horrible tragedy was made even more reprehensible by Johnson's escape from the scene. Leaving a friend and the dog injured in the car, he and the two others extricated themselves from the wrecked vehicle and ran. Johnson was captured a short time later and charged with two counts of manslaughter in the second degree, felony hit and run, assault in the fourth degree, and DUI. He was sentenced to 18 years in prison.

What remains at this location that may be paranormal? Sensitives who walk the path of the Kneppers' car perceive an imprint, or residual, of the horrible impact. Some actually perceive the sound of two vehicles colliding, which, at the time of the accident, was heard blocks away. At the utility pole, a female presence has been detected. This woman is terribly sad and seems confused and in need of help. Some ghost hunters have speculated that this is the ghost of Hazel Knepper mourning the loss of her son, Paul. Only a few weeks earlier, Hazel had lost another son, John, to cancer. It is also possible that the female presence at this site is an imprint of intense emotions experienced by a horrified resident who raced from her house to the scene hoping to save one of the victims.

GHOSTS OF THE POOR FARM

McMenamins Edgefield
2126 SW Halsey Street
Troutdale 97060
503-669-8610
ww.mcmenamins.com/edgefield

After decades of operating under deplorable conditions, the county's first poor farm, Hillside Farm, located in Portland's West Hills, was shut down in 1911 and its 211 inmates were transferred to a new facility in Troutdale. Located 16 miles from the heart of Portland, it was within reach of county administrators and sheriff's deputies but far enough away that the derelicts it housed would not trouble affluent citizens. Despite its purpose, the place was constructed in a grand style that included fancy brickwork on the exterior, spacious hallways with intricate woodwork, large dining rooms, recreation rooms, an infirmary, library, and facilities for teaching inmates crafts and skills they might use to regain a productive lifestyle. In addition, several outbuildings were erected to support farming operations. Edgefield was constructed to house vagrants, but many of its inmates were skilled or educated people who had simply had a run of bad luck due to illness or injury. During its 71 years of operation, however, the place also housed emotionally disturbed children, adults with mental illness, alcoholics, addicts, tuberculosis patients, released prisoners who had no means or support to live a law-abiding life, the blind, deaf persons, and anyone deemed to be a social deviant.

Despite this seemingly deprecating description of Edgefield's inmates, those who worked the farm created a hugely successful enterprise. Inmates provided themselves and the staff with all of the fruit, vegetables, dairy, pork products, and poultry they needed. In some years, they produced a surplus of food, which was sent to the county's hospitals and jails.

During the Great Depression, Edgefield's population grew to more than 600 residents. With the onset of World War II, greater opportunities for employment reduced the population to about 200. However, many inmates who entered Edgefield in the 1930s were never able to leave. As the residents grew older, portions of the facility were converted to a nursing home. Undoubtedly, several inmates died here, and there are rumors that many bodies were buried on the grounds.

By 1972, other social programs to assist the indigent made Edgefield obsolete. Still, the last patient did not depart the old home until 1982. Suffering attacks by vandals and abuse by the homeless, the vacant place faced demolition by the county. Fortunately, the Troutdale

Edgefield started as a poor farm but now offers guests a full range of services, including a chance to encounter ghosts.

Historical Society stepped in and mounted a campaign to save it. Several prospective buyers passed on the development opportunities until the McMenamin brothers saw its great potential and invested the time and money to make Edgefield the spectacular resort that it is today. With a theatre, winery, brewpub, indoor and outdoor dining, comfortable overnight accommodations, and beautiful gardens, Edgefield is an ideal destination for visitors to the Portland region.

If you are looking for ghosts, this place may be the most haunted hotel in Oregon. In fact, a log is kept at the front desk in which guests may record their paranormal experiences at the old poor farm. The log indicates that room 215 is one of the most active paranormal sites, although many entries suggest that the entire second floor is haunted. The third floor, the winery, the Black Rabbit Bar, rooms that once housed the infirmary, the old power station, and the Distillery Bar have ghosts as well.

Guests who have slept in room 215 have had encounters with a "spirit dog" that licks their feet or touches their face with its cold nose. A short, elderly woman has also been spotted shuffling across this room with an unsteady gait. In several rooms, guests have left personal items on a bed or table while they were out. When they returned, some items were missing or rearranged in patterns.

A woman dressed as a nurse has been spotted walking the hallways in broad daylight. Other females dressed as inmates wander the corridors, show up in the women's restrooms, and glide up and down the stairs. A little girl descends the front stairs and walks toward the parking lot but vanishes after passing the fountain. Some of the female ghosts serenade guests with hymns or recite nursery rhymes.

The Power Station Pub was once Edgefield's power plant and laundry. Today, the popular eatery is haunted. Staff members have said they often feel a presence in the room that hovers close by and creates that creepy feeling of being watched. In the Black Rabbit Bar, some staff members have encountered an angry ghost, but this spirit does not harm the living.

I could not find any credible reports of abuse of inmates by poor-farm staff members or attacks on an inmate by other residents. A housekeeper told me she had heard that a girl had been murdered in the old laundry (now the Power Station Pub), but I found no corroboration in historical records. Given the high probability that

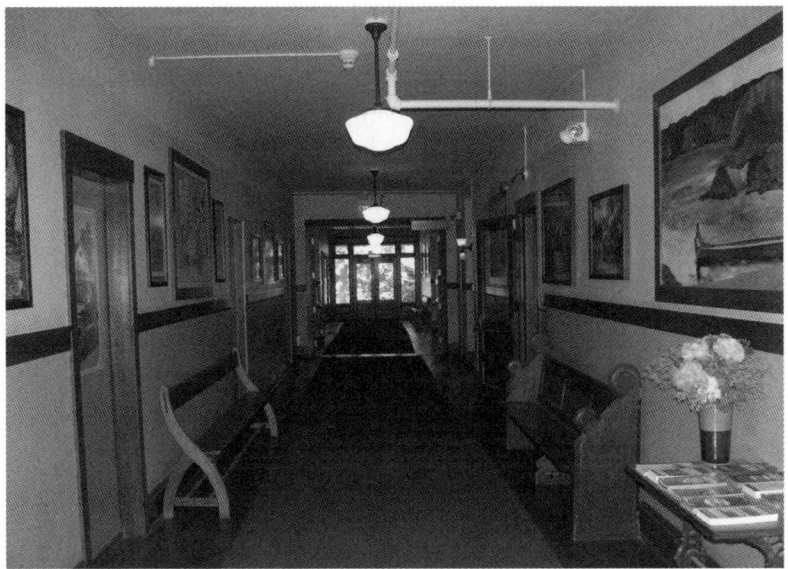

Paintings and other architectural features enable ghost hunters to get in touch with an earlier era that produced hundreds of imprints and ghosts.

many inmates were mentally unstable and, perhaps, prone to violence, I would not be surprised if unnatural deaths occurred at the old poor farm. Some sensitive visitors have encountered intense cold spots and places where strong negative energy creates perceptions of fear, rage, and pain. Several guests have heard unexplained sobbing, crying, and screams and called the front desk to report their impression that someone was in distress. The most fascinating thing about the paranormal activity at Edgefield is that much of it occurs in daylight hours. If you want the full-blown paranormal experience, however, plan to spend at least one night.

Other places to hunt ghosts:

CRASH RESIDUAL

Aviation Disaster
NE 157th at East Burnside Street
Portland 97203

On December 29, 1978, United Airlines flight 173 departed Denver with 189 people onboard, bound for Portland International Airport. The DC-8 carried a fuel reserve of nearly 50 percent, but a failure of the right landing gear required the aircraft to stay in the air much longer than planned. Less than three miles from the Portland airport, the aircraft fell from the sky. Fortunately, Capt. Malburn McBroom found open ground and guided the plane to a crash landing, with only moderate damage to an unoccupied house. He survived, but flight engineer Forrest Mendenhall and flight attendant Joan Wheeler were killed. Eight passengers died, 21 had serious injuries, and, miraculously, 152 had only minor or no injuries.

About 200 feet from the intersection of East Burnside and NE 157th Street is a vacant lot believed to be the site where the DC-8 hit the ground. At various places in the surrounding neighborhood, people often hear a loud crash yet find no obvious cause. The perception of sound may be a residual of the aircraft's impact on the ground.

RESTLESS MURDER VICTIMS

4523 NE 60th Avenue
Portland 97218
503-288-9771

In 2013, the city of Portland recorded 16 homicides. Two fatalities were the result of officer-involved shootings in which police acted to protect the public. The victims ranged in age from 15 to 61. Most of them were men; only three were women. Two fatalities occurred outside of bars. In every case, astute paranormal investigators recognize that the locations of these tragic events invariably retain imprints of sound, emotion, and images created by the victim, perpetrator, or horrified witnesses. The ghost of the victim often remains at the site as well. This may happen if the victim is unaware he or she is dead, or the transition from life to death is so devastating that the spirit stays at the location, deeply confused and awaiting help.

I discovered all of those paranormal phenomena outside the Skinn Club. On May 8, 2013, Anton Leshawn Hill, 33, died here from a gunshot wound to the head. If you visit this location, do not go alone. Stage an initial visit in daylight hours to familiarize yourself with the area. Take precautions to ensure your safety and do not be obvious in your paranormal investigation. A report of other murder sites may be found at http://www.oregonlive.com/portland/index.ssf/2014/01/portlands_2013_homicide_list_d.html.

A HAPPY PRESENCE

The White House
1914 NE 22nd Street
Portland 97212
503-287-7131
www.portlandswhitehouse.com

    Built in 1911 by lumber baron Robert Lytle, this house is not a replica of the executive mansion in Washington, D.C., but it is a spectacular place deserving of a moniker that attracts attention. For decades, the Greek Revival mansion was known as the most expensive home built east of the Willamette River, and given its restored elegance, which includes Qing Dynasty porcelain vases, 17th-century Danish furniture, and 18th-century bronze sculptures, it may be the finest inn to be found in this part of Portland. Its massive columns and spectacular porte-cochere give visitors a preview of the amazing interior of this manse. They don't raise suspicions of a ghost, but the place may be haunted by the man who built it. I detected a male presence who seems quite happy with the condition of the house. He stands in the foyer and other rooms on the first floor surveying the furniture and art, emits a melodic "hmmm . . . mmm," and then fades away.

CHAPTER 4

Vancouver and North Portland

North Portland, Oregon, and Vancouver, Washington, are distinct political entities but they have many economic, social, cultural, and historical ties that, in several ways, unite them as a single community. The two major bridges that cross the mighty Columbia River make travel between Vancouver and Portland easy for commuters and also others who wish to enjoy countless opportunities for shopping, recreation, entertainment, education, and sporting events. As early as 1846, Dr. John McLoughlin, superintendent of the Columbia District of the Hudson's Bay Company at Fort Vancouver, realized that the region comprised a unique place. Perhaps it was this idea that prompted him to found a city in Oregon and support the American annexation of Oregon Territory, which included land that would someday be Washington State.

Visitors who arrive at Portland's International Airport will find that they can, in a few minutes, cross the Columbia and begin their ghost investigations at historic Fort Vancouver and Vancouver Barracks, where the ideas of a city on the Willamette and the beautiful state of Oregon were first conceived. Stops at modern entities such as a fast-food restaurant, park, deadly intersection, and historic house that has become a wine-tasting venue will keep you grounded in the 21st century, but always be on the lookout for fascinating ghosts who lived during the early history of this region.

MURDER OF ANNA SVIDERSKY

McDonald's Restaurant
2814 NE Andresen Road
Vancouver, WA 98661
360-693-8481

Late in the afternoon of April 20, 2006, schizophrenic sex offender David Barton Sullivan grew increasingly captivated with the idea of violence against anyone. He would later admit that his greatest desire was to "hurt a female." Described as a level-two registered sex offender with a criminal history that included an assault in 2001 and incarceration in a state facility for mental illness, Sullivan was not under the supervision of social workers or law-enforcement officials when he decided to kill a female.

After sunset, Sullivan walked alongside busy Andresen Road for several minutes before deciding that he would find a victim inside the McDonald's restaurant. With a long kitchen knife concealed by his coat, he entered and spotted Anna Esther Svidersky.

Born in the Soviet Union in 1988, Anna immigrated to the U.S. as an infant and grew up to be a typical Western teenager. Eager to fulfill her American dream, she worked three jobs during her senior year at Fort Vancouver High School. Her goal of going to college may have been on her mind as she worked at McDonald's, unaware that her murderer had entered the place and was walking straight toward her. According to witnesses, the attack was brief. Sullivan pulled the knife from his coat and stabbed Anna in the chest with a single, strong thrust. Covered with blood, he ran from the restaurant as Anna fell to the floor. She died a short time later at a local hospital.

As Sullivan ran down the street, he dropped the knife. Several patrons of the restaurant ran after him as police rushed to the scene with a canine unit. Moments later, Sullivan was surrounded and taken into custody. On June 26, 2007, Sullivan was acquitted by reason of insanity. He now resides in a mental hospital.

It is difficult to enter this McDonald's restaurant without feeling the negative energy that remains there. In particular, the table for two near the half-wall dividing the dining area from the counter, where Anna was stabbed, still harbors an atmosphere of mental chaos and pain. Does the ghost of Anna Svidersky haunt this place? I was unable to capture any evidence that the 17-year-old girl was still there, but there is undoubtedly an intense, paranormal residual of her murder that sensitives can easily detect.

Aside from imprints, and possibly ghostly manifestations, there is something quite unique and paranormal at this location. When news of Anna's murder poured through news and Internet outlets, people all over the world became captivated by her biography, the dreams she pursued, and the tragedy of her death. Web sites such as MySpace were filled with messages of condolence and testimony of Anna's passion and kindness. The British newspaper *The Guardian* compared the widespread interest and outpouring of emotion to the world's reaction to the death of Princess Diana in 1997.

This unusual response to the death of an otherwise obscure American teenager was due, in part, to the nearly immediate dissemination of bad news around the world. In addition, Stephen Coleman, professor of political communication at Leeds University, explained that the tragic word that spread so quickly touched young people deeply because of the concept of "shared space" fostered by social networks. The news made many people feel vulnerable and frightened and, thus, created a confluence of emotions almost simultaneously. An interesting form of mass empathy—grief over the death of a stranger—created an emotional energy in millions of people worldwide that became focused on that McDonald's restaurant on Andresen Road in Vancouver, Washington. The result is a kind of nexus that may give us a paranormal experience of fear and sadness in a busy fast-food restaurant.

DOUBLE MURDER IN "DARK PARK"

David Douglas Park
1016 North Garrison Road
Vancouver, WA 98664
360-487-8311

This park was named for Fort Vancouver botanist and scholar David Douglas (1799-1834), who distinguished himself by identifying hundreds of species of plants indigenous to the American Northwest that were unknown in Europe, but few people remember the man or his role in discovering the natural treasures of the Portland area. In fact, since 1989, David Douglas Park has been known as "Dark Park" due to a horrific double murder that occurred there. The details of this tragic event are well known because the perpetrator kept a diary of his actions that included his speculation of ways he might improve his techniques for kidnapping, rape, and murder. Shirley Lynn Scott's compilation of many excerpts from the diary and excellent analysis of the event can be found at www.crimelibrary.com by entering "Westley Allan Dodd" in the search window.

Be aware that the details of this grisly double murder will be quite disturbing. Ghost hunters who visit this area can perform investigations with a few essential facts, however.

Early in the evening of Monday, September 4, 1989, 11-year-old Cole Neer and his 10-year-old brother, Billy, raced their bikes through the wooded area of David Douglas Park, anxious to get home for dinner. They found the dirt path blocked by a young man, Westley Allan Dodd (1961-93). Instantly achieving control over the boys, he ordered them to leave their bikes in the brush and walk with him. Finding a secluded spot far from the ball fields, Dodd tied the boys' hands, molested them, and then stabbed them with a crude knife. According to Dodd, all of this occurred while the boys cried and begged to be allowed to go home.

Barely alive, Billy was found at the edge of the woods near Topeka Lane. He died an hour later at a local hospital. Police initially believed that the crime involved only one victim but soon learned that Cole was missing. At two o'clock Tuesday morning, Cole's lifeless, bloody body was found.

Knowing the tragic story of Cole and Billy Neer, it is impossible to walk the wooded area of this park without feeling the energy of their horrific ordeal. For me, the experience becomes more deeply depressing when I recall that the frightened little boys repeatedly asked their molester, "Will it hurt?" and "When can I go home?"

Sensitives who walk the shaded trails of the park will hear the laughter of two boys. These are not sounds carried on the wind from the distant ball fields but rather joyful sounds that seem to move past astonished visitors, starting quietly, getting louder as they pass by, then becoming soft and distant again. Psychics get the impression that the Neer boys are reliving a happy moment in their lives, riding their bikes through the beautiful, mysterious forest as they head home for dinner. I truly hope that is what they are doing. Standing amid the shadows of this park, I can shake myself out of my empathic awareness of their pain and agony only by focusing on a moment of joy experienced by these little ghosts.

OLD CITY CEMETERY IN VANCOUVER

Mill Plain Boulevard at Grand Boulevard
Vancouver, WA 98661
360-696-8156
www.ccgs-wa.org

Contrary to popular opinion, cemeteries are rarely haunted by the ghosts of people interred under fancy monuments or in elaborate mausoleums. The vast majority of ghosts prefer to reside in a place that was important to them when they were alive. Homes, businesses, boats, and even airplanes are far more attractive places than a grave, and they offer emotional stability, a sense of familiarity, and opportunities to stay close to loved ones. No matter how ornate a headstone may be, a graveyard is not the kind of place that could entice a ghost to take up spiritual residence. Certainly, there are instances when a ghost becomes attached to a cemetery, but it is rare for even large graveyards to harbor more than a few ghosts. Cemeteries, however, are covered with imprints created by the emotions of grieving family members. This is certainly true of the Old City Cemetery in Vancouver.

Family members who may have visited a grave several times a year for decades could easily create intense imprints of emotions that remain intact and quite strong for a century or more. Each grave may have several imprints, creating a veritable mantle of paranormal energy that can be detected with audio recorders, EMF detectors, infrared imaging, and psychic sensitivities.

Opened in 1867, the Old City Cemetery currently contains about 650 monuments, but local historians believe that more than 1,000 bodies are buried there. Some of the dead worked for the famous Hudson's Bay Company at nearby Fort Vancouver. Later additions were pioneers who traveled West on the Oregon Trail. Despite the noisy traffic on Mill Plain Boulevard, the place has a creepy ambience almost any time of day. Tall trees cast long shadows and keep the air cool, giving the place a chilly atmosphere.

Orbs often have no validity as evidence of the paranormal, but when they occur in a cemetery they may signal a ghostly presence.

Look for the grave of Arthur Haine. Kicked out of New York by his family after a torrid affair with a showgirl, he arrived in Vancouver in 1871 and became prominent in the town's society. Never far from scandal, Haine became even more famous by arranging his own funeral that included a brass band. En route to the City Cemetery, his casket slipped off the wagon, giving onlookers a last look at the rather pale gentleman.

The best places to find intense imprints in this cemetery are at the graves of children. If you seek ghosts, look for damaged or vandalized headstones. Ghosts tend to know if a monument is damaged, and they become quite active as they seek the attention of anyone who might make repairs.

If you are visiting Vancouver near Halloween, join the cemetery tour to learn about pious and scandalous citizens who are buried here. Reenactors portray the dead, adding entertaining and macabre elements to your visit. Contact Vancouver Heritage Ambassadors at 360-695-5602.

HIGH AND DANGEROUS

100 Block of SE Columbia Way
At intersection with freeway off-ramp
Vancouver, WA 98661

On Sunday, November 17, 2013, after hours of drinking and smoking marijuana, Ian Cole put on a deadly demonstration of reckless driving on Columbia House Boulevard. According to witnesses, he drove his 2003 Ford Mustang both east and west on the road, swerving around other cars at a high rate of speed. Apparently, this was done to entertain his three passengers. At one time, he performed 360s at the intersection of Columbia House Boulevard and Columbia Way. Approaching the corner where the freeway off-ramp joins Columbia Way, he lost control of the car and hit a power pole and transformer box.

Cole staggered from the vehicle and wandered away to call for a friend to pick him up. With a blood-alcohol level of 0.97, he admitted to being "buzzed" and feeling "slow, relaxed, and mellow" from the marijuana. Apparently he was buzzed so high that he ignored his passengers. Inside the car, his friend, Jesse Orellano-Leister, 20, was dead, while Maxwell Borders, 19, and Benjamin Folk, 25, were unconscious and seriously injured. Folk later died at a local hospital. Cole was arrested and tried for vehicular homicide while driving under the influence, hit and run resulting in injury, and hit and run resulting in death. After learning of the deaths of Folk and Orellano-Leister, and recognizing his culpability, Cole stated, "Suicide doesn't sound like a bad idea."

What remains at the scene today? I discovered some fascinating imprints and a ghost. The atmosphere surrounding the power pole is dense, and there is a sensation of being pulled downward, as if gravity is stronger at this site. Sensitives also hear an audio imprint of a crash. A ghost at the site wanders about but stays close to the power pole. This ghost is confused and in pain. I captured an EVP at this site of a man sobbing.

Imprints of the horrific crash that occurred at this intersection are easily perceived by psychics.

GHOST OF THE CHILDLESS MATRON

Slocum House Theatre
605 Esther Street
360-696-2427

From 1966 to 2012, the Slocum House was a popular boutique theatre seating 65 patrons in an intimate setting. With six to eight shows a season and more than 160 season ticketholders, the theatre was well supported and recognized by many as a centerpiece of a revitalized neighborhood. Its creative atmosphere attracted a number of spirits, including the ghost of Laura Slocum (1838-1914). I've included old theatres on my list of the top five places to find ghosts, so it's no wonder that this marvelous place is haunted.

After achieving success as a merchant, Charles Slocum (1834-1912) started construction of this Italianate-style home in 1867 about one block from its current location. In 1966, the house was moved to make way for a redevelopment project.

Reportedly, Laura could not have children, but she enjoyed inviting neighborhood kids into the house for cookies, and she sometimes hosted parties for them. Her affinity for children may explain the frequent appearance of a cloudlike apparition when children's plays or parties were later held in the building. Witnesses described the apparition as being humanoid while revealing very little detail. Many feel that it was a female spirit, most likely that of Laura Slocum. This apparition appears at several places within the house, most often in the space used as a theatre.

Writer Jeff Davis recounted the experiences of a caretaker who encountered a menacing presence in the basement. While searching for costume items, she caught movement at the periphery of her vision. At one point, she spotted a humanoid figure that quickly faded away, leaving only a growing feeling that the spirit was malevolent or, at the very least, upset that a human had invaded its private space. This ghost

Charles and Laura Slocum built this large house and hosted parties here for children of the neighborhood.

may be the spirit of Charles Slocum. Reportedly, he was not as fond of children as his wife. During theatre productions for children, a male presence was frequently noted moving about among patrons, creating annoying sounds while generating negative energy. He was known to stand at the rear of the theatre and laugh or cough. Apparently, he left an indelible mark on seats B-6 and 7, because patrons often reported extreme discomfort in those seats and moved, leaving them empty for many performances.

In 2012, the Slocum House was investigated by the cast members of *Dead Files*, psychic Amy Allan and retired police detective Steve DiSchiavi (episode 2.4, "Final Curtain Call"). Amy discovered a male spirit she described as "seven feet tall and broad" who was annoyed with living persons in the house. Steve interviewed several staff members of the theatre, all of whom had paranormal experiences with the Slocums.

It is possible that the menacing ghost of the Slocum House is actually that of Amos Short, who died in 1853 at sea while returning to Vancouver from San Francisco. Amos and Esther Short had owned the land on which the Slocum House came to rest in 1966. By 1848, the Shorts had built a cabin and established a profitable farm at the site. By 1850, disputes with the British led to a gunfight in which Amos shot and killed two men at a place now known as Esther Short Park. The ghost of feisty Amos Short may still be on guard, protecting the property on which the Slocum House now sits.

The Slocum House is now home to the Ridgefield Winery tasting room (www.eastforkcellars.com). This business will provide you with an opportunity to taste spirits after searching for ghosts.

GHOSTS OF THE PALLBEARERS

The Academy
400 East Evergreen Boulevard #213
Vancouver, WA 98660
360-694-3271
www.NWvancouveracademy.com

Orbs on the stairs may signal a spiritual presence of Charles Slocum or Amos Short.

This magnificent building resembles the great Georgian halls I've investigated on the East Coast. Constructed in 1871 by the Sisters of Providence and opened as the House of Providence in 1873, it boasts brick walls, balconies, ornately framed windows, and a tall cupola that stand in stark contrast to nearby modern buildings. The architecture and the impression of antiquity it evokes also raise suspicions of ghosts.

The stately building served as a boarding school for girls from 1873 until shortly after World War II, when it accepted boys and discontinued housing. After the school closed in 1966, the rooms were reconfigured into a café, studio, gallery, and office space, and the beautiful chapel was restored to its 19th-century grandeur. The chapel may be the most haunted place in the Academy.

From 1890 to 1950, funerals and memorial services were staged in the chapel for military personnel from Vancouver Barracks. Naturally, many of these ceremonies were somber affairs complete with grieving survivors, comrades-in-arms, and officers decked out in ribbons and medals. In every case, the casket containing the deceased was carried slowly into the chapel and afforded all the honors the military could muster. Often the pallbearers were soldiers who performed that duty as part of their day-to-day service. One of those soldiers seems to be on the job to this day, floating down the center aisle of the chapel in a lock-step fashion, his blue jacket and its brass decorations clearly apparent to sensitive witnesses. On some occasions, more than one pallbearer has been spotted. After sitting quietly in the chapel for several minutes, I caught the transparent, partial image of at least four soldiers in formal uniform. They appeared halfway down the aisle, moving slowly toward the sanctuary. As they approached the steps, they vanished.

Other writers have reported sightings of children in the hallways of the building and on the stairs. At times they pass quietly, but there are reports of disembodied laughter flashing down the corridor. The ghost of a housekeeper who supposedly had a heart attack on the stairs may also haunt the Academy. This ghost appears to be wearing a long gray skirt partly covered by a soiled apron. A restroom near the café is haunted by the spirit of an angry girl who casts a discomforting stare at women who enter alone.

At the northeast corner of the grounds stands a two-story brick

Standing tall and stately, the Academy hosts the ghosts and imprints of several funerals.

The old Academy annex stands derelict and intrigues local ghost hunters.

building that was probably apartments for high-ranking faculty. The place looks derelict, and during my last visit, I found no one who could allow me entry. It may be a hotspot for an investigation.

VANCOUVER BARRACKS

Fort Vancouver National Historic Site
612 East Reserve Street
Vancouver, WA 98661
360-816-6230
www.nps.gov/fova

Despite its location in the state of Washington, on the north shore of the Columbia River, Fort Vancouver has close historical, social, economic, and even political links with Oregon and the city of Portland that provide a basis for research of paranormal phenomena anywhere in the region. Founded in 1825 as a fur-trading center and Western headquarters of the Hudson's Bay Company, the fort initially housed military personnel and explorers but later became a destination for immigrants moving westward along the famed Oregon Trail. In the Great Migration of 1843, as many as 1,000 Americans arrived at the fort before moving on to homesteads throughout the territory. After an arduous five-month trek on the Oregon Trail, many of the people who would later develop the city of Portland found much-needed refuge at the fort, facilities for repair of wagons, and stock to replace their draft animals. Without that assistance, Oregon and the Rose City may have grown very differently from what we know today.

During the 21 years that he served as Fort Vancouver's first manager, Dr. John McLoughlin, a subject of the British Crown, was a beneficent supporter of American immigration into Oregon Territory. While maintaining peaceful relations between the American and British, he also dealt fairly with local Indians by promoting lucrative trade. In 1846, McLoughlin retired and moved south to a beautiful spot on the Willamette River where he founded Oregon City. There, he promoted the political organization of Oregon Territory, which would ultimately lead to statehood in 1859. Known today as the "Father of Oregon," he built a home that still stands in Oregon City and attracts tourists and ghost hunters. His legacy at Fort Vancouver is represented by a full-scale replica of the military and trade facilities he founded in 1825.

Nothing of the original Fort Vancouver remains today aside from artifacts recovered through archeological digs. The fort replica, comprised of 10 buildings and a 10-foot-tall log fence, includes a museum that contains more than 2 million objects found in the excavations. This fascinating historic site is not a venue targeted by ghost hunters, but many investigators have searched the area for the fort's elusive graveyards. Records are incomplete and conflicting, but it is believed that the fort had at least three cemeteries. One of them is thought to be near the parade ground and Officer's Row at the U.S. Army's Vancouver Barracks. Another possible site is at the Old City Cemetery, on Mill Plain Boulevard.

By the mid-1840s, American settlement and economic activity in the region pressured British interests into moving farther north. The resulting de facto reorganization of political control of the region was formalized in the Oregon Treaty of 1846, which moved the southern boundary of British territory to the 49th parallel. The treaty enabled local Americans to establish the Oregon Territory, including land that currently comprises the states of Oregon, Washington, and Idaho as well as parts of Wyoming and Montana. After officially recognizing it on August 14, 1848, as an incorporated U.S. territory, Congress authorized the construction of a military facility adjacent to the now-derelict Hudson's Bay fort.

Opened in 1849, the facility was originally known as Camp Vancouver. In the 1850s, various publications referred to it as "Columbia Barracks" and "Fort Vancouver." Ghost hunters who research the history of buildings in the area may be confused by the U.S. Army facility and the earlier Hudson's Bay fort both using the name Fort Vancouver. The army facility and nearby Pearson Field sprawl over land once occupied by parts of the Hudson's Bay settlement, but they are distinct historical entities.

Through the second half of the 19th century, Vancouver Barracks grew to include more than 100 buildings, barns, and shops and several corrals. Among the remaining buildings are several mansions that comprise Officer's Row. Each one is distinctive, yet all of them reflect the architectural fashion of the time. Their styles include Second Empire, Italianate, Classical Revival, Queen Anne, and Colonial Revival. The largest mansions were constructed for field officers who held a rank of major or higher. Many of them were once occupied by famous generals, including Ulysses S. Grant, George B. McClellan, and George Pickett. In the 1930s, Gen. George C. Marshall served at the barracks. Throughout World War II, he was U.S. Army chief of staff and chief military adviser to Pres. Franklin D. Roosevelt. After the war, Marshall served as secretary of state under Pres. Harry Truman. He distinguished himself by developing and administering the Marshall Plan, which rebuilt Europe after World War II. His house, believed to be haunted, still stands on Officer's Row.

After World War II, military activity at the barracks was minimal. By 1949, most of the fort was transferred to the National Park Service. In 2012, the U.S. Army Reserve vacated all lands and structures within the East and South Vancouver Barracks, marking the end of military activity at the historic site.

Decades of U.S. Army activity, coupled with the dramatic history of early Yankee settlers and the struggles and early demise of Hudson's Bay explorers and fur trappers, have left an indelible paranormal mark on the landscape. Some of the buildings are not currently accessible, but the grounds offer many opportunities for dowsing, EMF and EVP sweeps, and exploration by empaths.

VANCOUVER BARRACKS HOSPITAL, BUILDING 614

Barnes Street at McClelland Road
Vancouver, WA 98661
360-816-6230

Most of the structures that comprise the Post Hospital at Vancouver Barracks were constructed between 1905 and 1907. The oldest portion of the hospital was built in the 1880s and served as an aid station and storage facility for medical supplies that were to be shipped out with troops dispatched to the Indian Wars and Spanish-American War of 1898. During its years of operation, buildings were joined together, porches were enclosed, and, in the 1970s, the southern wing was rotated 90 degrees and attached to the main building to make way for the I-5 widening project. At the height of its development, the hospital had 400 beds, several operating room and clinics, a morgue in the basement, and a large psychiatric ward on the third floor. Always busy with sick and injured soldiers, the hospital also served loggers from nearby mills and members of the Civilian Conservation Corps. During the Spanish flu epidemic of 1918, more than 21,000 patients were treated at this hospital. It is unknown how many patents died here, but through the decades during which sick and injured people sought help here, it is likely that thousands left the place by way of the morgue.

The army closed the Post Hospital after World War II but continued to use the building for storage and offices. Early in the 1990s, the last military tenants moved out, and the place has stood vacant since. With the exception of a few fortunate ghost hunters, only maintenance and construction workers have entered the building, trying to stop the ravages of time so that the place might someday be repurposed as an inn or offices. Despite their efforts, the building is in rough shape. I was allowed entry during my last visit to Vancouver Barracks. Aside from the basic creepiness of the place, it is dark with paint peeling from the walls, cracked and stained ceiling plaster, and some rooms filled with maintenance supplies or piles of dirt and dust. I was told many of the floor tiles contain asbestos.

The Vancouver Barracks hospital once had 400 beds serving wounded soldiers and thousands stricken with the Spanish flu in 1918.

Most of the credible stories about ghostly activity in this old hospital come from maintenance and construction workers. Doors to the building have been found unlocked when workers arrive in the morning, despite assurances that they were locked by the last person leaving the previous evening. Curious workers have left tape on the doors that would be torn if the doors were opened. When the doors were found unlocked on several occasions and the tape undisturbed, it seemed clear that whoever unlocked the doors did not enter or leave the place.

A ghost hunter visiting from Texas claims she was chased from the basement by an "aggressive" ghost. I encountered an angry spirit in the basement, but there were no gestures that caused me to flee. It was clear, however, that this ghost did not want visitors. His attitude did not change even when I told him that I work in a large hospital. A portion of the basement was used as a morgue, and I found it easy to identify areas where bodies were stored, because the air thickened abruptly and intense cold spots were discovered. One ghost hunter reported seeing an old autopsy table shake. Others have reported what they call "the smell of death" in the basement.

The women's restroom on the second floor has also been identified as a paranormal hotspot. Ghosts in this room raise and lower the toilet-seat lids. At several places throughout the hospital, workers have heard unexplained footsteps, keys jingling as if a ghost night watchman were walking about, coughing, moaning, loud bangs that echo down hallways, tapping sounds emanating from the walls, muted whispers, and creaking noises as if doors were opening on old, rusty hinges.

Today, the Fort Vancouver National Trust hopes to partner with other civic organizations and fully renovate the Post Hospital into a center for the arts. Glass-enclosed porches that once housed tuberculosis patients may be repurposed as artist studios, and large rooms that were once busy wards may be suitable for performance arts or meetings. When the place does reopen to the public, ghost hunters should be among the first visitors to learn what the ghosts think of the renovation and modern amenities

HOWARD HOUSE

750 Anderson Street
Vancouver, WA 98661
360-992-1820
www.fortvan.org

Strange things have happened in this house, causing many people to conclude that it is haunted. No one has identified the ghosts that occupy the mansion, but it is clear that at least one spirit has the power to break glass.

The house was constructed in 1879 as a residence for Maj. Gen. Oliver Otis Howard (1830-1909) and his family. A Medal of Honor winner, General Howard fought in several major battles of the Civil War, including Gettysburg, and lost his right arm in 1862 after suffering two gunshot wounds at the Battle of Fair Oaks. After the war, he played a major role in Reconstruction. In 1874 he assumed command of the Department of the Columbia and established his headquarters at Fort Vancouver. Over the next six years, he fought in several Indian wars, which nearly wiped out formerly peaceful tribes of the Pacific Northwest, including the Nez Perce led by Chief Joseph.

The ghost of Civil War hero Maj. Gen. Oliver Howard still paces the second-floor rooms of his former home.

Dubbed the "Christian General" because of his religious beliefs, Howard was known for considering spiritual issues in the development of his military policies, including battle plans. For several days after his return to Fort Vancouver from a battle, he was often seen pacing the mansion's wide porch or walking past the large windows on the second floor. This suggests he was deeply affected by the destruction of a culture that, at times, he defended against bureaucrats in Washington, D.C. Perhaps it is his ghost that witnesses have spotted passing by the large windows on the second floor.

The most reliable report of this ghostly manifestation is that of a former fort commander who walked past the Howard mansion one night with his son. At the time, the house was awaiting renovation after a fire, and much of it was boarded up. Both witnesses saw a white, humanoid figure pass by several second-floor windows. It moved from one end of the house to the other numerous times over a five-minute period.

Ghostly activity seems to have occurred on the first floor of the mansion as well. One morning in 1999, workers entered to find that an exhibit composed of 20 large glass panels had been vandalized. One panel, measuring four by eight feet, lay in pieces on the floor. The initial suggestion that a ghost was responsible was dismissed as a joke. However, a few years, later a similar event occurred. During a recent visit of mine, a person who works in the house told me that strange things happen "all the time." Usually, these are doors that swing open and closed, muffled footsteps, and unexplained cold spots. Once, a security system that tracked movements captured someone moving from a second-floor room to the hallway and into another room before disappearing from the surveillance.

General Howard resided in this beautiful mansion only two years before his appointment as superintendent of the United States Military Academy at West Point. Upon his retirement from the army on November 8, 1894, at the age of 64, he established his residence at his daughter's home in Portland, where he wrote his memoirs. Today, the Howard House is headquarters of the Fort Vancouver National Trust. Rooms may be rented for meetings and small receptions and the courtyard for weddings.

ARTILLERY BARRACKS

Fort Vancouver
600 East Hatheway Road
Vancouver, WA 98661
360-828-5237

Constructed in 1904, the artillery barracks were designed to house a battalion of up to 240 men. A Spartan military facility, the 40,000-square-foot building had a few architectural flourishes, such as a pressed-tin ceiling and fancy white-oak floors. These features were restored to their original glory when the entire building was renovated and reopened as a conference center. Today, meeting and banquet rooms can be rented by the hour.

Despite the modern conveniences, the place still has a military atmosphere, which includes a few ghosts. No one knows how many soldiers may have died in the building, but it seems certain that some

These barracks at Fort Vancouver were once home to an artillery battalion of 240 men, but it became a temporary hospital during the flu epidemic of 1918.

would have during the Spanish flu epidemic of 1918 here. When members of a battalion came down with flu or other contagious illnesses, the men were usually quarantined in their barracks. During my visits to the building, I encountered shuffling footsteps, as though sick men were struggling to walk from their beds to the latrine. These odd footfalls were often accompanied by muted coughs. This building is large enough that a ghost hunter may get away from others and conduct EVP sweeps or use dowsing rods without attracting unwanted attention. A hotspot for paranormal activity is the center of the large conference room. In 1904, this area was the sergeant's walk, a path that noncommissioned officers walked while monitoring the troops whose bunks filled the space between the outer walls and the columns that still stand.

GHOST ON THE STAIRS

George C. Marshall House

1301 Officer's Row
Vancouver, WA 98661
360-693-3103

Built in 1886 as a residence for the barracks commander and his family, this spectacular mansion has been occupied by so many people that it is impossible to determine whose ghost haunts the place. EVP and psychic investigations have not led to an identification of the ghost, but I believe that it is the spirit of a maid who worked in the house for many years.

The mansion is named in honor of Gen. George C. Marshall (1880-1959), although he resided in the house with his wife, Katharine, for only a few years, from 1936 to 1938. Marshall is well known to history buffs as the U.S. Army chief of staff throughout World War II and secretary of state from 1947 to 1949. His greatest postwar accomplishment was the Marshall Plan, which rebuilt Europe and many of the Pacific nations. For this great service to humanity, he was awarded the Nobel Peace Prize. During his three years at Vancouver

Army generals and staff officers attended to the command of the general's Fifth Infantry Brigade in the dining room of the Marshall House.

Named for U.S. Army Chief of Staff Gen. George C. Marshall, this house harbors the ghost of a maid who hums while walking up and down the stairs.

Barracks, he commanded the Third Division's Fifth Infantry Brigade and organized the region's Civilian Conservation Corps camps.

The interior of the Queen Anne-style Victorian mansion is nothing short of spectacular. Elegant mirrors and fireplace surrounds, distinctive inlaid hardwood floors, period furniture, and amazing wood paneling create a fascinating 19th-century atmosphere. I found the general's study on the first floor and the staircase to be the most active sites for paranormal activity.

For nearly 30 minutes, I sat on the small bench on the staircase landing between the first and second floors, detecting the presence of a female ghost who walked up and down the stairs while humming. At times, I also heard a distinct grunt, as though she had lost her breath while carrying something heavy. I believe that this ghost was a maid in the house who is eternally bound to continue her duties, cleaning the place and carrying heavy loads of laundry from the second-floor bedrooms to the basement.

In the general's study, I detected the presence of a very old gentleman who sits quietly at the desk, watching people who tour the place. He does not seem to object to strangers in the study, but he is quite curious about why they are there and not wearing military uniforms.

Today, this Victorian mansion is a museum open for self-guided tours, providing easy access for ghost hunters. Rooms are available for rent for special events and, on the second floor, as office space.

GHOST OF GENERAL SULLY

Grant House
1101 Officer's Row
Vancouver, WA 98661
360-906-1101
www.thegranthouse.us

Although Gen. Ulysses S. Grant never lived in this house, it bears his name in recognition of his service at Fort Vancouver from 1852 to 1853. He resided in the Quartermaster's Ranch while at the fort, but it is likely he spent a lot of time in this building. Constructed in 1848

Constructed as a log building in 1848, the Grant House is haunted by one of its most illustrious residents, Gen. Alfred Sully.

as a log building, the place was used briefly as the fort commander's residence before renovation as the officer's club. With the addition of wide verandas surrounding the first and second floors and wood panels over the logs, the house's architecture became reminiscent of a mid-Atlantic mansion, which was probably quite appealing to the many officers who were thousands of miles from their homes in Virginia and the Carolinas. During the Civil War, the building returned to use as a residence for commanding officers, one of whom was Gen. Alfred Sully (1821-79), who gained fame in the Indian Wars of the 1860s.

General Sully arrived in Monterey, California, in 1849, enthused by his assignment to such idyllic country. Soon after his arrival, at the age of 28, he married a 15-year-old Mexican girl and contemplated leaving the army for the life of a farmer and rancher in this pristine land. Tragedy struck, however, when his young wife succumbed to cholera and his child died of strangulation. Deeply embittered by their loss, he thrust himself into his military career, which culminated in his appointment as commander of Fort Vancouver from 1874 to 1879.

In his book, *No Tears for the General: The Life of General Alfred Sully 1821-1879*, Sully's grandson, Langdon Sully, noted that the general never recovered from the loss of his young family. Other biographers suggest that this personal anguish accounts for Sully's reputation as "a hard-bitten, unemotional soldier." It also explains why the general's ghost haunts the Grant House, a place where he may have found solace from the misery of losing his wife and baby.

Later in life, Sully was described in newspaper accounts as a somber and stoic fellow. In 1877, the Vancouver Independent described his appearance as he reviewed troops: "The General looks venerable with his silver locks, and gives the command with a stern dignity born of a long experience in Army life." Ghost hunters who search the Grant House for General Sully should be on the lookout for a man of stern demeanor with long, gray-silver hair.

Ghostly activity attributed to Sully includes cold spots, footsteps on wood floors, doors opening and closing, windows rattling, telephones and other electrical devices turning on, and disembodied voices whispering in the ears of surprised visitors. Sully also seems to like coffee. Restaurant staff have found coffeemakers turned on when they arrive in the morning. Sometimes, they discover a half-cup of coffee on a table and a chair pulled away.

Local author Jeff Davis has visited the Grant House often and believes that the general was sick for a long time before he died. "I think he may have had stomach cancer," Davis noted. "Others think it was kidney problems. Sometimes he couldn't get out of bed and other times he'd pace the hall all night because of the pain." It is worth noting that General Sully died in this house on April 27, 1879.

One of the owners of the restaurant that now occupies the Grant House has reported seeing a black apparition in a hall on the second floor. Others have spotted a tall man standing on the balcony. This fellow reportedly had a beard and wore an old-fashioned long coat that resembled a military coat.

I have spotted an apparition each time I visit the Grant House. Hotspots include the second-floor hallway outside the room where Sully died, the west balcony, the bar and fireplace, and the first-floor corridor where the building's original log structure is exposed.

EVP investigations may be more productive if you use the general's personal information to elicit a response. You might mention the loss of his young wife in Monterey or ask about his service in the Indian Wars. It has been reported that, in 1862, the general married a French-Yankton Sioux girl because she resembled his late wife. Questions about his Native American wife may evoke responses that suggest this is a sensitive issue.

Today, ghost hunters have easy access to the Grant House by patronizing the restaurant. Staff members may be willing to share stories of recent encounters with General Sully. The building is also home to the Grant House Folk Art Center.

GHOST OF THELMA TAYLOR

Cathedral Park
6636 North Baltimore Avenue
Portland 97203
503-823-7529

Thelma Taylor died near the St. Johns Bridge in the 1940s, but her tragic story continues to fascinate people in the neighborhood. Some of them are quite advanced in age, yet they clearly remember Thelma as a quiet, shy girl who worked hard in school and availed herself of every opportunity to make a little money by picking beans or cleaning houses. Their recollections in recent interviews have introduced Thelma to a new generation of people who are fascinated by tragic crimes and the ghosts they produce.

Fifteen-year-old Thelma was murdered on August 6, 1949, by 22-year-old Morris Leland after a miserable night huddled in the tall reeds and shrubs that covered the ground near the St. Johns Bridge. Thelma was kidnapped early in the morning on August 5. Leland admitted that he initially tried to befriend Thelma and, despite her misgivings, she made no attempt to escape. After driving around for an hour, Leland parked the car and kept Thelma in a secluded area near the Willamette River for the remainder of the day. Intending to rape her, he deferred when he learned she was a virgin. Throughout the day, long periods of silence were interrupted by brief conversation. Eventually, Leland grew tired of Thelma and the dangerous predicament he had created. With a long criminal record that began when he was only 13 years old, he knew that one more encounter with the Portland police would end with a significant prison sentence. Previous arrests for assault, rape, car theft, and robbery should have deterred him, but the prospect of more jail time had not been sufficient to stop him from committing one more heinous crime. Perhaps his beguiling demeanor and the seven-inch hunting knife he carried gave him the confidence to follow his baser instincts.

Sometime in the evening, Leland realized he could not release Thelma because she was a responsible girl who would promptly report the incident to the police. It was also clear that she would be able to give police a good description of the car and Leland himself. Concerned about being seen, he moved Thelma to another vacant lot about eight blocks north of the St. Johns Bridge.

After hours of pleading and crying, Thelma fell asleep as Leland sat brooding about the inevitable murder of a girl he wished he had never encountered. He fell asleep just before dawn, while Thelma awakened to the sound of railroads cars moving along a nearby track. Sensing an opportunity for help, Thelma started screaming. Leland, startled, grabbed a piece of steel rebar that had been discarded in the junk-strewn lot. After the first blow to her head, Thelma stopped screaming, yet Leland continued beating her. When it was clear she was dead, he plunged his knife deep into her abdomen.

Leland hid Thelma's body under logs and brush then escaped, only to be apprehended a week later while driving a stolen car. Police were aware of a missing person's report concerning Thelma Taylor but did not look upon Leland as a suspect. Plagued by guilt or simply tired of his miserable life, Leland asked to speak to a homicide detective about a murder he had committed. On February 7, 1951, Morris Leland was convicted of first-degree murder and sentenced to death. That sentence was carried out on January 9, 1953, in the gas chamber at the state penitentiary in Salem.

All of that horror and misery happened so long ago, yet something paranormal persists in the places where Leland held Thelma captive before murdering her. The ground under the St. Johns Bridge is now known as Cathedral Park, by virtue of the gothic design of the bridge's supporting structure. It opened as a beautiful park in the 1980s, and the tall reeds and weeds that once concealed Thelma from the help of passersby are now gone. Her ghost may still be there, however, screaming in the predawn air.

The proprietor of a nearby café, Pattie's Home Plate on Lombard Street, has heard a young girl's voice cry out, "Help me! Help me! Somebody, please!"

Others in the neighborhood told me they have heard two voices, a

Locals believe that the ghost of Thelma Taylor still haunts Cathedral Park, the site of a terrifying kidnapping and tragic murder.

male and a female, arguing in the middle of the night.

People who live near Cathedral Park also report strange lights moving around in the darkness and unexplained cold spots. Sensitives feel dread and anguish in the stand of trees that fills a depression slightly northwest of the bridge. This is likely the spot where Thelma spent the last night of her life.

These sounds and impressions may be imprints left behind from that harrowing night on August 5, 1949, because it seems unlikely to me that Thelma would remain in a place where she was held captive at knifepoint and sexually abused. It is possible, however, that her ghost remains in Cathedral Park, unaware that she is dead or unable to accept the notion that she is free to leave.

It is important to note that Thelma was not killed in Cathedral Park. Based on Leland's confession, her body was found a few blocks north of the park close to the Willamette River. I explored that location by walking north on North Bradford Street until I reached the eastern boundary of a large container yard. As I headed to the shore of the river, my dowsing rods became extremely active. At one spot about 15 feet from the water, near a pile of logs similar to those that once concealed Thelma's body, the rods began spinning and continued to do so for more than two minutes. They stopped when I asked, "Thelma, are you here?"

HISTORIC COLUMBIAN CEMETERY

1151 North Columbia Boulevard
Portland 97211
503-622-1615

Creepy yet beautiful, this old cemetery contains the remains of some of Portland's earliest pioneers. Among them are key players in the city's evolution from a muddy, backwater logging town to a major Pacific Rim port. Despite the efforts of dedicated volunteers who provide 100 percent of the funds necessary for the cemetery's maintenance, many headstones are covered with fallen leaves and branches from the canopy of trees. Others are simply worn by the climate, making the inscriptions almost illegible. Opened in 1857 at the shore of the Columbia Slough, the tiny cemetery is now surrounded by freeway ramps that convey traffic to and from I-5. A dense tree canopy provides a barrier to the sound of cars and trucks and creates still air and shadows that enable sensitive visitors to get in touch with the spirits of Portland's pioneers who await help clearing or repairing graves. Many visitors have reported experiences with a ghost of Lydia, who seems to have assumed the duty of cemetery hostess. She whispers in the ears of fascinated visitors and sometimes appears as a partial apparition. I could not find a headstone engraved with Lydia, but many monuments in this cemetery were obscured by piles of leaves and tall grass. As I walked the alleys between rows of graves, I did encounter cells of thickened air that was much cooler than the surrounding atmosphere.

The graves of Andreas Schmidt (1827-1910) and his wife, Amelia (1830-1908), are particularly fascinating because they are surrounded by the graves of their children and grandchildren. The graves of the Adams family are just as compelling and thought-provoking. Little Frankie (1876) lived less than a year, while Sethie (1873-79) lived to age six.

Opened in 1857, beautifully creepy Columbian Cemetery contains the remains of some of Portland's earliest pioneers.

Patriarch Asa Adams (1804-77) lived a long life but had to endure the passing of his wife, Hannah (1816-73), and grandson Frankie. Strong imprints may be found here, undoubtedly created by Adams family members who visited the graves on birthdays and other important dates.

As I walked around the cemetery, I perceived several strange sounds. Being completely alone and blocking out the noise of nearby traffic, I heard the muted tones of musical instruments, horse's hooves on the muddy ground, and a gunshot that echoed off the wall of a warehouse that stands adjacent to the east border of the cemetery.

Other places to hunt ghosts:

OLD GLORY ANTIQUES MALL

2000 Main Street
Vancouver, WA 98660
360-906-8823

Antiques stores are hotspots for ghostly activity and strong imprints that are generally easy to detect. The Old Glory Antiques Mall offers much more than memorabilia, old clothes, art, household items, and used junk. From the street, it looks like a small neighborhood shop. Inside, however, astounded customers find a vast collection of unusual antiques. People who are sensitive to paranormal phenomena also detect the intense imprints and ghosts that fill the place.

By their nature, antiques stores contain items that were used many years, sometimes even decades, before finding their way to the stores' shelves. Repetitive use coupled with strong emotions create imprints on these objects that may, when handled, be detected as fragrances, images, or sounds or feelings ranging from happiness to fear and rage.

In addition to imprints, many items in the Old Glory Antiques Mall have ghosts attached. It is challenging to investigate ghosts at this or any other store without attracting unwanted attention. It is possible, however, to place an audio recorder next to a compelling object and let it run for 30 minutes or more as you browse the shop. After discounting background noise and the voices of customers, you may find some fascinating audio phenomena that indicate a ghostly presence.

PEARSON AIR MUSEUM

1115 East Fifth Street
Vancouver, WA 98661
360-816-6232
www.pearsonairmuseum.org

Old airplanes are similar to old ships: they almost always have something paranormal attached to them. Both may attract spirits that died elsewhere because they offer a familiar, emotionally stabilizing place. Despite a fatal crash or sinking, ghosts of pilots and sailors tend to have an undying affinity for an airplane or ship that enabled them to fulfill their dreams and experience some of the greatest thrills life can offer. So it shouldn't surprise us if ghosts take up residence in aviation museums and historic ships.

Located adjacent to historic Fort Vancouver, the Pearson Aviation Museum is a worthwhile place for ghost hunters to visit. The historic hangar, built in 1918, stands next to a modern structure that houses most of the exhibits. An ongoing dispute between the National Park Service and the Fort Vancouver National Trust resulted in the removal of all privately owned artifacts. The few remnants of historic aircraft in the hangar are prime targets for ghost hunters. The hangar itself seems to have numerous imprints dating from World War I, when soldiers worked there producing millions of board feet of spruce, which was used to build planes.

GHOST OF THE RECKLESS DRIVER

NE Highway 99 at 72nd Street
Vancouver, WA 98665

On November 27, 2012, Anastasia Morrison, 20, of Vancouver, took the 78th Street exit and turned right onto busy Highway 99, heading south. Surveillance video revealed that she continued driving her 2006 Mazda MX6 well above the speed limit. Then, something distracted her, causing her to lose control of the car, swerve across two lanes of oncoming traffic, collide with a pedestrian, and finally slam into a pole in front of My Dad's Automotive and Exhaust Shop at 7205 NE

Highway 99. Anastasia died on impact, precluding any assessment of her perspective. Equally tragic was the resultant injury of 21-year old pedestrian Joseph Reilly. Anastasia's vehicle struck him with such force that he was thrown across 72nd Street into the parking lot of Collins Plaza, a distance of more than 40 feet. Reilly required several surgeries and months of rehabilitation before he could return home in May 2013. According to accident investigators, his survival was truly a miracle.

I believe that the ghost of Anastasia Morrison remains at the site of this terrible crash. At the light post on the corner of 72nd Street and Highway 99, I detected the presence of a distraught female entity. She was in pain, both physical and emotional, and totally confused by her current status. She asked, "What happened?" and then added, "Did I do that?"

EVIL PRESENCE

Nelson Residence
Officer's Row
Fort Vancouver
Vancouver, WA 98661

This house has severely restricted access, but some ghost hunters have been able to enter it and post fascinating reports. It is the current residence of Adm. Paul Nelson, Ret., the great-grandson of Pres. William Howard Taft. It has been reported that the admiral does not kindly receive ghost hunters' requests to investigate his home. Some Web sites warn that anyone who rings the doorbell and asks permission to take a look around will be charged with trespassing. There are times, though, when the place is opened for tours. If you visit Fort Vancouver, it may be worthwhile to stop at this house for such a tour.

Some say that the grass in front of the residence fades from green to brown and then returns to green over a period of four days. This cycle repeats every week or two year round. Visitors have reported that the walls are marked with a substance believed to be blood. Efforts to clean it have not been successful. There is much speculation about the source of these bizarre phenomena and the likelihood that the home is haunted by a malevolent presence. No EVP or other technical evidence has been posted on the Web. Furthermore, I found no historical documents that offer insight into these reports. The place is delightfully creepy, though, even when viewed from the street.

DOWSING AT VANPORT

Site of Vanport Flood
North Lake Avenue at Mud Slough
Portland 97217

The Blue Heron Golf Club and Portland International Race Way now occupy a site that was once the town of Vanport. The 648-acre town was constructed at the onset of World War II to house shipbuilders. Once the second-largest city in Oregon, with more than 40,000 residents in 1943, Vanport saw its population drop to about 18,000 by 1948. The town was essentially composed of hastily built shanties, constructed without regard to their location on a floodplain, in order to accommodate workers desperately needed for Henry Kaiser's shipbuilding industry.

On May 29, 1948, the general manager of Vanport announced that the city was "not in any foreseeable danger" of flooding, despite the Columbia River having risen several feet above its normal level. By the next afternoon, the river reached 15 feet above normal, undermining a dike that had held the mighty river in check for eight years. At 4:05 P.M., a 200-foot-long section of the dike was breached, allowing water to rush into Vanport and destroy every house. No warning had been issued to the residents, yet the official death toll was only 15. Unofficial estimates say that as many as 150 lost their lives in the Vanport Flood, which also left 18,000 homeless.

It is unlikely that ghosts of the victims inhabit the golf course, raceway, and parks here, but sensitive visitors have strange experiences. Dowsing rods are known to be very active in West and East Delta parks and on the golf course. This may be due to disturbed patterns of energy caused by the flood. Ley lines may also have been disrupted or amplified by the rush of millions of tons of water in 1948.

Several archival images of the Vanport Flood may be viewed online.

CHAPTER 5

Oregon City and Communities South of Portland

Oregon City, Salem, Eugene, and other communities linked by I-5 are often visited by travelers heading to or away from Portland. This modern highway makes transit easy, leaving you time and energy to stop and spend an hour or two touring the many historical sites. Ghost hunters who take the time to look into the histories of these communities will find fascinating tales of pioneer families who traveled for months on the arduous Oregon Trail, arriving a decade or more before Oregon became the 33rd U.S. state on February 14, 1859. The homes they built, the towns they founded, and the cemeteries they filled remain as intriguing sites for those who wish to experience the ghosts of some of Oregon's great families. Modern tragedies have created a fresh crop of ghosts, but it is particularly fascinating to seek out spirits from some of Oregon's pioneers, such as Dr. Forbes Barclay, Dr. John McLoughlin Asahel and Eugenia Bush, Gen. Cyrus Reed, the McMurphey daughters, and little Josephine Hunsaker, who died at the tender age of 12. Visit the Ermantinger house, where Francis Pettygrove and Asa Lovejoy flipped the coin that decided if the booming, muddy city to the north should be called Boston or Portland. Enjoy the scenery and ease of travel on I-5, but do take the time to visit with Oregon's historical ghosts.

GHOST OF THE FATHER OF OREGON

McLoughlin House
713 Center Street
Oregon City 97045
503-656-5146
www.mcloughlinhouse.org

The McLoughlin House stands today as an iconic structure that calls to mind Oregon's greatest pioneer, Dr. John McLoughlin (1784-1857), and his effect on the history of Fort Vancouver, Oregon City, and Oregon. Originally constructed in 1845 on a steep hillside by the Willamette River, the grand two-story house was slated for demolition in 1909 until concerned citizens stepped forward. They founded the McLoughlin Memorial Association and quickly mustered the resources to move the house to its current location on a bluff subsequently named McLoughlin Ridge. After a lengthy restoration process, the place opened as a museum that contains many pieces of furniture used by the McLoughlin family.

Despite its distinction as the grandest home in Oregon City, the McLoughlin House has a dark past. Ten years after the doctor's death in 1857, his daughter, Marie Eloisa McLoughlin Harvey (1817-84), sold the mansion, and it reopened as a hotel. Its location near the rapidly growing industrial part of town fostered its transition into a dormitory for workers at a nearby woolen mill and then into a brothel. Ultimately, it was abandoned to vagrants, who nearly destroyed the place. The McLoughlin Memorial Association saved it only weeks before its planned demolition. Today, the McLoughlin House is the oldest museum in Oregon. It is notable that McLoughlin and his wife, Marguerite (1775-1860), both died in the home. Their graves, located in the backyard, were moved from the original site.

Born in Quebec in 1784, McLoughlin was a quintessential pioneer who literally created a new civilization in a land thousands of miles from his home. From the age of six, he lived with his great-uncle, who generously supported the boy's education. McLoughlin received a medical degree at a very young age in 1803. As a physician working for the Northwest Company, a fur-trading enterprise, he traveled extensively throughout Canada and mastered several Indian languages. In 1824, Hudson's Bay Company hired him as chief factor (superintendent) of the Columbia District. Arriving in Oregon country in 1825, he established Fort Vancouver, where he regulated trade in the region, kept peace with the Indians, and developed salmon fisheries and the timber industry as well as export businesses that sent goods as far as Russian Alaska, Mexican California, and Hawaii. He also maintained amicable relations between American and British fur trappers, whose numbers increased rapidly throughout the 1830s. By the 1840s, friction between British and American interests in the region had escalated, and McLoughlin found himself favoring Yankee immigration and settlement, despite

The graves of Dr. John McLoughlin and his wife, Marguerite, may be found in a quiet, shady spot behind their home.

orders from his superiors to discourage such encroachment. In 1842, he supported the formation of Oregon as an independent nation, but this notion was dropped when American settlers called for a provisional government that would ultimately create Oregon Territory as part of the United States. McLoughlin favored that movement, and in 1846, representatives of the British Crown joined American representatives in signing the Oregon Treaty.

McLoughlin immediately resigned from the British-owned Hudson's Bay Company and founded a town about 30 miles south of the Columbia River on the banks of the Willamette. Possibly as a demonstration of his true allegiance, he named the town Oregon City.

In many accounts of Oregon's history, McLoughlin is described as an able administrator, skilled and caring physician, shrewd politician, wise diplomat, visionary, and congenial host to both white settlers and local Indians. He stood six feet five inches tall and, in his later years, wore long white hair and a stern countenance. Local Indians, who revered him for his fairness, called him the "Silver-Haired Eagle." His marriage to Marguerite, a half-Cree, half-Swiss woman, not only reflected his attitude toward Indians but enhanced his popularity with them.

This old house is reportedly full of spirits. In addition to the spirits of McLoughlin and his wife, ghosts may be found here that were "created" when the place was a hotel, brothel, and vagrants' flophouse.

McLoughlin's presence has been detected at several locations within the mansion. Visitors and museum staff members have heard unexplained footsteps on the stairs, in the parlor, and in an upstairs bedroom. A tall shadow believed to be the doctor has been spotted on the stairs, in the parlor, and in the dining room. A portrait of McLoughlin hangs over the fireplace in the parlor, where he died. It is said that every year on September 3, the anniversary of his death, the doctor's painted face glows eerily.

An apparition, unmistakably identified as McLoughlin, has been seen sitting on the bed in the master bedroom. This ghost often sits in a rocking chair, making it rock and back and forth.

Passersby on the street have reported seeing the image of a woman, identified as Marguerite McLoughlin, looking out an upstairs window. Marguerite was known for smoking a pipe, and several people have

Once the home of Dr. John McLoughlin, known as the Father of Oregon, this 1845-vintage house is now a museum that harbors several ghosts.

detected the peculiar odor of pipe tobacco in an upstairs bedroom. She has also been known to hover close to or touch visitors and staff members and move out-of-reach objects such as her china tea set.

In the 1880s, Chinese workers at the nearby woolen mills were housed in the building. There is no historical record of deaths, but it seems likely that several of them died there, because psychics have detected a number of spirits in the office who are frightened of something. They create an aura in the room that some psychics sense as quite disturbing or negative.

Some writers have reported that a murder occurred in the parlor, probably during the time that the place was a brothel or vagrants' camp. Sensitive people who enter the room experience an abrupt and intense impression of foreboding. Some break into a sweat and feel they must get out of the house immediately.

The most frequently sighted ghost in the McLoughlin House has been dubbed the "red-haired boy." Judged to be six to eight years old, he appears as a lifelike apparition at several locations there and in the nearby Barclay House. He has been spotted playing near the stairs, in the dining rooms, and in the offices of these homes. Often, the boy is accompanied by the partial apparition of a dog, which leaves muddy footprints. This kid has been so active in the houses that, at times, the police have been called to investigate an intruder. His antics include hiding objects needed by staff members and watching visitors as they tour the houses. It seems likely that the red-haired boy was a child of Eloisa McLoughlin. However, I was unable to locate any historical records that describe the hair color of her three boys.

Sensitive people who tour the house detect fascinating and sometimes unpleasant sensations. A group of Native Americans once entered but stopped abruptly when they encountered something that they described as "unpleasant." It is difficult to imagine what may have created that impression, because McLoughlin was known for his kindness toward local Indians and he was highly respected by them. One psychic reported that she detected the presence of a protective Indian who was once a servant in the McLoughlin House. The spirit of the servant may still be on duty, safeguarding his fortunate position within the household.

GHOST OF UNCLE SANDY

Barclay House
719 Center Street
Oregon City 97045
www.mcloughlinhouse.org/the-barclay-house.html

Built in 1849 as a residence for Dr. Forbes Barclay and his family, this house now stands next to the McLoughlin House, part of a cluster of historic homes once occupied by Oregon City's greatest pioneers. The house stood at the Oregon City waterfront until the 1930s, when it was moved to its current site on McLoughlin Ridge. It no longer commands a view of the Willamette River, but shaded by tall trees, it is still a popular venue for ghost hunters.

In his early life, Dr. Forbes Barclay (1812-73) was somewhat of an adventurer. He embarked on several Arctic expeditions, including one that ended in a shipwreck from which he was saved by Eskimos. Deciding to settle down, he took his medical degree from the Royal College of Surgeons in 1838 and entered into service with the Hudson's Bay Company, based in eastern Canada. Still longing for adventure, Dr. Barclay headed west to Fort Vancouver, arriving June 4, 1839. There he met Dr. John McLoughlin, the famed superintendent of the fort who, years later, enticed Barclay to move to Oregon City.

While at Fort Vancouver, Barclay married Marie Pambrun (1826-90), who was not yet 16 years old. The eldest daughter of Chief Trader Pierre Chrysologue Pambrun and Catherine Humpherville, the French-speaking beauty was widely known for her fine character and trace of Indian blood. She and Barclay had seven children together. Their first child, Jean Jacques, died of diphtheria in 1847, at age two. Their two other boys, Peter Thomas (1847-unknown) and Alexander (1851-1908), moved with the Barclays into their new Oregon City house in 1849. The couple had four more children, all of whom were born in the Barclay House: Adrianna "Katie" Catherine (1852-1934), Hattie (1854-1926), William Charles (1856-1926), and Edmund (1859-63).

Numerous relatives visited the house often, some staying for several months. It has been reported that Barclay's seafaring brother, "Uncle Sandy," stayed there whenever his ship docked in Portland and that his spirit now haunts the place. I wonder if this is an error perpetuated by the retelling of a popular ghost story. I could find no record of Barclay's nine siblings, aside from James, who was a teacher at Larwick, in the Shetland Islands. Barclay's son William Charles was an accomplished sailor, however. Beginning his career on windjammers, he sailed the world, experiencing eight shipwrecks and accumulating a large collection of guns he confiscated from Chinese pirates. He retired from the transport service of the United States Navy with the rank of captain and died on March 10, 1926, at the Marine Hospital in San Francisco. I wonder if he is the ghost that has been spotted sitting in a chair at the Barclay House, glaring at people who enter his room.

William may have been "Uncle Sandy" to Hattie's children, who resided elsewhere in town but were constantly in the house visiting their aunt Katie. Though childless, Katie had taken over the house as her residence after her father's death.

Ghost hunters may resolve this issue of identity by performing an EVP sweep in which questions are posed regarding childhood,

Now used as a visitor's center, the home of Oregon pioneer Dr. Forbes Barclay is haunted by several ghosts.

encounters with Chinese pirates, and rank achieved. If audio recordings capture a disembodied voice that claims to be a captain born in Oregon (while denying a childhood in Scotland), we might conclude that "Uncle Sandy" is Barclay's son.

The ghost of a red-haired little boy has been spotted in the Barclay House, too. Estimated to be six to eight years old, he is playful. He hides tools and other small objects and often plays near the front door. He shows up next door in the McLoughlin House as well.

The Barclay House was used by family descendants until 1934, when it was deeded to the city and moved from its original location at the waterfront. It is now used as a gift shop, featuring unique books about Pacific Northwest history, and as a National Park Service visitor's center. Psychics claim to have encountered the spirits of Barclay and his wife here, who seem to be unaware of visitors and changes that have occurred inside the home. The couple died in the house, as did their daughters, Hattie and Katie.

ERMANTINGER HOUSE

Sixth Street at John Adams Street
Oregon City 97045
www.orcity.org/parksandrecreation/ermantinger-house

At least one ghost haunts this fascinating home, but the Ermantinger House's historical significance is due to a momentous event that took place in its parlor in 1845. During a dinner party hosted by Francis and Catherine Ermantinger, Francis Pettygrove and Asa Lovejoy began a spirited discussion about land they owned downriver at a spot often referred to as "the clearing." Lovejoy argued that it should be called Boston, after his hometown, while Pettygrove insisted that a better name was Portland, like his own hometown in Maine. A coin, tossed into the air three times by Ermantinger, settled the issue. Pettygrove won two out of three tosses, and today, the city in "the clearing" is called Portland.

The Ermantinger House is one of the oldest in the state of Oregon and is distinguished as the only two-story Federal-style home

The Ermantinger House was the scene of a famous coin toss in 1845 that granted the winner, Francis Pettygrove, the right to name a muddy village downriver "Portland."

originally built with a flat roof sheathed with tin. Born in Portugal, Francis Ermantinger (1798-1858) obtained an education in England before immigrating to Canada, where he found employment with the Hudson's Bay Company in 1818. In 1825, he transferred to Fort Vancouver and worked for Dr. John McLoughlin. He met and married McLoughlin's granddaughter, Catherine Sinclair, and secured a transfer to an outpost on the Willamette River that would later be named Oregon City. In 1844, McLoughlin deeded to Ermantinger the land on which this house was built in 1845. Francis and Catherine lived there only a short time before he was transferred to another Hudson's Bay enterprise. In 1849, the house was sold and, for the next 60 years it was occupied by various families. It was moved from its riverfront location to Center Street in 1910. Years later, it was moved again, to its current site in the McLoughlin Historical District. Historical records do not help us determine who may be haunting the house, but it is clear that something paranormal is attached to the place.

The last time I toured the home, it was undergoing extensive renovation that had attracted the attention of at least one ghost. I detected a spirit who seemed angered that a fireplace was missing. Historical records show that two fireplaces once existed on the first floor, but they were removed to facilitate the move from the riverfront location. The fellow I encountered seemed quite agitated about the changes.

STEVENS-CRAWFORD HOUSE

603 Sixth Street
Oregon City 97045
503-655-2866

Constructed in 1908 by Oregon pioneer Harley Stevens and his wife, Elizabeth Stevens Crawford, this fascinating Craftsman-style house is now a museum. Stevens (1847-1924) arrived in Oregon in 1862 at the age of 15 and worked for the railroad as a telegraph operator and depot agent. In 1871, he married Mary Elizabeth Crawford (1850-1932), with whom he had two children, Harley Jr. and Muriel "Mertie" (1872-1968). At the age of 36, Mertie moved with the family into the new house and resided there until her death. Diagnosed as a "sickly child," she was advised not to marry or attempt to have children. Thus she lived a spinster's life, but she enjoyed great popularity in Oregon City. Appreciating the historical value of the home's furnishings and other artifacts, Mertie bequeathed the entire property to the Clackamas County Historical Society upon her death. The house, including the Stevens family's cherished possessions, is now open to the public.

Is this charming old home haunted? Many ghost hunters in the area believe that spirits wander through the parlor, dining room, and quaint kitchen. Northwest Ghost Tours includes this grand old house in its popular two-hour tour. Numerous artifacts most certainly contain imprints of Mertie and others who spent time in the home. The ghost of Harley Stevens may occupy the house, looking after family heirlooms, including pictures of his little girl, Mertie.

When I toured the home and grounds, I felt strangely familiar with the place. The house is similar to many in my hometown, Alameda,

California. Beyond that, I sense that the spirits who remained in the house were quite at ease. None of them felt threatened or bothered by modern persons who staffed the place or tourists who wandered from room to room, expressing curiosity about the way people lived in the early 20th century.

JOSEPHINE'S ROSE

Mountain View Cemetery
500 Hilda Street
Oregon City 97045
503-657-8299
www.oregoncity.org/cemetery

    Mountain View Cemetery is the quintessential Oregon landscape, with rolling green fields, a creek full of water, and tall trees standing against a brilliant sky. The monuments placed here by loving family members to commemorate the lives of deceased spouses, parents, or children, however, remind us that life is precious and often cut short by unforeseen tragedy. Aside from durable granite headstones with fascinating epitaphs, other offerings, far more ethereal, may arouse a visitor's emotions. These mark a spot where century-old imprints may produce a paranormal experience.
    The most fascinating of these fragile offerings is Josephine's rosebush, which has flourished at the grave of a young girl since the 19th century. After an arduous journey on the famed Oregon Trail, Josephine Hunsaker's family arrived in Oregon City in 1846. The bountiful land enabled them to flourish and help others newly arrived in town and desperate for aid. In the winter of 1853, however, the Hunsaker family found itself in need of help, as 12-year-old Josephine became ill with diphtheria or typhoid fever. Throughout February, she lay in her bed, gazing out the window at green hills and, perhaps, spotting other children at play. Dr. John McLoughlin visited often and, one day, realized that Josephine should have something special to gaze upon. He pulled a rosebush from his garden, potted it, and placed it outside her window. It was winter and the plant was not in

bloom, but the good doctor probably hoped that its graceful little branches and few remaining leaves might give Josephine hope that she and the rosebush would flourish in the spring. Sadly, she died on March 10, 1853. This tragedy was soon followed by the death of Josephine's 14-year-old brother, Horton.

After burying her two children side by side, so that they could be together for eternity, Mrs. Hunsaker realized that Josephine might be comforted by having her rosebush at her grave. Thus, it was transplanted and nurtured for many years until Mrs. Hunsaker passed away. The rosebush remains there to this day, despite considerable damage inflicted by groundskeepers who were unaware of its significance. Now protected by a fence, it stands as if something exceptional or paranormal has kept it alive. Psychics who visit the grave sense an energy there that may be an imprint created by Mrs. Hunsaker, who doubtless visited it often, or Josephine, lending her spiritual vigor to the beloved rosebush.

The children's gravesite is on the left as you enter the grounds (in the pioneer section of the cemetery), surrounded by a black fence.

Another fascinating site within this graveyard is the McCune

The crumbling McCune family tomb in Oregon City's Mountain View Cemetery has aroused a ghost who seeks help in restoring the monument.

family tomb. Also located in the pioneer section at the north side of the cemetery, this tomb is larger than nearby monuments and is crumbling apart. Several bricks seem to be missing, and the mortar is decayed. As I approached, I sensed a wall of energy, as if a spirit was quite disturbed by the current state of this tomb. Typically, whenever headstones or other monuments are damaged by storms or fallen trees, ghosts are aroused and may stand at the tomb, awaiting the help of anyone who may replace the bricks.

Many graves in this cemetery will capture the imaginations of ghost hunters who also love history. The first grave to be placed here was that of John Barclay, who died at the age of two in 1847 while residing at Fort Vancouver. Another old grave is that of Dr. William Allen, who died June 9, 1851. Graves with the most intense paranormal activity seem to be those of children.

MASS MURDER HOUSE

2580 Fisher Road NE
Salem 97305

While staring at the vacant lot at the corner of Beverly Avenue NE and Fisher Road NE, sensitive ghost hunters may become overwhelmed by the energy that lingers here. A house once stood at this place that seemed to be a happy home for Nikolay and Natalya Lazukin and their three daughters. The tiny house, tucked into a modest but well-kept neighborhood, may have been occupied by something other than a happy family, however. At 6:03 on the morning of May 22, 2012, Nikolay Lazukin sent a text to his father-in-law that read, "Please forgive me. They took control of my body and did it. I begged them not to but they did. I'm so sorry. Please God forgive me. My last fight I have lost at Exit 174."

This bizarre message suggests Nikolay had been battling demons or some other malevolent force for some time. During the night, this powerful force overwhelmed him and he committed mass murder. Natalya died from two gunshots to her head. Three-year-old Angelica also died of two gunshots to the head, while Zoe, almost two, was shot once. Baby Sulamia, four month olds, died of traumatic asphyxiation. Before leaving the house, Nikolay doused the place with a flammable liquid and set it ablaze. Firefighters arrived at 5:28 A.M. as the neighborhood awoke to a horrible tragedy.

Later that morning, Nikolay was found at Exit 174 slumped in the backseat of his Jeep Cherokee, dead from a self-inflicted gunshot wound to the head. Toxicology reports ruled out a drug, alcohol, or neurological basis for his murderous behavior.

This tragedy may not have been limited to the Lazukin family. Investigators suspect that Nikolay may have killed 21-year-old Devin Matlock, whose body was found near Fisher Road only a few hours after the fire was extinguished.

By all accounts, Nikolay loved his family, yet it seems clear that some powerful, malevolent force gained control of his mind, causing him to murder his wife and children. As I stood at the periphery of the vacant lot where the Lazukin house once stood, I felt that I should not enter the space. I was unable to discover any indication of a burial ground or other spiritual significance of the lot linked to Native Americans. Something must be there, underground or in another dimension, however. The remains of the Lazukin house have been completely removed except for a portion of the driveway. No one has taken a chance and built a new structure at this site.

If you visit this vacant lot, take steps to protect yourself against any malevolent spirits who still reside there. Wear a St. Benedict's medal and a Christian cross, carry a packet of protective herbs and minerals, and cross your forehead with holy water. Do not actually enter the lot.

COMMUNITY OF MISERY

Fairview Hospital and Training Center
2250 Strong Road SE
Salem 97302
503-986-5050

The creepiest place in Oregon may be the Fairview Training Center in Salem. Unfortunately for ghost hunters, it may also be the most inaccessible place, since the grounds are closed to visitors, and ominous signs warn those who consider trespassing that they may face a speedy prosecution. It is possible, however, to get a good look at it and even feel some of the negative energy that remains there by approaching the broken fences or the single strands of chain that are intended to keep visitors out. Infrared imaging, either video or still, may capture the many spirits that roam this place at night. The history of this place and fascinating reports of paranormal activity posted by reliable investigators create a strong attraction to those who want to have an intense ghostly encounter.

Construction of this large collection of buildings, tunnels, wells, and farm facilities began in 1907, when Oregon created the State Institution for the Feeble-Minded. Late in 1908, the first 39 residents were transferred from the Oregon State Insane Asylum. The center had 670 acres for gardens, orchards, a dairy, and small farm animals, which provided stabilizing and instructional activity for inmates while enabling the place to be nearly self-sufficient in food production. By

Even when viewed from a distance, the creepy buildings of Fairview Hospital and Training Center fascinate ghost hunters.

1911, the inmate population was 181, with 25 awaiting admission.

In 1917, the state's commitment law was changed, and Fairview was no longer permitted to admit people who were legally declared insane. Inmates were described as "feeble-minded," but the community also included those with epilepsy and mental retardation. Elimination of an age minimum in 1921, allowing admission of infants, caused the population to rise from 389 to about 950 by 1928. In addition, admission was now open to orphans, hitchhikers, promiscuous girls, mongoloids, and drug abusers. Community sensitivities later changed, and in 1933, the facility became known as the Oregon Fairview Home. Throughout World War II, the place's population continued to soar, reaching a peak number of 1,235 inmates in 1948. The name was changed again in 1965, to Fairview Hospital and Training Center. Finally, in 1979, it was known simply as Fairview Training Center.

On February 24, 2000, the last resident left Fairview, ending a 92-year period of attempted altruism, medical treatment, and social experiments that, unfortunately, also included isolation of children who should have remained with their families. Treatment also included physical and emotional abuse, forced sterilizations, "time out" in cages, ice baths, and the liberal use of straitjackets, handcuffs, forced feedings, leg shackles, and psychotropic drugs. It's no wonder that numerous escape attempts occurred and an untold number of children and young adults died here. The official list of inmates who died at Fairview is short compared to the number of patients who simply disappeared from the roster of residents. It is known that, in 1970, two boys drowned in a small lake used by Fairview inmates for swimming and fishing. A cemetery once existed on the grounds, but some historians believe that several unofficial burial sites were filled between 1920 and 1950.

After Fairview's closure, a few former residents and staff members gave interviews to newspapers and TV news outlets or posted reports on the Internet about strange events they experienced in the residential units, common rooms, and the maze of underground tunnels that connect several buildings. Many of those reports suggested that the place was a site of intense paranormal activity.

Despite their mental incapacitation, it is likely that many residents were horrified to find themselves incarcerated there. Furthermore, many of them probably missed their families. It might be anticipated that, after death, residents would wait at Fairview for the day when a mother or father would arrive to take them home. Other spirits, having been given up during their lifetimes by their parents, might remain there because they feel they have nowhere to go. Still others may be angry about forced sterilizations or other physical abuse and are waiting for revenge on doctors and staff members.

Hollie Pollock may continue to haunt the cistern near Fairview's Withcombe Cottage because he is deeply distraught over the mutilation of his body. In November of 1923, Hollie was not present when roll call was taken. It was immediately assumed he had escaped from the facility, since such attempts were common. A few weeks later, pieces of skin and hair emerged from water pipes as staff members filled tubs for washing clothes. Someone suspected contamination of the cistern by a dead animal. When it was opened, the remains of Hollie's body were found. The paranormal activity at the site is said to be so intense that cars parked close by often fail to start. Others claim to hear a voice calling out from the now-covered cistern.

A Fairview doctor recounted his experience with a resident who suffered an epileptic seizure. At the time, the resident was alone, but he was quickly discovered by a woman who rushed to the adjacent building and alerted medical staff. After the patient was stabilized, questions were asked about the woman who had, in effect, saved the boy's life. No one came forward who could identify her. Days later, a photograph was found at the patient's bedside of his mother, who had died years earlier. The doctor was astonished when he realized that the person who had alerted staff to the medical emergency was the boy's dead mother.

After the training center closed, a team of security guards was employed to patrol the place all night, ensuring that vagrants and vandals did not enter the grounds. Several guards have reported seeing people, at a distance, wandering the grounds at night, yet on closer inspection, no one could be found. The figure most often sighted was that of a woman walking near the center's cottages.

Several people fortunate enough to get into Fairview after its closure have experienced screams, sobs, voices crying out for help, and even growls. Some fascinating EVP have been captured here that may be accessed online.

Fairview Hospital and Training Center is now closed, but many of its derelict buildings harbor the ghosts of inmates and staff who died there under miserable conditions.

A few years after Fairview's closure, a development group known as Sustainable Fairview Associates purchased 275 acres and several buildings. In 2004, the Pringle Creek Community was developed on 32 acres. So far, I have not discovered any reports of paranormal activity in the buildings that comprise this development. I would not be surprised if something strange occurs that residents simply don't feel inclined to reveal.

Go to Flickr.com and search for "Fairview Training Center." This site contains more than 800 photographs and a fascinating history. Also, on YouTube, you can view some amazing stories about Fairview residents who returned to the place many years after their departure.

GHOST OF THE CIVIL WAR VETERAN

Thompson Brewery and Public House

3575 Liberty Road South
Salem 97302
503-363-7286
www.mcmenamins.com

    Constructed in 1905 as a residence for Franklin (1841-1923) and Maria Thompson, this home has been transformed into a popular brewpub. Despite the modern equipment for producing and serving a vast array of drinks and food, the homey atmosphere of an early-20th-century house has been preserved. Old photographs of the town, a portrait of Franklin and Maria, low-angled ceilings on the second floor, and small rooms remind us that this place was once a dream home for a veteran of the Civil War who, on the day he moved in, was 63 years old. We can be certain that Franklin loved the house because it was built by his son, Fred Thompson, on 20 acres of lush pasture that fronted the market road to Eugene. Furthermore, when Franklin and Maria arrived in Salem at the invitation of their son, after they suffered through 40 years of frigid Minnesota winters, they surely found it to be a veritable paradise. It's no wonder, therefore, that Franklin's spirit remains in the house, usually in the second-floor room in which he died on November 23, 1923. Many staff members and astonished patrons have seen the apparition of a short man with gray hair at several locations within the house and at the rear of the building near the brewing facility.

    A photograph of Franklin taken in 1907 may be viewed online. At that time, his hair was dark, yet thin, with a receding hairline. Sixteen years later, at the time of his death, it is likely that his hair was gray and quite thin. The bedroom where he died is located at the front of the house, on the north side. Today, it contains three tables and chairs for private parties. Franklin appears in this space, on the stairs leading down to the first floor, and near the front door. At times, he appears to be completely lifelike, and busy staff members rush by him thinking he is a customer. When they are struck by something odd about the man, they turn to find he has vanished.

    A staff member told me that strange fragrances are often detected in many places within the house, including coffee. In the kitchen, coffee beans are sometimes found spilled on the floor, suggesting Franklin

The Thompson Brewery and Public House is haunted by Civil War veteran Franklin Thompson, who died in a second-floor room.

loved coffee. In his former bedroom, disembodied voices and loud banging are heard, and condiments move on the tables. In some areas in the brewery and the old house, paranormal activity is so intense at times that staff members working late at night insist on staying close to each other.

It has been suggested that Mrs. Thompson also haunts the place. Known as a jokester, she is believed to move kitchen utensils, generate unexplained odors, and create loud bangs.

GHOSTS OF THE PIONEERS

Salem Pioneer Cemetery
Hoyt at Commercial Street South
Salem 97302
503-588-6336
www.salempioneercemetery.org

Salem Pioneer Cemetery sits on a busy street, suggesting that daytime visits would be unlikely opportunities to experience anything paranormal. On a cold, dark day when the fog rolls in, however, this place, filled with looming monuments and massive trees, can be strangely quiet and quite freaky. As visitors move away from the Commercial Street side of the cemetery into the grove of madrones and oaks, older graves are found and an eerie atmosphere charges the air.

In 1853, the land now occupied by the center of this cemetery was the homestead of Rev. David Leslie and his second wife, Adelia. He established the first grave here when he buried his first wife, Mary A. Kinney Leslie, in 1841. Leslie added the graves of two daughters in 1854. That year, when the Independent Order of Odd Fellows purchased adjoining land for community burials, he sold his land, making this elevated spot, overlooking Salem, the town's foremost graveyard.

Among the notables in the graveyard are Asahel and Eugenia Bush (cemetery plot 66). Bush built the mansion that stands on Mission Street NE (see "Bush House," below). William Graves is also buried in this graveyard, and that seems altogether fitting since he was a well-known and successful undertaker and gravedigger. Unfortunately, the location of his grave has been lost. Perhaps this is the reason why his ghost walks the cemetery at night. Ninety-six Civil War veterans are interred here, including three sailors who served in the Union Navy. In plot 44, you will find Tabitha Moffat Brown (1780-1858), one of the earliest pioneers to travel the Oregon Trail. A founder of Tualatin Academy, which later became Pacific University, she was dubbed the Mother of Oregon by the state legislature. Nearby, in plot 106, is Charles H. Bennett (1811-55). In 1848, he stood near John Marshall in the American River mill trace at the moment gold was discovered in California. He later served in the U.S. Army as captain of a cavalry unit and died in the Indian Wars.

Few cemeteries have active ghosts, but this graveyard is regarded as a great place to experience spirits. Since 2002, when a paranormal group encountered an angry spirit that issued warnings to leave, several investigators have visited. They often seek an angry spirit that calls out to astonished visitors from an elevated place behind a tall monument. Some ghost hunters claim they have calmed this spirit and received his permission to continue touring the cemetery. During my investigations here, I got the impression this ghost is Graves. He may be frustrated rather than angry because the location of his grave has been lost. A colleague has suggested that the angry ghost may be Leslie.

At several locations, ghost hunters hear unexplained noises, such as a clanging sound that seems to emanate from a crypt. Audio recordings have captured footsteps, a baby crying, sobbing, a high-pitched male voice that says, "Hey, hey," and the sound of a violin.

GHOSTS OF THE SIBLINGS

Bush House
600 Mission Street NE
Salem 97302
503-363-4714
http://www.oregonlink.com/bush_house/

The magnificent Bush House, which sits on a hill in Salem's beautiful Bush's Pasture Park, gives us a glimpse of life and death more than a century ago. Today, the mansion is surrounded by a rose garden and wooded park bordered by busy streets. In the late 19th century, it stood in the center of a large tract of land as a symbol of the pioneer spirit, hard work, and great wealth that comes to those who are willing take a chance. The Italianate Victorian mansion was constructed in 1877-78 by Asahel Bush II (1824-1913), who had gained his wealth by establishing a newspaper in 1851, winning election to the office of state printer in 1859, becoming a powerful political figure in Oregon, and operating one of the most successful banks in the Pacific Northwest. The 12-room house had every modern convenience money could buy, including indoor plumbing, central heating, gaslights, 10 fireplaces with Italian marble surrounds, and running water in each bedroom.

The happy day on which Bush moved into the place was marred only by the fact that his wife, Eugenia, was not with him and their children, Asahel III (1858-1953), Estelle (1856-1942), Sally (1860-1946), and Eugenia (1862-1932). She had died 14 years earlier of tuberculosis. Despite that loss, the children grew up happy, well adjusted, and seemingly well prepared for the rigors of a university education. After high school, all of them left Salem for eastern universities and graduated, except Eugenia.

Apparently, the stress of life at a university in Massachusetts was too much for Eugenia and, in 1880 at the age of 18, she developed a mental illness diagnosed as schizophrenia. Urban legend says that her father moved her home to Salem and kept her confined in the basement. Historians dispute this claim and point out that wealthy Asahel II could afford the finest care available. In fact, Eugenia was sent to a hospital in Boston, where she received many years of treatment. Despite excellent care and frequent visits from her siblings, she did not return to the mansion in Salem until 1913, at the age of 51.

Biographers indicate that Sally and Eugenia had a special bond. Apparently, Asahel II preferred to keep Eugenia confined in a Boston hospital rather than endure the unpredictable and occasionally frightening behavior of a schizophrenic. Immediately after his death, Sally boarded the family's private railroad car and sped to Boston, where she retrieved her beloved sister and transported her home to Salem. The haste with which this dramatic event took place suggests that Sally had been forbidden to bring Eugenia home while Asahel II was alive. Under the constant care of a live-in nurse and Sally's watchful eye, Eugenia resided in the house until her death in 1932. After decades in a mental hospital, Eugenia must have been so thrilled to be home with her sister, in beautiful Salem, that even death could not take her from this cherished place. The bond between these sisters may be the basis for some of the paranormal activity that occurs in the house.

During the 19 years preceding Eugenia's death, Sally managed the household and acted as a hostess for social affairs. Well known in Salem as Aunt Sally, she was generous to vagrants who begged for a meal at the kitchen door and a benevolent keeper of 27 cats and a beloved cow. After her death in 1946, her brother, Asahel III, moved back into the mansion at the age of 90 and remained there until he died in 1953.

Long lives spent in a grand mansion, animosity between father and daughter, a strong bond between two sisters, and a number of unavoidable yet tragic deaths have all contributed to a ghostly atmosphere within the Bush House. Original furnishings, selected by Sally Bush, add to the beautifully creepy ambience that visitors experience as they tour the place, yet staff members either deny knowledge of any paranormal phenomena or simply refuse to comment. Apparently, people associated with the current management, the Art Association of Salem, don't want the place to become known as the proverbial haunted house. Many ghost hunters, however, believe that the place is haunted by the ghosts of Eugenia and her family.

Witnesses have spotted the apparition of a young woman as she descends the stairs and moves through several rooms on the main floor. Reportedly, this ghost plays with the thermostat controls. Several writers suggest that this ghost is Eugenia, who, after a 32-year stay in a mental hospital, has discovered a modern device that can make her home warmer. It is possible, however, that this apparition is Sally and that she roams the house as mistress of the place, checking on the work of the servants and proper setting of the thermostat. Ghost hunters who visit the mansion should use an audio recorder to elicit a response from both Sally and Eugenia. Call out to "Aunt Sally," to prompt some fascinating EVP.

Once the home of one of the region's wealthiest families, the Bush House is haunted by sisters Eugenia and Sally.

Upon the death of her husband in 1923, sister Estelle returned to live in the mansion. Her ghost may reside in one of the upstairs bedrooms and the parlor. She was known as an "elegant lady," and the swishing sound of a lady's long gown often heard in the parlor may signal Estelle's presence.

GHOSTS OF THE BALLROOM DANCERS

Reed Opera House
189 Liberty Street NE
Salem 97301
503-391-4481

It is rare for two people to experience a paranormal phenomenon simultaneously, but that is exactly what happened when my son and I entered the third floor of this venerable old building. As soon as we stepped off the elevator, it was apparent that the atmosphere was different from that of the first and second floors. As we moved about the large ballroom, we agreed that the air seemed less dense, or lighter. We also felt as though we were walking 12 inches off the floor, on a surface that supported our weight but seemed soft.

Today, the Reed Opera House stands in downtown Salem as a reminder of the city's earliest commercial development. Still a popular social and business venue, the tall brick building is only a few blocks from the State Capitol. Built by Gen. Cyrus A. Reed (1825-1910), adjutant general of Oregon during the Civil War, the grand opera house opened on September 27, 1870, for the inaugural ball of Gov. LaFayette Grover. A few days later, numerous gas lanterns were lit to illuminate the stage for the first dramatic performance, *Frances Carroll, a Picture of State Life*. Many traveling theatre groups performed here over the next 30 years. Among the famous orators who attracted large audiences were Mark Twain, Susan B. Anthony, and Presidents Rutherford B. Hayes and Benjamin Harrison. Other events included the Firemen's Annual New Year's Ball, gubernatorial inaugurations, political meetings, and community celebrations.

In addition to hosting these occasions, the building included a large

The third-floor ballroom of the Reed Opera House has a strong paranormal atmosphere that creates bizarre sensations in sensitive people.

hotel and a saloon that, in 1893, was hailed as the best in town. It was also the busiest gambling venue the city has ever known.

By 1900, the opera house faced competition from more modern and comfortable facilities, including the Grand Theater a few blocks away and the Chemeketa House. Dwindling audiences forced the owners to renovate the building into stores and offices. A major tenant, Miller's Department Store, remained in the building until 1970, when the place was sold. In 1975, new owners renovated it once again, creating the current configuration of shops and offices on the first and second floors and a huge ballroom on the third floor.

My review of the history of this grand old building did not uncover specific events that may have produced ghosts. In the saloon that once operated busy gambling tables, fights must have occurred, possibly leading to a fatality. In the hotel, an unfortunate traveler may have died, far from home, and lay in his room for a day or two before discovery. It was my impression, however, that the paranormal phenomena on the third floor include both imprints and ghosts.

The atmospheric anomalies are likely created by intense imprints

The Reed Opera House opened in 1870 as the city's premier entertainment venue. Today, it is a multi-use building that harbors ghosts on each floor.

that seem to fill the entire floor. These may be residuals from great events staged there, such as Grover's inaugural ball. The minerals in the thick brick walls may have created the right electromagnetic conditions to retain these imprints and, perhaps, even amplify them. The ghosts that seemed to swirl around the room in a counterclockwise fashion gave me the impression that they were happy and enjoying one of the greatest events of their lives. This gathering may be composed of people who died at various places in Salem but returned to the opera house to continue the dance that gave them so much joy.

GHOST OF THE ENTREPRENEUR

Elsinore Theater
170 High Street SE
Salem 97301
503-375-3574
www.elsinoretheater.com

Old theatres that presented live performances are among the top-five places to find ghosts. That's because musical performances, dramatic plays, and even comedy evoke so much passion from singers, musicians, and actors that a bond is created with the site that transcends death. Performers relish the adoration of audiences and, in many cases, the brilliance of their own accomplishments, so much that they cannot let go of that shining moment.

Audiences also contribute to the ghostly populations of old theatres. Captured by a sweet voice or powerful dramatic delivery, avid theatregoers sometimes fall in love with a favorite singer or actor. Attending performances night after night, they choose to remain in their reserved seats long after death, awaiting another chance to play out a one-sided love affair. Stagehands sometimes fall into this emotional chasm as well, but their passion for the theatre is most often directed at the machinery, lighting, elegant curtains, and stage props that they installed, maintained, and operated for many years. Falling from a high catwalk or succumbing to a heart attack while moving heavy backdrops, stagehands find themselves still on the job after death, caring for the one thing that made them a vital part of the theatre experience while they were alive.

Directors, producers, and theatre owners are often among the ghosts of old theatres because they are unwilling or unable to let go of the magnetic emotions of the creative process or lucrative business that made them famous and adored by their community. The man who built the Elsinore Theater in downtown Salem, successful attorney George B. Guthrie (1882-1957), was so deeply passionate about his glorious accomplishment that he decided to stay on the scene to guide it through a number of troubled times and essential renovations, despite his death.

When the Elsinore Theater opened on May 28, 1926, it was declared to be "the most beautiful theater in America" and "inspiring in aesthetic beauty." Designed to resemble the castle in the city of Elsinore in Shakespeare's *Hamlet,* its Tudor-Gothic architecture includes Povey Brothers stained-glass windows, 30-foot faux stonework walls, chandeliers, a decorative foyer, murals of Shakespeare's characters, and two grand carpeted staircases. The auditorium now seats 1,300 before a 30-by-60-foot stage framed by a decorative proscenium arch.

Initially a venue for live performances by notables such as ventriloquist Edgar Bergen and Charlie McCarthy, Otis Skinner, Clark Gable, and the John Phillip Sousa Marine Band, the theatre also presented silent films, accompanied by music from a Wurlitzer organ in 1929. For the next 22 years, it continued to operate as a movie theatre, in addition to holding twice-weekly auditions by aspiring performers, including Doc Severinsen, who went on to fame on the Johnny Carson TV show. At times, the old theatre faced the possibility of demolition, but concerned citizens, and perhaps, the benevolent spirit of George Guthrie, saved the place. A series of ownership changes and multiple periods of renovation that ended in 2004 brought new life to this magnificent theatre.

Many people have spotted a wispy apparition, believed to be George Guthrie, walk through several rows of seats. It seems likely that the seats now occupy a space that was originally an aisle, and Guthrie simply follows a familiar route. Some witnesses claim he appears with two young actresses on his arms. Maintenance-staff members often

The ghost of entrepreneur George Guthrie haunts his most glorious achievement, the stately Elsinore Theater in downtown Salem.

hear disembodied voices rise from the stage, as if invisible actors are rehearsing their scenes. Sound bursts of music, including notes from the old Wurlitzer organ, are frequently heard at night, when only a few staff members are present. Members of the audience, while waiting for a performance to begin, sometimes feel unseen beings pass close by as if ghosts are moving to their favorite seats.

As with most haunted theatres, isolated cold spots may be found onstage and in the wings. At times, staff members feel an unseen being rushing by between the stage and dressing rooms. Ghostly workers have been spotted on the backstage scaffolding dislodging dust that falls to the stage.

The best way to experience the Elsinore Theater and its spirits is to attend an event. Today, the theatre offers a range of entertainment, from a Queen cover band to ballet and standup comedy. A tour of the theatre may be booked by calling 503-375-3574.

GHOSTS OF THE OLD PLACES

Willamette Heritage Park
1313 Mill Street SE
Salem 97301
503-585-7012
www.willametteheritage.org

It is unfortunate that many cities in the U.S. have demolished hundreds of 19th-century homes and buildings that once housed historic businesses, laboratories, hospitals, courts, newspapers, and government offices in order to make room for freeways, malls, and stadiums. Places of worship, graveyards, and battlegrounds have been targeted by redevelopment agencies and dismantled or paved over to provide space for parking lots, factories, and office buildings. In my hometown, Alameda, California, many Victorian mansions built before 1880 were razed and replaced with small apartment buildings before anyone in government realized they had sanctioned the destruction of the town's history and cultural heritage. Before all was lost, some cities had the wisdom to establish heritage parks, where old buildings were moved, placed on sturdy foundations, renovated, and reopened as museums or rented as offices, meeting halls, retail space, or private residences. Oakland, California, established its famous Preservation Park, which contains 16 19th-century mansions gathered from various sites throughout the city and reopened as a dazzling upscale Victorian neighborhood that fascinates history buffs and ghost hunters. Salem created a similar venue at its Willamette Heritage Park. On this five-acre campus surrounding the 1895-vintage Thomas Kay Woolen Mill, 14 historic structures comprise a priceless museum depicting the life and development of the community.

Pleasant Grove Church: Built in 1858 near Aumsville, Oregon, this historic church was moved to its current location in 1984. It is believed to be the oldest remaining Presbyterian church in the state. Some historians refer to it as the "Condit Church" because it was founded by Rev. Phillip Condit (1801-56), who arrived in Oregon in 1854. Although construction started only two years after his arrival, the church did not open its doors until April of 1858. Sound bursts of a male voice preaching the gospel have been heard by astonished visitors standing just inside the vacant church. Some ghost hunters speculate that these are paranormal manifestations of Reverend Condit, but history indicates that he never preached there. He died November 21, 1856, and is buried in Pleasant Grove Cemetery.

Condit's church remained in use for 86 years before falling into disrepair. For a few years, the building was completely neglected and nearly destroyed by squatters and vandals. Restoration began in the 1940s, preserving a remarkable building constructed of hand-hewn logs held together by wooden pegs, as well as its pews, pulpit, and stove.

This old church is haunted, but the identity of the spirit is unclear. It is possible that Reverend Condit has located the church he envisioned and is conducting the services he intended to perform before death put an end to his plans. His sons, Sylvanus and Cyrenius, who were instrumental in the fundraising and construction, may haunt the place, looking after a beloved house of worship that they literally carved out of the wilderness. Condit's colleague, Rev. J. A. Hanna, may be at the pulpit as well. After founding a church in Corvallis, he assisted in founding the Pleasant Grove Church by contributing his first year's salary to construction costs.

A strange light, often described as the flame of a candle, has been seen drifting across the church in front of the pulpit. Unexplained

Moved from its original location in 1984, the Pleasant Grove Church contains paranormal imprints of weddings and funerals and some ghosts.

sounds include a violin, voices raised in song, boots tapping on the floor, and rattling of metal on the stove, as if an unseen hand were opening and then closing the tiny door to add wood to the fire.

Jason Lee House: Built in 1841 on the site of the woolen mill's current water tower, the Lee house has a reputation as a haunted place. It is a fascinating place, but I did not find it to be active in a paranormal sense. The rooms of both floors are filled with display boards depicting the history of the region, including Indian culture, wildlife, and Yankee pioneers. As a result, the house does not possess a mid-19th-century atmosphere. Ghosts may have attached themselves to some of the artifacts on display, but I did not get the impression that active spirits occupy the place. Other ghost hunters may have better luck finding ghosts in this house than I did. I interviewed people who had some compelling experiences on the stairs and in one of the second-floor rooms.

It is doubtful that Jason Lee's spirit occupies this house. In 1834, the evangelist led a group of Methodists from Missouri to Oregon to create a mission where local Indians would study the Bible. Arriving at a spot 13 miles north of present-day Salem, the group was plagued by floods and disease. Their relocation in 1841 to a spot called Chemeketa (a Native American word for "meeting" or "resting place") proved beneficial, as the missionaries built a gristmill, sawmill, and several buildings that would become the nucleus of Salem. A few years later, while visiting family in the East, Lee became ill. Recognizing the possibility that he might not recover, he made the arduous trip to his family home in Stanstead, Canada, and died there March 12, 1845, at the age of 41.

The families of Lewis Judson, Josiah Parrish, and W. W. Raymond also resided in this house over the years. EVP sweeps that invite these people to speak may be productive.

John D. Boon House: This may be the most haunted house in Willamette Heritage Park. With the exception of one room, this little building is a faithful representation of a family home from the 1840s. Believed to be the oldest single-family dwelling still standing in Salem, the place contains a kitchen, parlor, dining room, and bedroom, with period furnishings that include a cast-iron stove and organ. Built in 1847, it was home to the John D. Boon family. Boon (1817-64) arrived in the region in 1845 and achieved quick success in the lumber and wool industries. As a well-established leader in business and society, he became treasurer of Oregon Territory in 1851 and, in 1859, of the state of Oregon, serving until 1862. He constructed a brick building in 1860, still standing at 888 Liberty Street NE, for use as State Treasury offices. Today, it houses the popular McMenamin's brewpub known as Boon's Treasury.

John D. Boon died in Salem on July 17, 1864, at the age of 47. He is buried in Salem Pioneer Cemetery, but I suspect that his ghost still resides in his house. The bedroom has been converted to a media room with a few benches and a screen mounted on a wall. This modern intrusion has apparently aroused a spirit who does not like the alteration. When my son entered the room, he was immediately pushed backward by unseen hands. Upon crossing the threshold, he also felt an abrupt change in the atmosphere. After listening to his report, I attempted to enter the room but encountered a wall of energy a few inches inside the doorway. Moving ahead, I felt large hands push against my shoulders. Clearly recognizing a malevolent spirit or, at least, one that did not like a paranormal investigator intruding on its space, I decided to leave the house.

Methodist Parsonage: The Parsonage was built in 1841 under the

A small media room in the John D. Boon House, which was restored and furnished in 19th-century décor, has a ghost that seems unhappy with the modern intrusion.

supervision of Jason Lee and Gustavus Hines with lumber produced by the Methodist mission's sawmill. Originally designed as a duplex to house the families of two missionaries, part of the building was eventually used as the Indian Manual Labor School while a schoolhouse was under construction. The place originally stood at 1325 Ferry Street but was sold in the late 1840s, as the Methodist mission was disbanded. The building served as a boardinghouse for many years until falling into disrepair. Eventually, the house was moved to the heritage park, restored, and filled with artifacts from the Methodist mission period.

A docent told me that strange sounds are often heard in this house when no tourists or other staff members are present. These sounds include muted whispers, soft footsteps as though an unseen person walked about in bare feet or slippers, and doors opening and closing.

Aside from Jason Lee and his family, others who lived in the home with large families include the Reverends Gustavus Hines and Hamilton Campbell. Members of their families and numerous short-term residents may have loved the comfortable house so much that they remain there long after death.

Muted whispers and soft footsteps are heard in several rooms of the Parsonage, which was once used as an Indian school and a boardinghouse.

Murder Bridge: The ghostly image of a woman has been seen running across the bridge that spans Mill Creek adjacent to the dye house. Those who have observed this spirit claim she has a crazed expression on her face as though she is in fear of losing her life. A few people have reported that they spotted the woman's husband chasing after her. Both ghosts disappear as they complete their crossing. Some accounts state that in the early 20th century, a man murdered his wife on this bridge. Both were employed at the woolen mill, and the husband suspected that the wife had become infatuated with a man who worked in the dye house. I was unable to verify any of these claims, but I did speak to a docent and two locals who report having seen the frightened woman. A review of available newspaper and police records spanning 1900 to 1920 failed to reveal any information about a murder on this bridge. It is possible that a murder occurred here long before the mill and bridge were constructed in 1896 and the ghostly couple plays out their tragic event on the modern structure. It is interesting to note that the brick mill that stands today replaced an earlier structure that burned in 1889. The ghosts of a crazed woman and angry man spotted dashing across the bridge may be linked somehow to the historic fire rather than a lover's triangle that ended in murder.

Thomas Kay Woolen Mill: Among the defining elements of the 19th-century industrial revolution, with its large factories, were six-day workweeks, with a shift spanning 12 hours, and fatal injuries of unprotected workers caused by noisy, fast-moving machines. A tour of this fascinating wool mill reveals numerous machines that likely led to severe injury or death for workers who were sometimes as young as eight years old. After dying in this crowded, noisy place, spirits certainly would want to move on to some peaceful, cherished house or farm, but some may be trapped here, afraid to leave a job that saved their family from misery and starvation.

Today, visitors who tour this 1895-vintage mill find it quiet, yet there are ghosts around still at work. On the second floor, at the wool carding machines, a transparent figure sometimes appears with a dazed expression on his face. His legs are not visible, but his fingers look stretched and bloodied. On the first floor, the ghostly image of a man wearing a black vest, white shirt, and string necktie walks from one end of the building to the other, apparently overseeing invisible workers.

At times, astonished visitors hear the sounds of machinery start up or drive shafts overhead begin to turn. These sounds are brief and may be mistaken for those generated by trucks outside the building.

In the turbine room, adjacent to the mill, an angry spirit manifests in several ways, ranging from dark energy, perceived by sensitive people, to sharp screams in a masculine voice. It has been reported that a worker was killed by the water-driven turbine while attempting to perform maintenance on the device.

Wayne the Groundskeeper: Many reports on the Internet mention a groundskeeper named Wayne who haunts several locations at this park. Wayne Mentzer worked in the mill's machine shop until his retirement in 1968. He loved the place so much that he stayed on as a volunteer groundskeeper until his death in 1984 at the age of 79. Apparently, death hasn't stopped Wayne from going to work at the mill. His ghost has been spotted in the machine shop he loved so much and at various sites around the park. It has been reported that he used to leave food out for the mice. Ghost hunters might attract his attention and capture his voice on EVP recordings if this fact were mentioned.

The huge machines of the Thomas Kay Woolen Mill were noisy and dangerous and likely led to severe injuries and deaths that created the imprints and ghosts detected there.

The restored Thomas Kay Woolen Mill allows visitors to step back in time, to 1895, and experience the ghosts who labored 12 hours per day and died here.

THE SALEM HANGING TREE

Church Street at D Street NE
Salem 97301

The intersection of Church and D streets marks a place that was well known as Salem's hanging ground from about 1854 to 1866. Previous to the selection of this spot for public executions, the first hanging in Salem was staged on ground now occupied by a covered parking lot for the SAIF Building (the state-chartered workers'-compensation insurance company) at 400 High Street SE. At that site, murderer William Kendall was dispatched to the great beyond on April 18, 1851 for killing William Hamilton over a land-use dispute. Kendall's trial and execution were swift, because the town had no jail or other secure facility for keeping prisoners. Recognizing the problem, the County Board of Commissioners contracted for the construction of a jail on lower Church Street near Mill Creek. A nearby tree was used as a gallows for several hangings at this site until 1866, when the Oregon State Penitentiary was transferred from Portland to Salem. The new facility conducted executions by hanging and firing squad, but the general public was not permitted to witness these events.

The number of hangings that occurred on Church Street is uncertain, but two of them endure as local legends. Charles I. Rose has the distinction of being the first man executed after Oregon attained statehood. His guilt for the murder of his second wife, Angelica Carpenter, was easily established, as he confessed to the killing and two witnesses corroborated his admission.

A hanging staged in 1865 became entrenched in history because two murderers were executed simultaneously. On the night of January 9, 1865, saloonkeeper George Beale and his friend, butcher George Baker, approached the home of Daniel Delaney with the intention of robbing him of a large amount of money rumored to be stashed there. As Delaney resisted, the two shot him and fired at a boy who worked in the house. A speedy trial rendered a guilty verdict and May 17 was set as the execution day. Owing to Delaney's popularity and the unique double hanging, more than a thousand people crowded around the hanging tree at the corner of Church and D streets, eager for a view of the event.

Today, tall trees stand at the edge of Mill Creek, very close to the intersection of Church and D streets. Local ghost hunters believe that one of those trees served as the gallows for Beale, Baker, and Rose, largely because paranormal phenomena have been detected among them. Strange things do occur at this spot, but I doubt that a hanging tree stands amid the current grove of trees. A historical account published by Ben Maxwell in 1945 indicates that the court paid the Wilbur brothers to construct a scaffold and gallows, suitable for a double hanging, in a grove of small trees at the southeast corner of Church and Mill (later D Street) streets. Aside from that, an arborist told me that the trees that currently stand at the edge of Mill Creek are not old enough to have been of sufficient size and strength for a hanging in 1865.

Other places to hunt ghosts:

CLACKAMAS TOWN CENTER MALL

12000 SE 82nd Avenue
Happy Valley, Clackamas County 97086
503-653-6913

About 3:30 P.M. on December 11, 2012, 22-year-old Jacob Tyler Roberts arrived at Clackamas Town Center mall intent on killing as many people as possible. Armed with a stolen Stag Arms AR-15 semiautomatic rifle and extra magazines containing 145 bullets, he apparently entered the mall via Macy's and took a position outside the store's interior entrance in the mall's atrium, facing the food court. Straight ahead stood a kiosk operated by 45-year-old Steven Forsyth. Occupied with a phone call to his father, Forsyth apparently never saw Roberts raise the rifle to his shoulder and fire. A single shot to the head killed Forsyth. Moving to his left, toward the food court, Roberts then shot nurse Cindy Yuille, a 54-year-old mother of two. In the same area, he also shot 15-year-old Kristina Shevchenko in the chest. Though severely wounded, Kristina was able to move away from the gunman to safety. She taken to a nearby hospital and miraculously survived. Roberts also targeted others in the mall, firing 13 more shots before finding his gun had jammed. After 22 minutes of terror, police closed in on Roberts, only to find him dead of a self-inflicted gunshot wound in a service corridor near JC Penney.

Today, many who work at the mall feel strange sensations at the sites where Forsyth, Yuille, and Roberts died. None of these people consented to the use of their names in this book, but I was told that many people feel an uneasy presence in the service corridor and food court. It is unlikely that the ghosts of Cindy Yuille and Steven Forsyth are present, but Roberts' spirit might still be trapped in the corridor where he died. Added to that, there are imprints of emotions—intense fear and sadness—in many places around the atrium. These were probably created by the crowd of shoppers as they ran to escape the shooter.

GHOSTS OF WORLD WAR II

Formerly Camp Adair
E. E. Wilson Wildlife Area
29555 Camp Adair Road
Monmouth 97361
541-7454-5334

Established at the onset of World War II, Camp Adair was at one time populated by more than 50,000 officers, enlisted personnel, and civilian workers, making it the second largest city in Oregon. For many years after the war, the place was known as the largest ghost town in Oregon. The camp was named in honor of Henry Rodney Adair, a resident of Astoria who distinguished himself in the fight against Pancho Villa in 1916. During its four years as a military center, more than 100,000 troops received combat training here before shipping out to the western Pacific and Europe. To accommodate the camp's personnel, more than 1,700 buildings were constructed and roads and railroads were rerouted. To make way for the 50,000-acre facility, the town of Wells was demolished and its residents, together with those from many of the region's farms, were relocated elsewhere.

The relocation process also involved the dead. Graves at many of the farms and formal cemeteries were moved. It is doubtful that this process was fully completed, however, as some historians suspect that many graves were left behind without markers. Two cemeteries in the area—the Ridders Cemetery and Gingles Pioneer Cemetery—were left in place and remain fascinating attractions today.

Few buildings from the World War II era still exist, but those that do captivate local ghost hunters. The camp's firehouse is now open as the Firehouse Café. Located on NE William Carr Street, the old building contains many original features, including roll-up garage doors and a brick chimney. Some interesting EVP have been captured on the second floor that were interpreted as sounds of firefighters moving about.

The camp's hospital, which once contained beds for 3,600 patients, is currently used by the Santiam Christian School. Visitors to the main building have posted reports of squeaking bedsprings, moans and cries, sobbing, and an intensely uncomfortable feeling of being watched. Ghost hunters are discouraged from visiting this place, however, because the school does not want to become known for paranormal activity. One person I spoke to advised me not to question staff members or students about their impressions of the building's paranormal events.

A former barracks that once housed German and Italian POWs is currently undergoing renovation as a museum and visitors center. This place has already developed a reputation as a haunted venue. No official records of deaths are available, but many prisoners certainly died there thousands of miles from their home.

North of Adair Village, a large open space exists that has attracted a lot of attention from ghost hunters. Known as the E. E. Wilson Wildlife Area, visitors have heard unexplained screams as if some unseen person were trying to get attention. It is believed that several graves marked for removal in 1942 remain in this area.

GHOSTS OF DEVOTED PARISHIONERS

First United Methodist Church
600 State Street
Salem 97301
503-364-6709

Established in Salem in 1841, the First United Methodist Church held services in tents, cabins, and rooms in the Oregon Institute until 1852, when a modest structure was erected at the corner of State and Church streets. By 1870, that building could no longer accommodate the church's congregation. Construction began on a larger church, but finishing touches to the steeple were not completed until 1878. Today, the church stands as the tallest building in town (185 feet above ground level) and is listed on the National Register of Historic Places. Pews, doorknobs, ornate woodwork, a huge circular stained-glass window, and other features create an ecclesiastical atmosphere, but sensitive psychics detect something else in the stately old church.

Considering its long history of benevolent pastors and devoted parishioners, I wouldn't be surprised if a few spirits find this beautiful old church irresistible. In addition, numerous intensely emotional events—including funerals, baptisms, and weddings—would most certainly leave imprints that psychics can detect.

GHOST OF THE GYPSY'S SON

Masonic Cemetery
Mineral Springs Road
Lafayette 97127

Sitting only a few miles west of I-5, the town of Lafayette and its spooky Masonic Cemetery are worth a visit. A gruesome murder, a hanging, an angry ghost, and a gypsy's curse can make your short detour truly fascinating. It all started in 1886 when a 27-year-old loafer named Richard Marple came under suspicion as the perpetrator of several burglaries in town. Apparently, an attempt to rob David Corker's store on November 1, 1886, went terribly wrong, ending in the axe murder of Corker. Marple was quickly apprehended and tried, and then hanged on November 11, 1887. His angry ghost may haunt the town's cemetery, waiting for revenge on the town's people, because his execution was botched. The noose was poorly fashioned and failed to slip tightly against Marple's neck. As a result, he dangled at the end of the rope in excruciating pain for 18 minutes as he slowly suffocated. His body was buried in an unmarked grave, possibly adding to his anger.

During the hanging, Marple's mother, Anna Marple, went into frenzy, shouting threats at the crowd. Known as a gypsy who often claimed to have supernatural power over people, she cursed the town with destructive fires and other disasters. Residents were astounded when a fire occurred in 1888, wiping out 19 buildings. Two more fires occurred in 1904 and 1934. In addition, a smallpox epidemic swept through the town in 1890, causing many deaths.

Many people believe that the most active ghost in this cemetery is that of Anna, but historical records show that she moved to Jacksonville, Oregon. She lived there until she died on March 11, 1916, of liver cancer at the age of 73. Her body was interred in the Jacksonville Cemetery. Suspicions run high, however, that her spirit returned to the Lafayette cemetery, searching for the body of her son. Many people claim to have heard a bloodcurdling scream echo through the night.

The cemetery is now in private hands and closed to visitors, due to a history of vandalism and inappropriate use of the grounds. Go to YouTube to see some interesting videos about this cemetery (*The Lafayette Cemetery #3* and *The Curse of Lafayette*).

THE FIRE STARTER

Capitol Building
900 Court Street NE
Salem 97301
503-986-1388

Multiple fires that occur in a building designed to be fireproof always arouse my suspicions of paranormal activity, particularly when accidents and arson are firmly ruled out. In many of my investigations throughout the U.S., unexplained fires are often linked to construction on hallowed ground or a curse invoked by indigenous people or someone with a grievance. The first fire at this site quickly followed a protracted debate over which city would be the territorial capital. In 1852, Pres. Millard Fillmore decreed that Salem would be the capital of Oregon. As construction of a statehouse continued, members of the territorial legislature staged a political battle that ultimately moved the capital to Corvallis. U.S. Secretary of the Treasury James Guthrie intervened and declared the move illegal. Thus, on December 18, 1855, the state legislature reconvened in Salem. Two weeks later, the newly completed capitol building was destroyed by fire. As it was made of stone, the destruction was initially attributed to arson, but no proof of a crime was found.

In 1873, construction began of a new state house patterned after the U.S. Capitol. This building opened in 1876 and stood until April 25, 1935. Again, fire consumed most of the combustible material inside the massive stone building. Witnesses described smoke rising from an elevator shaft, but no cause of the fire was identified. The current capitol building opened in 1938 after a dedication by Pres. Franklin D. Roosevelt.

Sensitive paranormal investigators have identified two phenomena that may be linked to the destructive fires. An unseen man has been detected by psychics as he walks from one end of the building to the other, passing through the rotunda on the main floor. He emits anger and frustration, perhaps aimed at placement of the state capitol in Salem instead of Corvallis. The second phenomenon has been described as the ghost of a Native American shaman. Apparently, this spirit resists the placement of the building over hallowed ground. Perhaps this angry entity is the Kalapuya goblin mentioned in the legends and lore of local Indians. Named Chuchonnyhoof, this "ironhide" spirit was said to cause the disappearance of troublesome people.

GHOST OF THE DESPONDENT STUDENT

Sackett Hall
2901 SW Jefferson Way
Oregon State University
Corvallis 97331
541-737-1000

Many colleges and universities throughout the U.S. have a dormitory on campus that is said to be haunted. In most cases, the victim is female, murdered by a young male who was not a student. A little research usually reveals that the stories are fabrications, perhaps inspired by an accident or natural death. At Sackett Hall on the campus of Oregon State University, however, the story of a murder has some basis in truth. Although many students I spoke to in Sackett Hall were quick to recount highly variable versions of the story, all of them insisted that the ghost of the victim still haunts the dorm. Accomplished paranormal investigators have looked into the haunting of Sackett Hall, clearly establishing the elements of the crime while pointing to reasons why the victim would remain at OSU.

In May of 1974, notorious serial killer Ted Bundy roamed the campus looking for another female he could abduct, terrorize, and then kill. The evening of May 6, he found her. Roberta Kathleen (Kathy) Parks, despondent over a May 4 argument with her father that may have precipitated his heart attack on May 6, left Sackett Hall to meet friends for coffee. Preoccupied with concerns for her father, Kathy headed to the student union, unaware of people around her or anyone who might be following her. Available evidence indicates Bundy abducted Kathy from campus, although no witnesses came forward to verify this event. The next morning, Kathy was noted as missing by campus police. Her disappearance remained a mystery until 1975, when her skull was discovered in Ted Bundy's "dump site" near Seattle.

Clearly, Kathy was not murdered in her dorm room or the maze of hallways in the basement of Sackett Hall. Her ghost seems to have returned to the dorm, however, the last place where she experienced comfort, security, and the friendship of roommates. Many students have reported seeing objects fall from shelves and slide across the floor, and doors swing open and then close. Others have told me of strange cold spots that seem to move through the hallways.

Some of the paranormal activity of Sackett Hall has been attributed to another murder victim. In 1972, Nancy Wyckoff was murdered in her room in Poling Hall, across the street from Sackett Hall. Her murderer, Marlowe James Buchanan, lived one floor below and had stalked her for days before entering her room late one night. Buchanan first claimed the intrusion was a practical joke but later admitted his intention was rape. Whatever his plan, he ultimately stabbed Nancy at least three times.

Why Nancy's ghost would move across the street to Sackett Hall has never been explained by local ghost hunters. Another mystery is the name given to this ghost: Brandy. Some accounts suggest the victim was promiscuous and always ready for a party. In my research, I found no verification of this. The name "Brandy" may have been a nickname, however. Regardless of her reasons for taking up residence in Sackett Hall, this ghost is far more rambunctious than that of Kathy. "Brandy" has been heard yelling, singing, and running in the hallways.

GHOST OF OPAL

Fox Hollow Elementary School
5055 Mahalo Drive
Eugene 97405
541-790-3177

This school offers a French/English bilingual program housed in modern buildings. I found no record of a fatality, either from accident or criminal activity. So why do locals believe that a ghost roams the playgrounds and hallways?

Students, parents, faculty, and staff members of this school have reported hearing an unseen entity call out the name "Opal." This has occurred most frequently on the playground equipment, but the mysterious voice has been heard in the parking lot and at the entrance to the school as well. No one has reported seeing an apparition or other paranormal phenomena such as moving doors or light anomalies. I did speak to one person who frequently encounters isolated cold spots at the playground.

Who is Opal? Some of the people I interviewed believe that the ghostly entity is Opal. A few insist that the entity is searching for a friend named Opal. The fact that this audio phenomenon occurs most often on the playground raises suspicions that a fatal accident occurred there, leaving the ghost of Opal to roam about looking for classmates to play with. My search of local records turned up no reports of a tragic schoolyard death. In addition, I found nothing in the history of Eugene that suggested that a person named Opal may have lived on the land now occupied by Fox Hollow. Another possibility is that Opal died elsewhere, only to return to a cherished place, the playground.

As I walked about the campus, I did not hear a disembodied voice call out "Opal," but I did discover an intense, clearly defined cold spot at the bench on the east side of the play area near the red slide.

If you visit this school, or any other school in Oregon, abide by rules governing visitors. It may be best to explore this site on a weekend or evening.

GHOST OF THE FALLING JANITOR

Lane Community College

4000 East 30th Avenue
Eugene 97405-0640
541-463-3000
www.lanecc.edu

Virtually every paranormal book about Oregon's haunted places includes mention of the haunted elevator at Lane Community College. Servicing the basement and two main floors of the Center Building, the elevator is said to be haunted by the ghost of a janitor who died after falling down the shaft or from a crush injury caused by a door malfunction. Various sources say this accident happened in the 1960s. The first classes were held at Lane College in September of 1965, narrowing the period of time when this may have occurred. It is possible, however, that a fatal accident happened during construction. If that is the case, we must wonder why it is said to involve one of the college's janitors.

I searched county and state accident records from 1960 through 1975 but found no mention of a Lane College incident. I also searched the University of Oregon archives for the *Eugene Register-Guard* over the same period. No headlines included the key words *Lane College, accident, fatality,* and *elevator.* Despite the lack of evidence, sensitive people who ride the elevator will have some bizarre experiences.

Most sources I reviewed stated that sensitives standing inside the elevator may hear the janitor's cries for help. I heard something that may be interpreted as a moan or sob accented with a higher-pitched sound similar to an animal's "yelp." I was also overcome with a terrible foreboding, as if something awful was about to happen.

Stepping out of the elevator, I decided to take the stairs to basement. I did not find a bank of lockers mentioned by previous investigators, but the place was creepy. Gathering my courage, I rode the elevator several times between the basement and the top floor, noticing that it often stopped at floors I had not selected. In some cases the doors did not open before the elevator moved to the next floor. Sometimes, the doors opened and remained so, despite my pushing the *door close* button several times.

One sensitive claims to have discovered a locker in the basement that contained a collection of photos described as a shrine. Supposedly, the pictures revealed the history of a man who was married yet infatuated with a female student. The sensitive surmised that the man's wife discovered his obsession or affair and pushed him into the elevator shaft. There is no corroborating evidence, however.

Is this elevator haunted? As a sensitive, I affirm that there is something quite strange about it.

GHOST OF ROBERT GRANKEY

South Eugene High School
400 East 19th Avenue
Eugene 97401-4162
541-790-8000

Unlike most reports of ghostly activity, the identity of the spirit that haunts South Eugene High School is known. Robert Turnbull Grankey died at the school on March 11, 1958. A record of his life and death may be found in that year's March 12 edition of the *Eugene Register-Guard*.

During his sophomore year, Robert became involved in theatre productions at the school. His duties as a stagehand included adjusting the lights that hung high above the stage. On March 11, 1958, while moving about the catwalks, Robert lost his balance and fell 55 feet to his death. Thirty students witness the horrible event. Landing on seats 10 and 11 in row G, Robert suffered a broken neck and severe head injury. It is believed he died instantly. The seats that Robert fell upon remained in use for many years, revealing dents from the impact of his body, until they were replaced in 1994 in an effort to dispel superstition.

Soon after Robert's death, faculty and students became aware of a strange atmosphere in the theatre. Some actually saw a translucent, indistinct figure on the catwalks, while others perceived footsteps on the stage or a disembodied voice practicing dialogue or calling out names of students. Other phenomena attributed to Robert's ghost include creaking sounds on the catwalk, strange shadows in the balcony, and the sound of a piano.

Author Kent Goodman recounts the experience of a teacher who once spotted Robert's apparition. Noticing someone on the narrow planks suspended over the stage at a time when no one was supposed to be working, the teacher climbed to the dark and dangerous catwalks thinking someone was playing a prank. Chasing the ghostly image, the teacher saw the features of a young boy wearing a white shirt. As he came to the end of the catwalk, the apparition disappeared into a wall, leaving the teacher certain he had encountered the spirit of Robert Grankey.

Why this ghost would run from a teacher is a mystery. None of the reported encounters with this apparition suggest anger of malevolent intent. The sightings and creepy feelings experienced by so many people have been so intense, however, that the place now has a very firm reputation as a haunted high school.

GHOSTS OF THE THREE WOMEN

Shelton-McMurphey-Johnson House
303 Willamette Street
Eugene 97401
541-484-0808

This stately mansion was once known as the "castle on the hill." Though not occupying the highest spot on Skinner's Butte, it could be seen from just about any place in old Eugene. Conversely, inhabitants of the house had a commanding view of the town including the busy train station, which no longer exists. Today, the grand old mansion is open to the public as a museum and is available for special events. Most of the people who wander about the place have no idea it is haunted by at least three ghosts.

Arriving in Eugene in 1873, Dr. Thomas Shelton established his practice and acquired sufficient wealth to hire architect Walter Pugh to begin construction of the mansion in 1887. Before the family could move in, however, an angry workman set fire to the place, requiring another year to rebuild the house.

Thomas and Adah Shelton raised their daughter, Alberta, in the mansion. When Thomas died at the age 49, she became the owner of the property and mother Adah moved to Portland. Alberta married Robert McMurphey in the parlor, in the alcove formed by the bay windows. Three of their four daughters were married in this same spot.

Music was a prominent pastime for the four McMurphey daughters and two sons. Having graduated from the piano conservatory of the University of Oregon, Alberta was an accomplished pianist and music teacher. As the children became adults, they moved in various directions, eventually leaving Alberta and Robert alone in the house until his death in 1921. Alberta continued a solitary lifestyle another 28 years before passing away in a Portland nursing home in 1949. Her childhood friend, Eva Johnson, purchased the home for $30,000 and began the Johnson era in this grand mansion.

A graduate of Rush Medical School of Chicago, Eva Johnson and her husband, Curtis Johnson also a physician, moved into the place in 1950. Though she was finally realizing a dream she had held since childhood, the move into the grand mansion was marked with bad luck. A fire broke out during renovations that eventually required extensive reconstruction of several rooms. This event, together with post-traumatic stress from serving in both world wars, left Curtis depressed and caused him to become a recluse. Spending much of his time in the tower, Curtis stored his memorabilia there, perhaps inadvertently creating a depository for a lot of negative energy emanating from his war souvenirs and his emotional state. It is said that he spent long hours in the cramped space. He died in 1967, leaving his wife, Eva, in the house until her death in 1986 at the age of 97.

It is likely that Curtis's ghost occupies the tower, moves up and down the stairs, and paces the kitchen. Sensitives detect his presence by the wave of negative energy he produces. This is most intense in the

Over the course of a century, the Shelton-McMurphey-Johnson mansion was home to three families. Some of those residents have stayed behind as ghosts.

tower, where he spent much of his time surrounded by souvenirs of his career as a military physician. Visitors to this space are sometimes overwhelmed by his depression arising from his wife pressuring him into moving to Eugene.

In contrast, ghosts on the main floor of the house seem pleased that the old place has been preserved. Apparitions of three women have been spotted standing together in the alcove of the parlor where three of the McMurphey daughters were married. One visitor reported he had captured the three women in a photo, but I could view the evidence myself. Others have seen one to three apparitions of women, quite translucent and partial, move about the parlor and foyer. All of the McMurphey children played at least one musical instrument, so it isn't surprising that musical notes are often heard in the house.

Many believe that Alberta also haunts the mansion in which she lived as a child, was married, and raised her six children. That kind of history and strong emotional attachment are the kind of ingredients that may create a lingering spiritual presence a century or more after death.

GHOST OF THE WHITE LADY

Eugene Pioneer Cemetery
Corner of East 18th Avenue and University Street
Eugene 97403

Surrounded by the high-energy atmosphere of the University of Oregon, the tall trees and grass scattered about this cemetery create a peaceful oasis for more than 5,000 of Oregon's dead, including some notable pioneers. Opened in 1872, the cemetery covers 16 acres and includes a special plot established by the Grand Army of the Republic. This ground contains 51 graves of Civil War veterans, including that of Louis Renninger (1841-1908), a Union soldier who was awarded the Medal of Honor. Renninger volunteered to lead an assault on the Confederate heights at the Battle of Vicksburg in May of 1863. Two-thirds of his brigade were killed, despite his bravery and repeated supporting attacks led by Gen. U. S. Grant.

The GAR plot also contains six graves for women and three for children who were, apparently, buried here because their husbands and fathers could not bear to be separated from them in death. In other sections of the cemetery, you will find the graves of people who fought in the Spanish-American War, World War I, and World War II.

The cemetery has attracted the attention of local ghosts and the curiosity of many UO students who regularly pass through the place. In the 1970s, the discovery of an apparition of a woman was highly publicized. The report described a thin woman, wearing a long white gown similar to a wedding dress, floating above ground on a thick fog. Apparently, many people witnessed this apparition on several occasions. At times she was seen hovering over a GAR grave, but most often she floats over the cemetery pathways, traveling up to 50 feet before disappearing.

Every cemetery I've investigated has a legendary "woman in white" assumed to be a bride who died on or soon after her wedding day. In this cemetery, I found a number of graves that contained young females, but I could find no information in cemetery records or local newspapers about a specific event that might identify this ghost.

The apparition of a man dressed as a traditional Scottish bagpipe player appears near the GAR plot. Witnesses have noted insignia and colors of his uniform that identify him as a member of the "Black Watch," the Royal Highland Regiment founded in 1881. Several ghost hunters have captured the sound of bagpipes with audio recorders. This fellow plays before disappearing before astonished witnesses. At times, only the mournful notes of bagpipes are heard. During two of my visits to this cemetery, I caught the sound of bagpipes on my audio recorder. I suspect that this audio phenomenon is a residual or imprint created by repetitive emotional events, such as the playing of the bagpipes during funerals. As expected, the two EAP I captured were near graves marked with Scottish names.

On October 12, 2009, three men and a woman desecrated several graves, dislodging the headstones to build a fire pit. They were captured and convicted, but their vandalism disturbed many spirits and increased paranormal activity in the cemetery.

MORTUARY GHOSTS

Bijou Art Cinemas
492 East 13th Street

Eugene 97401
541-686-2458

I love old theatres. They tend to smell of past ages, in a good way, and the fragrances bring to mind fancy people dressed for a night of entertainment. In the case of the Bijou, however, the scents may be something left over from when the place was a mortuary. Described by many writers as Spanish mission style, the architecture is actually late 19th and early 20th century Mediterranean, as executed by the renowned architect Walter Wilcox (1869-1947). He designed and constructed the building in 1925 to house the First Congregational Church of Eugene. It remained in use as a church until 1956, when it was sold, remodeled, and reopened as the McGaffey and Andreason Mortuary. For nearly 25 years, bodies were brought here and prepared for burial while friends and family mourned the dead through wakes and funerals. So it's no any wonder that something paranormal remains within the walls of the old church and mortuary, refusing to relinquish the attachment despite its current use as a theatre.

Renamed the Wilcox Building in 1980, perhaps to rid the place of its reputation as a mortuary, the Bijou now operates there, offering patrons independent films in an intimate setting. Architectural elements of the old church and mortuary persist, including a tranquil patio separating the two viewing rooms that take patrons back in time while creating an atmosphere conducive to ghost hunting. Yes, it is easy for sensitives to detect something paranormal in the Bijou.

In 2010, members of the Pacific Paranormal Research Society conducted an investigation in the Bijou. Using a digital camera, a trainee captured the image of an apparition in the lobby. Others have not been so fortunate, but light anomalies are frequently found in digital images snapped by visitors.

Both viewing rooms are believed to be haunted, but reports do not specific any identifying information about the spirits. Generally, the experience is limited to an isolated cold spot or sensation of a presence hovering close by. Room number 2 was used to store and prepare bodies for burial. Paranormal activity here may be generated by a spirit who is looking for its body. Room number 1 may have been used for funeral services. Consequently, that room probably contains a large number of imprints of emotion created by people in mourning.

CHAPTER 6

Oregon's Coastal Communities

The magnificent Oregon Coast extends 363 miles southward from the Columbia River to the California border. Long stretches of desolate beauty are interrupted by tiny hamlets, quaint towns with spectacular beaches and popular resorts, and cities such as Coos Bay, Brookings, Lincoln City, and Astoria. Separated from Portland and the cities of the Willamette Valley by the Oregon Coastal Range, Highway 101 runs the length of the coast, providing ghost hunters with easy access to many fascinating haunted places, charming inns, beautiful beaches, placid bays, and seafood restaurants. Numerous shipwrecks, disastrous floods and storms, plane crashes, and other accidents have populated the region with many active ghosts and created intense imprints that lead to paranormal experiences. Old buildings in towns such as Astoria, Lincoln City, and Seaside provide a tangible link to the early 20th century and a glimpse of life in towns that were essentially isolated from Portland.

In addition to ghosts, travelers along the Oregon Coast often spot bizarre creatures. Near the mouth of the Columbia River, close to Fort Stevens and Astoria, a creature named Claude swims the turbulent waters. The first published report of a sighting occurred in 1937 and described Claude as "mean and snaky." Reportedly, this monster had an eight-foot-long, serpent-like body with a 30-foot tail. In 1935, another sea monster was spotted south of Newport at Seal Rock. Several witnesses reported that its head was three feet wide and its snakelike body was 40 feet long. Over the years, many people have seen this creature play in the surf before disappearing beneath the waves. Naturally, no photographs or films of these monsters are available. It is fun to keep an eye out for them, though.

Near Cannon Beach, a humanoid creature dubbed "Bandage Man" jumps in the back of pickup trucks or dashes across the road, frightening astonished travelers. Wrapped in bloody bandages and appearing like a mummy, he often shows up near the intersection of Highways 101 and 26. Some witnesses have described him as a ghost, while others believe he may be a Sasquatch that has wrapped discarded clothing around its body for warmth.

Aside from ghostly experiences, travelers along the coast may have the delightful experience of a "Wheeler Moment." Something about the beauty and tranquility of Nehalem Bay and charms of the town of Wheeler have created a supernatural atmosphere that leads to wonderful coincidences, unexpected fulfillment of hopes and dreams, astonishing visions, and fortuitous twists of fate. Described as a "spiritual vortex," the region causes locals and visitors to frequently experience this benevolent effect. A Wheeler Moment may be the sudden appearance of a long-lost friend, answer to a perplexing question, or discovery of information that changes a career or travel destination. Whatever the basis of this fantastic experience, a Wheeler Moment is most likely to occur outdoors, close to the ocean or bay, during a period of quiet introspection.

Other weird and wonderful places you should visit include the ghost forest of Neskowin, the Forbidden Cliffs of Neahkahanie, and the mystical peace of Nye Beach.

GHOSTS OF THE THEATRE PATRONS

Liberty Theater
1203 Commercial Street
Astoria, Oregon 97103
503-325-5922
www.liberty-theater.org

After many years of paranormal investigations, I have come to believe that old theatres are among the most haunted places we may find. In fact, I rank them as number three in my list of the top-five locations most likely to harbor ghosts and retain imprints. This is because the devotion and passion of successful actors, musicians, directors, writers, and producers are characteristically intense and likely to persist with a high degree of energy after death. As ghosts, these talented people refuse to let go of their stardom and tenaciously hold on to the place where they experienced the greatest moments of their lives in front of admiring audiences. Many remain onstage trying to achieve that special performance that would finally make them a star. Some would die elsewhere but, as spirits, would find their way back to the spot where they felt most alive, achieved their greatest success, or received the deepest admiration of an audience.

The mix of ghosts in old theatres becomes more eclectic when we include patrons who became emotionally involved with actors or actresses, and stagehands who suffered fatal accidents while working with heavy curtains, scenery, and electrical equipment. In many of the old theatres in the U.S., fires cut short the lives of actors and musicians.

Old playhouses almost always retain hundreds of imprints of great performances, accidents, and personal relationships as well. The repetitive nature of rehearsals and shows invariably creates intense and highly durable imprints that are easily detected by audio recorders, infrared cameras, and psychic sensitivities. The old Liberty Theater in Astoria is a great example of the proverbial haunted theatre that will captivate every ghost hunter.

The Liberty Theater virtually rose from the ashes left by the great fire of 1922. The fire destroyed hundreds of businesses and residences on 36 city blocks in central Astoria, including a theatre that stood at 11th and Exchange streets. This place was officially the Astoria Theater, but many historians, including paranormal researchers, call it the First Liberty Theater. Following the fire, civic leaders supported the reconstruction of buildings that would quickly restore businesses and the social life of the city. One of those projects was the Liberty Theater destined to stand at the corner of 12th and Commercial streets. It was state of the art. Equipped with electric lights and a Wurlitzer organ, the theatre could seat 1,000 and provided space for offices, several shops, and a restaurant. Although they started with silent films and live vaudeville performers, the owners installed speakers as a technical upgrade when talking movies came to Astoria in the early 1930s.

In later years, the theatre was closed for major renovations. It reopened in 2005 after a multimillion-dollar restoration. The renewed brilliance of this amazing theatre may be one reason why the ghosts there have become so active. Prominent local writers repeat stories of three ghosts without offering documentation that the persons described ever existed. Contemporary ghost hunters and some employees, however, told me that they firmly believe the place is haunted, due to ongoing paranormal activity that sometimes includes partial apparitions.

It is said that a ghostly couple, Paul and Mary, haunt the theatre's second-floor restroom and passageways. Identified as "Handsome Paul" in some accounts and described as a pimp in others, this man controlled Mary, who worked as a prostitute. An argument over working conditions started in the restroom and moved onto the balcony, where Paul threw Mary over the railing to her death. It isn't clear if Paul also died in the building, but ghost hunters seem certain he is still there, perhaps searching for Mary. Visitors to the restroom have reported bizarre experiences, including intense cold spots, eerie presences, and images in the mirror of a woman in early-20th-century clothing. Paul's partial apparition has been spotted in the basement as well as in the passageways on the second floor.

A third ghost, named Lily, remains attached to the main-floor seat on which she died from a knife wound to the neck. Reportedly, her

The old Liberty Theater in Astoria literally rose from the ashes of the disastrous 1922 fire, but its ghosts are linked to crimes committed decades ago inside the building.

boyfriend killed her while she watched a vaudeville matinee. Her apparition is often seen in one of the back rows. I found the last two seats to the left, in the row second from the last, to be strangely cold. Sitting in these seats elicits Lily's attention, causing her to generate a cold cell of sadness that makes you feel that you should move.

The Liberty Theater has been investigated by AGHOST (Advanced Ghost Hunters of Seattle-Tacoma), known as one of the best paranormal groups in the U.S. One of its psychic investigators encountered an oppressive spirit in the theatre's basement. This ghost manifested by standing close or leaning on her shoulder. As this occurred, a shadowy figure was captured on video. The figure moved about, giving investigators the impression that it was trying to get photographed. The pimp, Handsome Paul, might not welcome this kind of attention, but an actor certainly would recognize an opportunity to appear in front of a camera. Some fascinating EVP have been captured in the basement and several other locations. The best way to become familiar with the ghosts of the Liberty Theater is to attend a film festival or other event and meet some of the staff members.

GHOSTS OF THE HOTEL FAMILY

Hotel Elliott
357 12th Street
Astoria 97103
503-325-2222
www.hotelelliott.com

The ghost of a former owner of this hotel, Jeremiah Elliott (1859-1929), roams the building, marveling at the amazing improvements and spectacular décor. Every part of this vintage hotel probably amazes him as he moves through the lobby and each floor with a benevolent demeanor, trying not to disturb guests. There is evidence that the ghosts of his son, John, wife, Margaret, and daughter, Flora, also haunt the place.

Soon after downtown Astoria was destroyed by a fire in 1922, construction began on a four-story building to be called the Niemi

Hotel. Before its completion, Jeremiah Elliott leased the place, changed its name to Hotel Elliott, and instructed builders to add a fifth floor. He installed his family's kitchen and living room in the basement but insisted that they use bedrooms on the fifth floor. During the many years that the Elliott family resided within the hotel, a number of them died there or close by.

After seven years in a coma, Margaret (1869-1950) died in a bedroom that is now part of the presidential suite. Flora (1886-1970) also died in this suite at the age of 84, of a heart attack. Psychics have detected the presence of an unseen female there.

Jeremiah died on the morning of May 6, 1929, while conducting business in the Fix It Shop on Exchange Street, only a block from the hotel. His body was transported to the hotel, where grieving family members awaited the arrival of a mortician.

Many local ghost hunters believe that Jeremiah has resumed residence in his hotel. The translucent apparition of an elderly man dressed in a suit has been spotted sitting in a chair in the lobby. While it is possible this is the ghost of Jeremiah's brother, John L. Elliott, it is more likely that it is the spirit of Jeremiah himself. Jeremiah has also appeared in room 405 and walking the hallways on each floor.

Since the hotel's opening in 1924, Jeremiah's son, John L. Elliott (1892-1984), worked with his father and his uncle John in its management, learning the trade and becoming a central figure in Astoria's business community. He took full control of the business in the early 1960s, only to discover that he could not stop its financial decline. John sold the hotel in 1969 and settled into a house at 1140 Franklin. From the upper floor of his new home, he could see the Hotel Elliott, to which he had devoted nearly 50 years of his life. Heartbroken from the loss of the hotel and longing to return to his family's home, John died on January 8, 1984. The house in which he died is now the Franklin Street Station B and B.

Hotel guests, staff members, and curious visitors have reported a variety of paranormal experiences. Unseen hands have touched guests in rooms on the third and fourth floors, and whole-body imprints have appeared on beds soon after housekeepers have changed the sheets. In the hallway, near room 307, many guests have reported seeing the shadows of children and hearing their voices, as if they are playing. In rooms 306 and 307, an unseen benevolent presence creates a feeling of being watched.

A cigar and wine bar once operated in the basement that may have attracted the attention of John Elliott, who was known for his affinity for cigars. Images of persons wearing clothing from the 1940s often appeared in glass partitions. This space has since been renovated and converted to a gym, and the wine bar was moved to the first floor, where guests can enjoy a view of the revitalized Liberty District of Astoria. Translucent images of 1940s-era cigar-bar patrons are sometimes spotted in this popular bar.

Writer Jeff Davis has raised the possibility that a curse fell upon the Hotel Elliott after the Elliott family gave up ownership. Apparently, the next two owners each died about six months after they sold the property.

GHOSTS OF THE FAMILY THAT DIED AT HOME

Flavel House
Eighth Street at Duane Street
Astoria 97103
503-325-2203
www.oldoregon.com/visitor-info/entry/flavel-house-museum/

There are two houses in Astoria known as the "Flavel House." One of them is well preserved as a fascinating museum, while the other remains derelict, evoking an atmosphere of oppression and evil. Both are believed to be haunted.

The museum known as the Flavel House was built in 1885 by Astoria's first millionaire, Capt. George Flavel. The captain made his money by serving as a Columbia River pilot, guiding ships from all over the world through the entrance of the treacherous river so that they could make their way to Portland and Oregon City. He was also known as a shrewd businessman who accumulated a great deal of property in Astoria, including wharves, warehouses, and a fleet of small craft that hauled cargo to local destinations and serviced large ships moored along the shore. The mansion, built with the captain's fortune, is over 11,000 square feet and features very tall ceilings, ornate woodwork, and a flush toilet.

Unfortunately, the captain enjoyed the elegance and comfort of the home for only eight years. He died in his great bedroom in 1893. His daughter, Nellie Flavel, enjoyed the grand house for many years, but she died in 1933 while traveling in New York. Many believe that her spirit resumed residence in the mansion. Nellie's sister, Katie (1864-1910), died in her own bedroom of a crippling illness, probably rheumatoid arthritis. Their mother, Mary Flavel, died in the captain's bedroom in 1928.

Nellie and Katie enjoyed a privileged lifestyle, complete with tutors from San Francisco and Europe and instruction in music. They must have been closely supervised because neither one ever married. They relied on their brother, George Conrad Flavel (1855-1923), to carry on the family line.

The house remained in the hands of the captain's great-granddaughter, Patricia Jean, for several years until she donated it to the Clatsop County Historical Society. It opened as a museum in 1951 and remains a popular attraction today. If you visit Astoria, I suggest you start at this house to learn something about life in old Astoria and get some clues as to where you can find ghosts.

Psychics who visit the Flavel House have posted some interesting reports. One said the captain's bedroom was the "center of all evil." Others have simply experienced sadness and the low-frequency energy of a life slowly ebbing away. Some lucky visitors have spotted the captain's apparition in the bedroom, standing away from the bed and fully dressed in a fine suit.

The captain's ghost may also manifest in the tower that caps this stunning mansion. Captain Flavel spent many hours up there keeping watch over the ships sailing the Columbia River. It is likely he considered this part of the mansion his personal space, completely off-limits to his wife and children. Psychics who climb the narrow steps to the tower often feel a terrible foreboding, as if an unseen force wished to deny them entry.

Apparitions believed to be Nellie, Katie, and Mary have been spotted in the music room and other locations throughout the mansion. Ghostly activity attributed to these women is not threatening but

The mansion constructed by Capt. George Flavel is now open as a museum, but he and his family continue to haunt the rooms in which they died.

often playful. In addition to these apparitions, electrical devices get unplugged, a music box plays, and unexplained cold spots occur.

The other Flavel House in Astoria was built in 1901 by George Flavel, Jr., the son of Capt. George Flavel. Upon the death of the former, son Harry M. Flavel (died 1951) took ownership of the house as well as his father's position as president of a local bank. Young Harry moved in with his second wife, Florence, with whom he had a son, Harry Sherman Flavel (1927-2010) and daughter, Mary Louise Flavel (1929-). The house's peculiar history is based on the behavior of young Harry, otherwise known as Hatchet Harry.

Known for his eccentric and, at times, angry behavior, Harry Sherman Flavel received his strange moniker in 1947, when neighbor Fred Fulton heard Mary Louise screaming for help from inside the house. After breaking in, Fulton raced to an upstairs bedroom, only to encounter Harry wielding an axe. The encounter left Fulton wounded on the arm. Harry avoided a prison sentence by arguing that Fulton was drunk and the axe was used only for self-defense. Despite the favorable opinion of the court, Harry was thereafter known as Hatchet Harry. Notoriety of this event, rumors of Harry's bizarre behavior,

Built by George Flavel, Jr., in 1901, this derelict Flavel home has been the site of bizarre events attributed to an evil presence.

occasional gunshots heard from within the house, and the declining appearance of the property gave rise to stories of an evil presence.

Despite a steep decline in his family's prominence, Harry continued to live in the house with Florence and Mary Louise until 1983. In February of that year, Harry got into another altercation that ended in Harry stabbing a man. Harry was convicted in 1985 and, once his appeals were exhausted in 1990, he became a fugitive with Mary and 90-year-old Florence, leaving the house abandoned. Months later, Harry and Mary were arrested in Pennsylvania for stealing towels from a motel. After paying bail, the pair disappeared again until Harry's death on May 31, 2010. Mary's whereabouts remain unknown, but many believe she returned to Astoria and died in the house. In October of 2010, black funerary bunting mysteriously appeared draped over an exterior balcony.

Mysteries surrounding the bizarre Flavel family and the abandoned home became even more intriguing when city officials entered the place. Overcome by the stench of rotting food and soiled clothing, they found that most of the rooms were filled with stacks, up to three feet tall, of old newspapers and magazines, leaving space on the floor only for little trails from one door to the next. The officials discovered clothing hung from ropes as if to dry, a dead dog in a refrigerator, unopened mail dated 1979, a huge collection of unopened toilet paper and adult diapers, and numerous other items wrapped in duct tape. (See the *Daily Astorian,* Tuesday, July 3, 2012, and December 11, 2013.)

Today, the once-grand mansion stands derelict and in the hands of the city. If Mary Louise fails to come forward, the place will probably be demolished. Until that happens, fascinated ghost hunters would welcome the opportunity to explore the house. Even from the outside, psychics may have bizarre impressions that emanate from the suspected incestuous relationship between Harry and Mary, Mary's disappearance, Harry's criminal behavior, and the possibility that an evil presence drove the young Flavels far from the refined course set by their revered ancestor, Capt. George Flavel.

RESTLESS SOLDIER OF BATTERY RUSSELL

Fort Stevens State Park
100 Peter Iredale Road
Hammond 97121
800-551-6949
www.visitftstevens.com

Historic military installations converted into museums and historical sites may be found all over the U.S. Many of them were established in the mid-19th century and, thus, possess what may be called several strata, or layers, of history, including the paranormal remnants of America's wars and other military events. We may find, hidden among the obvious relics of military history, imprints of great moments experienced by heroic and ordinary individuals and their ghosts. Fort Stevens, in the westernmost corner of Oregon, is one of those places, harboring spirits while offering countless opportunities to touch the past.

Established in 1863 as an earthwork battery designed to protect the mouth of the Columbia River, the facility was later named for the former territorial governor of Washington, Isaac I. Stevens, who was killed in action during the Civil War. Throughout the remainder of the 19th century, the fort was expanded as its technology and artillery were upgraded. By 1930, huge guns and concrete bunkers dotted the landscape, along with observation towers, munitions bunkers, barracks, a hospital, and various other military facilities. After 84 years of military service, the fort was closed in 1947, only to later reopen as Fort Stevens State Park. Today, many buildings and military installations exist within the 4,200-acre park, providing ghost hunters with opportunities to explore past eras and connect with the spirits of men who served there. A good place to start your exploration of this amazing fort is the military museum.

Fort Stevens may be best known as the site of the first mainland attack by Japanese forces during World War II. Late at night on June 21, 1942, the Japanese submarine I-25 fired on the fort, believing it was a navy base for submarines and destroyers. The enemy submarine fired 17 shells at the fort from eight miles offshore, some of them landing close to Battery Russell but failing to create significant damage. Soldiers at the fort rallied from their bunks and manned all of the operational guns. Expecting a massive invasion, anxious soldiers stood ready to engage the enemy, but no orders were given to return fire because officers decided that the blasts from the big guns would reveal the exact location of the fort's batteries. This frightening night of bombardment ended without fatalities but was sufficient to create intense imprints of emotions in the concrete and metal fittings of Battery Russell.

Today, Battery Russell stands as a stark reminder of one of America's most challenging moments in military history. All of its guns have been removed, but the weathered concrete, dark and damp tunnels, rooms never illuminated by the sun, and dense shadows create a fascinating and eerie atmosphere, giving rise to stories of a ghostly soldier who is always on patrol.

Some describe him as a watchman, while others insist he wears an army uniform. At times he appears as a translucent apparition, revealing remarkable detail to psychics, but most often he manifests as a shadow, an anomalous cold spot, or a light resembling a flashlight. Some witnesses add that these ghostly sightings are accompanied by the sound of rattling chains, boot steps, or doors in motion. This spirit's identity will likely never be known, unless some lucky ghost hunter can entice him to say his name as an audio recorder runs.

Fort Stevens was fired upon by a Japanese submarine on June 21, 1942. No fatalities occurred in that event, but ghostly soldiers are still on duty there.

At the fort's guardhouse, a ghostly figure described as a tall, thin man walks through the rooms, creating loud crashing sounds as if he is slamming cell doors. Ghost hunters have captured pictures of orbs at the cell doors, in the office, and in the narrow hallway.

Orbs have also been readily captured at Battery Pratt. Ghost hunters report that the hotspot for these light anomalies is in the rooms below gun emplacement number 2. Orbs may indicate a spirit presence or simply be the result of operating deficiencies of digital cameras. Corroborating evidence such as concurrent EVP, movement of objects, or visual sightings may authenticate these light anomalies.

The site of the fort's hospital is believed to be occupied by both benevolent spirits and ones that create a sense of fear and foreboding. Some investigators have stated that these are evil spirits. This blend of energies may be the result of unmarked graves that contain the remains of soldiers who died during the worldwide flu epidemic of 1919. Some spirits may be attached to this place because they are unaware they are dead and await medical attention, or they have no desire to leave the last place where they received care and comfort.

The soldiers of Fort Stevens never suffered fatalities by enemy attack, but many who lost their lives in heroic battles overseas may have returned here seeking comfort, safety, and the comrades with whom they served. Like the aircraft carrier USS *Hornet* in Alameda, California, Fort Stevens may be a spiritual gathering place for military ghosts.

WRECK OF THE *PETER IREDALE*

Fort Stevens State Park
Clatsop Beach at Iredale Road
Hammond 97121
800-551-6949
www.visitftstevens.com

Destined for Portland with a crew of 25 and two stowaways, the iron-hulled sailing ship *Peter Iredale* faced rough seas and unfavorable winds as she approached the mouth of the Columbia River on the night of October 25, 1906. By 3:00 A.M., a heavy mist obscured the Columbia River light ship, an essential beacon to any vessel entering the great river. When that vital navigation aid was lost, it was clear to captain and crew that the 275-foot-long vessel was doomed. A short time later, the sound of the hull scraping on sand echoed through the ship and confirmed their worst fears. As the vessel plowed into the sandy shore, there was little relief on board. The greatest threat to the lives of the men would be to capsize in the pounding surf, tossing everyone into the sea. Despite losing her top spars and headway through the choppy water, the *Peter Iredale* was driven high onto the beach by gale winds and huge waves. She came to rest nearly upright, saving the lives of all on board. The crew was rescued by men from Hammond and taken to Fort Stevens for respite.

Today, the *Peter Ireland* is little more than a rusting collection of iron beams and fragments of the foredecks stranded on the beach near Hammond. Still, it is a popular attraction, arousing the wonder of those who explore the remains. Those who visit the shipwreck on foggy days or near twilight have had bizarre experiences that give the impression that there is something paranormal about it. Standing inside the wreck, I've heard the sounds of straining ropes and cables, wind rustling canvas sails, and heavy boot steps on a deck. These may be imprints left by the crew on that frightening night in 1906.

Others have told me of sounds that they described as "creaking," like the noises that the crew may have heard when the ship ran aground. Digital images have also captured strange lights at the location.

The best time to visit the wreck of the *Peter Iredale* is at sunset, when the sea is calm and the wind absent. Those are rare conditions on this beach, but they may prove to be essential if you want to detect imprints of a dying ship and desperate crew.

NEHALEM BAY WINERY

34965 Highway 53
Nehalem 97131
1-888-368-WINE

One of more than 350 wineries in Oregon, Nehalem Bay Winery is unique not only for its bottled spirits but also the kind of spirits that roam about in the still of the night. Patrick McCoy founded the winery, which released its first vintage in 1974. Today, under the ownership of Ray Shackelford, the winery sells about 4,000 cases of wine per year, ranging from divine white wines, including Riesling, Gewurztraminer, Chardonnay, and Pinot Gris, to very impressive reds, including Merlot and Cabernet Sauvignon. Being from the heart of California's wine country, I have to admit I was surprised and awed by the character of the red wines produced in a climate that is much cooler than Sonoma and Napa. Nehalem Bay Winery also offers a collection of wines made from peach, plum, and blackberry, and a honey-mead creation that Sonoma wine aficionados would call a dessert wine.

Yes, the wines are impressive, but the history of the place and reports of ghostly activities make this winery a must-see for any ghost hunter traveling on Highway 53. The building was constructed around 1907 and housed the Mohler Creamery from 1909 to 1959. The place sat nearly vacant for many years, serving as a storage facility for farm equipment, until Shackelford bought it. After extensive renovation, which probably aroused a lot of old spirits, the place took on the character and charm of a coastal winery.

Employees and locals who often visit will tell you that the winery is haunted. In fact, reports of ghostly activity there may be found in much of the Internet literature focused on Oregon's haunted places. Some of the earliest paranormal experiences occurred in the mid-1970s, soon after the winery sold its first cases of wine. The usual experiences are fairly common: unexplained incidents of floors creaking, doors moving, missing objects discovered in odd places, cold spots, and gusts of wind.

More exciting experiences have also occurred. An EVP has been captured in which a disembodied voice repeated, "Kill me." In other recordings, both male and female voices have been heard uttering unintelligible words that, nonetheless, gave the impression that unseen persons were going about their daily lives. Employee Angi Wildt reportedly saw a shadowy figure in the narrow corridor behind the winery's stage. A dark, translucent apparition has also appeared upstairs in one of the guest rooms. Ghost hunters who have staged investigation at the winery reported that they were touched and pushed, though not in a malevolent manner, and they felt an unseen entity walking or standing behind them.

In the tasting room, employees have witnessed objects move. For example, the sound of wineglasses clinking is a frequent occurrence. Doors move without explanation, and souvenirs vibrate.

Ghost hunters who visit the Nehalem Bay Winery should rely on digital audio recorders. In addition to active ghosts of unknown origin, this place seems to have paranormal imprint phenomena in virtually every room.

RENOVATION GHOSTS

Old Wheeler Hotel
495 North Highway 101
Wheeler 97147-0555
877-653-4683
www.oldwheelerhotel.com

The ghosts of this historic seaside hotel stand as a good example of the precept that spirits tend to be aroused by changes in the environment to which they are attached. Furthermore, paranormal activity tends to correlate to the extent and duration of renovations. Since renovations of the Old Wheeler Hotel have been continuing since the 1930s, it is no surprise that its ghosts have been aroused and, indeed, intrigued by the never-ending changes. The place has so much ghostly activity that it has attracted investigations by local and visiting paranormal groups. In April of 2013, a group called "Paranormal Insights" staged a class in the old hotel. Participants gained skill and knowledge of the psychic method of paranormal investigation in a venue known to harbor highly active spirits.

The current structure was built in 1920 as a replacement for two buildings, the Rector Hotel and the Hotel Annex, that simply deteriorated so badly in the marine climate that they became unusable. When it opened in 1921, the place was called the Old Wheeler Hotel. For the next 10 years, the booming logging industry brought a steady stream of customers, keeping every room occupied. The great fire of 1933 (the Tillamook Burn), which devastated the lumber industry, and the Great Depression took a severe toll on the hotel's business and changed the economy in the region for decades.

The hotel barely kept its doors open until 1940, when Dr. Harvey Rinehart arrived. With a firm belief that the climate was favorable for people afflicted with arthritis, Rinehart renovated the building and opened a clinic based on his unique treatments. Patients were housed on the second floor, while treatment rooms were established on the ground floor. Rinehart's treatments were so successful that the clinic remained in business until the 1980s. There is no record of patients dying in the building, but many paranormal experts suspect that the ghosts that haunt the place died elsewhere, then returned to the clinic where they had received care and comfort.

In the ensuing decades, the building changed hands many times. Each owner improved the infrastructure and décor, often changing the street front, yet a slow deterioration continued. This process was halted in 1998 when the place was transformed into a modern inn. Current owner Katie Brown made additional improvements in 2009. These may have triggered an increase in paranormal activity because, according to Brown, several unexplained experiences occur every day.

It is common for staff and visitors to feel an unseen person place a hand on their shoulders or stand very close. Sounds of a Victrola playing music from the 1920s, sudden changes in the volume of the TV, and the tapping of BBs dropping on glass are frequent occurrences. Each room in the hotel has a characteristic paranormal activity that is probably linked to the ghost that either died there or returned there after death to seek additional treatment from Dr. Rinehart.

Room 3 is inhabited by a spirit named "Walter." This fellow leaves indentations on the bedding, indicating that he has stretched out for a nap. He also causes the TV to change channels or emit a snapping sound. No historical record has been uncovered that could verify that a person named Walter died on the premises. Given the many years Dr. Rinehart operated his clinic at this location, it is quite possible that he treated someone there by that name. Walter may have died elsewhere but, upon achieving spiritual form, chose to return to the only place where he received comforting treatment.

The basement is the creepiest place in the building and a prime target for local ghost hunters. Apparently, this space was used as a morgue and lab. The atmosphere there is quite different from that of the guestrooms. The air is still and thick and creates a sensation that the place is full of trapped spirits. Some of those ghosts are upset or angry.

Go to YouTube and enter the words *Old Wheeler Hotel*. You will find two videos. One offers a good view of the interior of the hotel. The other is the ghostly image of Walter as he passes in front of an illuminated TV.

PHANTOM OF THE BIJOU

Bijou Theater
1624 Northeast Highway 101
Lincoln City 97367
541-994-8255
www.cinemalovers.com

The simple but classic marquee, tiny ticket office, and quaint lobby clearly reflect this theatre's pedigree as a 1930s-style movie house. Opened as the Lakeside Theater in 1937, the single-screen theatre has retained its charming atmosphere from decades past and, perhaps, a few ghosts. One of them seems to like organ music and traditional themes from the 1930s.

When the Bijou opened, the era of silent films accompanied by a live organist had ended nearly a decade earlier. In 1937, "talkies" were the standard, but soundtracks often included organ music to support transitions from one scene to another or to highlight the actor's emotions. In the 1940s and 1950s, many films were produced as musicals to engage audiences that still remembered vaudeville, the popular live performances that had died out about 1930. It is possible that the ghost of the Bijou Theater was a regular who enjoyed films with strong musical tracks, especially organ music. I say that because an intriguing report of a ghostly presence is linked to music.

In 2000, Joe Svogar was alone in the theatre practicing on the organ in preparation for a silent-film festival. As he played, Joe noticed a woman standing near the last row of seats. He also saw that there was something very odd about her. She was dressed in white, appeared to glow, and seemed translucent. As Joe watched, the woman glided down the aisle, heading straight for him. Joe stopped playing, astonished as the bizarre apparition approached him. When the echo of the last note faded, the ghost disappeared.

These days, the Bijou's projection equipment is digitized and the musical tracks of contemporary films lack the classic style of the 1940s and 1950s, but the phantom of the theatre still shows up from time to time. As I watched *The Hunger Games* from a seat at the far right, in the second-to-last row, I spotted a pale cloud, roughly shaped like a human. It moved a short distance down the aisle, from the last row toward the screen, and then disappeared. As I sat through the movie, I noticed the cloud appearing several times, always when the music was soothing yet full of emotion.

There is no record of anyone dying in the Bijou Theater, but it seems likely that the ghost that haunts the place was a regular audience member who enjoyed musical films. She may have been a vaudeville performer who became enamored with talking films, especially musicals. Your best chance of seeing her there would be to attend a movie that is likely to have a beautiful music track.

In addition to the draw of witnessing a ghost in this charming old movie house, the theatre's Web site offers an enticing note that "couples have broken up and fallen in love under the bathe of our silver screen."

MATILDA

Wildflower Grill
4250 Northwest Highway 101
Lincoln City 97367
541-994-9663

If it weren't for the Wildflower's sign, set back from the highway and nearly hidden by tall grass and shrubs, strangers to the area might think they've simply driven past a beautiful shingled house set amid spectacular foliage. Those who are fortunate enough to see the sign and turn into the parking area will be surprised to find a great restaurant with an ambience that truly reflects the character of this coastal town. They may have an encounter with a ghost named Matilda, too.

Constructed as a large cottage, the bright and airy Wildflower Grill raises no suspicions that a spirit is present. The large windows that stretch from floor to ceiling and the spectacular views of the pond and dense forest attract the attention of patrons, causing many to miss an encounter with a ghostly lady. People who work in the restaurant, however, are well acquainted with this pleasant spirit. They've named her Matilda, and she seems to like that.

Matilda appears lifelike but quite translucent as she floats around the restaurant and onto the deck. I was told that there is no record of anyone dying in the house, but it seems likely that a death occurred there, creating the attachment of a former female resident. Alternatively, it is possible that Matilda died nearby, perhaps on the highway. After her death she may have decided to reside in the house because of its beauty and comforting ambience.

People who have encountered this ghost describe her as pleasant and benevolent. She does not break dishes or hide things, but she has been known to move glasses and silverware if they are out of place on a table.

A ghost named Matilda floats around this charming café.

ROWDY RALPH

Spouting Horn Restaurant
110 Southeast Highway 101
Depoe Bay 97341
541-765-2261

Most of the people who patronize this restaurant love the food and find the service to be great. According to a Web site called Travel Advisor, however, a few people have a contrary opinion. I can't help but wonder if these dissatisfied customers have had an encounter with the lifelike ghost of a disgruntled former employee, Rowdy Ralph. I say that because I found the food to be very good, the service pleasant and prompt, and the atmosphere in keeping with the marine ambience of the town.

Rowdy Ralph has been described as a tall, burly man whose facial expressions suggest he is angry, frustrated, or insulted. Clues to his identity may be found in his apparel. He wears a cook's apron, sleeveless shirt, and dirty jeans. Some witnesses claim he wears a traditional chef's hat, while others report that Ralph's head of dark, curly hair is uncovered. He has been seen standing with his arms crossed on his chest or hanging at his sides with fists clenched. He shows up in the kitchen, the bar, and spaces where servers prepare drinks. Some people don't see Ralph but do feel his presence. Sensitives immediately become aware of his unhappy demeanor. Many people heading to the restrooms notice a thickened atmosphere and feel a little nervous or tense for inexplicable reasons.

Despite hundreds of encounters with Ralph's anger, witnesses have not sustained emotional or physical injury. Furthermore, he does not break dishes or glasses, cause the restaurant's appliances to malfunction, or disturb staff members to the extent that they quit. Ralph may be rowdy and angry, but his attitude seems to have little to do with the restaurant. After my visit to the place, I got the impression that Ralph is a frustrated cook. He may have died on the premises when the building was occupied by another business. A colleague suggested that Ralph may have applied for a job at the café that preceded the Spouting Horn Restaurant but suffered the indignity of rejection. He may have died elsewhere and then, frustrated and angry, decided to take the position he once sought. He may appear aggravated because he feels ignored by the live people who work at the restaurant.

The Spouting Horn Restaurant offers a spectacular view of the harbor and friendly wait staff who are willing to talk about Rowdy Ralph. To me, this is a winning formula for adventure and one that ghost hunters should not pass up. In addition, Depoe Bay is the only town on the coast with a real blowhole or "spouting horn" within city limits. Fissures in the rocks forming the seawall funnel the breaking waves into a narrowing tunnel, increasing the pressure until the water blasts through a hole into the air, as high as 40 feet.

GHOST OF THE HAPLESS TEENAGER

Yaquina Bay Lighthouse
Yaquina Bay State Park
740 SW Government Street
Newport, Oregon 97365
541-574-3100
www.yaquinalights.org

All of the lighthouses that I have visited have intriguing stories of lonely light keepers, disastrous shipwrecks whose survivors are pulled from the sea, threats of destruction by massive storms, and ghosts. Whether I explore the New England coast, the Caribbean, Southern California, or the Pacific Northwest, I consistently encounter such tales. Naturally, I am most interested in ghost stories, and Yaquina Bay Lighthouse has one that is well known.

Yaquina Bay Lighthouse was opened in 1871 but used for only three years because its location inside the entrance to the bay limited the light's projection out to sea. In 1873, its replacement was completed at Yaquina Head, and Yaquina Bay Lighthouse was closed the next year. The facility is similar to Point Pinos Lighthouse in Monterey, which opened in 1855. The Yaquina Bay light tower projects from the roof of the keeper's house, an interior circular stairway providing easy access in foul weather. The house consists of a basement and two floors with a kitchen, a parlor, and bedrooms.

After the light was extinguished in 1874, the house was used as a residence for a few years before entering into a long period of neglect and decay in the harsh marine environment. Sitting derelict at the edge of the bay, it became known as a spooky place. Naturally, it attracted the interest of local teenagers. The widely known ghost story attached to this lighthouse tells us that about 1915, a teenager named Muriel Travenard, and her friends decided to visit the abandoned lighthouse. Finding the first floor full of discarded junk and bird droppings, they climbed the stairs to the second floor. There, they discovered what looked to be a trapdoor covered with an iron plate. The boys lifted the plate and trapdoor and found a small opening to a tunnel or chute that they believed led to the basement. Apparently, they decided not to explore the shaft but, instead, ascended to the lantern room and then exited the building. When the friends gathered outside, Muriel discovered she had dropped her scarf somewhere inside the lighthouse. Her friends waited while she entered the house. Moments later, they heard a scream. Frightened and perplexed, the teenagers waited for Muriel to appear, running from the house. Several anxious moments passed before the boys reentered the building to search for her. It is said that, on the second floor near the chute, the boys found only a warm pool of blood and Muriel's scarf. Curiously, the heavy iron plate was shut.

Local police searched the lighthouse but found no trace of Muriel. Not long after her disappearance, stories began to circulate of a ghostly woman walking the paths near the lighthouse and standing in the lantern room.

This story attracted visitors to Yaquina Bay Lighthouse for nearly a century. Unfortunately, it may be a work of fiction. The authors of *Weird Oregon*, Al Eufrasio and Jeff Davis, are certain it is nothing more than local legend inspired by the derelict appearance of the lighthouse early in the 20th century. In my research, I found no record of a trapdoor, iron plate, or chute to a concealed compartment. Furthermore, I could discover no documentation of a Muriel Travenard residing in Newport, nor could I locate a police record or newspaper story of a teenager's disappearance at the place. People who believe the story point to a dark stain on the floor, claiming it was created by Muriel's blood.

Despite this lack of provenance, several people have had paranormal experiences at this lighthouse. Lighthouse Association staff members have heard unexplained footsteps on both the first and second floor. Others have watched as a ghostly figure appears inside the lantern room

Local legend tells of a bizarre disappearance at the Yaquina Bay Lighthouse linked to a presence that may still haunt this place.

or walks the narrow ledge outside the glass. Whether you believe in the tale of Muriel Travenard or not, this lighthouse is worth a visit. Period furnishing and a 19th-century ambience, together with knowledgeable docents, make this a good place to seek a paranormal experience.

Yaquina Bay Lighthouse is open to the public every day except major holidays. There is no entrance fee, but a donation is requested. The lantern room is not generally accessible, but the watch room, living quarters, and basement offer plenty of places to perform an EVP sweep.

GHOST OF A LONELY MAN

Yaquina Head Lighthouse
750 Northwest Lighthouse Drive
Newport 97365
541-574-3100

Initially called Cape Foul Weather Lighthouse, the Yaquina Head Lighthouse opened in 1873 as a replacement for the lighthouse on Yaquina Bay, which failed to project its light far enough to ensure safe navigation on this part of the coast. Standing 93 feet above ground level and 161 feet above sea level, this lighthouse is the tallest in Oregon. For more than 60 years, it was staffed by keepers hired by the U.S. Lighthouse Service. The U.S. Coast Guard took over management of the facility in 1939. During World War II, a large contingent of U.S. Navy and Coast Guard personnel were stationed at the lighthouse to keep watch for Japanese ships and planes.

The original facility included only the tower and adjoining oil house. Apparently, the keepers lived in town. In 1923, a single-story keeper's house was constructed near the tower. That was replaced with a two-story house in 1938 to accommodate a large number of military personnel who would conduct coastal surveillance in anticipation of growing hostilities between Japan and the U.S. The two-story structure was demolished in 1984. Today, the tower and its adjoining oil house intrigue ghost hunters because the place may harbor two ghosts, one of them the quintessential lonely light keeper.

Assistant Lighthouse Keeper Henry Higgins is believed to haunt the tower. Sometime in the 1930s, the head keeper left him and another man in charge of the light for an extended period. Higgins' helper was apparently a drunk and became completely useless when the oil reservoir at the top of the tower was nearly empty. Dedicated to his duty, Higgins began carrying cans of oil up the 114 steps. After several trips, the man was overcome by the grueling work and died of a heart attack at the base of the stairs. The ghost of Henry Higgins has been active at this lighthouse since that day. Legend says that, for decades, workers would not go into the tower alone for fear of encountering this spirit.

In 2011, lighthouse staff received a letter reportedly from Higgins' relatives asserting that he died in Portland many years after retiring from the lighthouse service. If this claim is true, it takes the drama out of the ghost story but does not discount the possibility that Henry haunts the lighthouse. I've encountered many spirits at locations far from the sites at which they died. It seems clear that after death, a ghost may gravitate to a place that is cherished, such as a home, or one that is comforting. Furthermore, a spirit may have a desire or feel obligated to continue to perform a vital duty, like lighthouse maintenance. So, Higgins may have died in Portland, but many visitors, including myself, feel certain he is still on duty at this lighthouse.

The other ghost said to haunt this place is that of a man who died in 1873, during the lighthouse's construction. I could not locate official records of accidents that may have occurred during construction, but legend says that a man fell into the narrow space between the outer and inner walls of the building as tons of sand were poured inside. The process could not be stopped in time to rescue this poor fellow, so he was buried alive. His ghost is apparently trapped inside the walls and creates a tapping sound. Generally, spirits don't stay in a disagreeable place unless they are unaware they are dead or unwilling to leave their corpse. This ghost may be trying to attract the attention of anyone who might recover his body and give him a decent burial.

GHOST OF THE GRIEVING MOTHER

Heceta Head Lighthouse State Park
92072 South Highway 101

Yachats 97498
866-547-3696

Of all the haunted lighthouses on the Oregon coast, the Heceta Head Lighthouse has the best documentation of paranormal activity. Many unbiased witnesses have reported experiences that appear to be genuine encounters with ghosts.

Construction of the lighthouse began in 1892, establishing a powerful light 205 feet above sea level that could project its beam for 21 miles. A crew of dedicated keepers maintained the oil-burning lamp that aided navigation on the coast for 42 years before electrification in 1934 and automation in 1963 transformed the lighthouse into a lonely bastion, seldom visited by living persons. Its isolation and position on a windswept and wave-pounded promontory gave rise to a reputation for ghostly activity that still attracts the attention of ghost hunters.

The original facility included two large Queen Anne-style houses constructed a few hundred feet away from the lighthouse tower, along with several outbuildings. One of the homes was the residence of the head keeper, while the other, a duplex, accommodated two assistants and their families. The head keeper's house is now a B and B inn. By 1900, a large community was established at the facility that included three large families, pens for small animals, corrals for horses, and vegetable gardens. After complete automation, buildings were demolished, leaving only one house and the light tower.

The most active ghost at this place has appeared at several locations in and around the home that is now used as an inn. She is widely known as the "Gray Lady." Ghost hunters who performed a Ouija-board session on the property claim they learned that her name is Rue.

It is said that Rue was the wife of one of the keepers and lost a baby girl to an unspecified illness. The child was buried somewhere near the keeper's house, but ghost hunters have not yet found her. Some reports say the grave is concealed by vegetation, but I observed only a few shrubs near the inn, none of which would make the discovery of a headstone impossible. A grave marker may have been covered by mud created by heavy rains or simply removed by a souvenir collector sometime in the distant past.

Apparently, Rue remains at this site searching for the grave of her daughter. The best documented encounter occurred in 1970, when a man was working in the attic. It is said that he noticed the reflection of a woman in a window, and upon turning around, he saw a wispy apparition float a few inches above the floor. She appeared to be old and wrinkled and wore a gray dress with a hood or shawl over her head. She made no threatening gestures, but the man was so frightened that he ran straight through her and left the attic, refusing to return. Rue has been seen staring out the windows of the first and second floors, causing visitors to inquire about the woman who appears to be a reenactor dressed in period clothing. She also wanders the grounds, apparently searching for the lost grave. Witnesses report that her facial expressions convey grief and anxiety. EVP sweeps directed at this ghost might be highly successful if inquiries are made about the tragic death and lost grave of a child.

Other paranormal activity includes doors and cupboards opening and closing; the sounds of disembodied screams, sobbing, and footsteps; dishes and glassware rattling; and missing objects turning up in inexplicable places.

Other places to hunt ghosts:

SEASIDE AQUARIUM

200 North Promenade
Seaside 97138
503-738-6211
www.seasideaquarium.com

This popular, privately owned aquarium may be haunted by ghosts from the early 20th century. The current building was constructed in 1924 and served as a saltwater bathhouse. The structure contained a natatorium that consisted of a large concrete swimming pool filled with frigid seawater. The possibility of a drowning seems likely, since the icy water could easily cause muscle cramps or drain even a strong swimmer of strength, causing the victim to slip beneath the surface.

In the early 1930s, the building was remodeled and reopened as an aquarium in 1937. Construction continued soon after the aquarium opened, adding several apartments on the top floor. These remained in use until 1970, when they were vacated and the spaces entered a period of demolition and renovation that went on for 35 years. There is no information available about the residents of the apartments or the deaths or other tragedies that may have occurred and formed the basis of paranormal activity at the aquarium. Despite that, many people believe that the building is haunted by spirits.

For many years, employees have heard disembodied voices on the top floor and in other locations throughout the aquarium. No one has reported seeing an apparition, but several spots evoke that "totally creepy" feeling.

GHOSTS TO GO

Twisted Fish Steakhouse
Formerly Girtle's Restaurant
311 Broadway
Seaside 97138
503-738-3467

This restaurant may be haunted by ghosts who moved into the building when their original haunt, the old Hotel Seaside (a.k.a. The Seasider), was torn down. Apparently, the ghosts of the old hotel were attracted to Girtle's Restaurant and took up residence in the popular eatery. Over the years, several employees, and owner Bob Girtle, witnessed astounding paranormal activity in the building, including the apparition of feet, a coffeepot flying from the kitchen to the dining room, utensils disappearing only to reappear in bizarre places, chairs moved by invisible hands, disembodied voices, and isolated cold spots. Some of the restaurant's staff had seen identical incidents at the old Hotel Seaside.

Today the building is occupied by the upscale Twisted Fish Steakhouse. I was told that paranormal activity continues at the place, but management doesn't want employees to encourage ghost hunters to drop in looking for spirits. The place gained more notoriety on January 8, 2014, when a couple tipped a waitress by leaving an envelope containing crystal meth.

ROSEBRIAR OF THE HOLY ORDER

Formerly The Rosebriar B and B
636 14th Street
Astoria 97103
503-325-7427

This elegant 1902 historic Georgian mansion is the home of several ghosts. It was constructed for local banker Frank S. Patton, who resided there until his death in 1952. Over the ensuing 20 years, a Catholic order used the mansion as a nunnery before its transition into the Phoenix House, a home for girls. In 1980, the building was fully restored to its early-20th-century elegance and opened as a B and B. The inn stayed in business until 2010, when the Rosebriar became a facility for the treatment of substance abuse. The place is not readily accessible to ghost hunters, but limited access may be granted.

Residents of the girls' home, guests of the B and B, and staff members of both had a fascinating collection of experiences. The ghostly image of a nun has been seen in the kitchen, room 9, and a second-floor hallway. Always a benevolent presence, this spirit also manifests on the kitchen stairs, where a psychic perceived a tragic event.

An unseen entity opens and closes the front and other doors in the house and may be responsible for items that go missing. The ghost of a man, probably Frank Patton, has been spotted in the living room. At times, he looks completely lifelike, but most often his image appears detailed but quite translucent before disintegrating into a cloud of smoke.

The anxious ghost of a girl has been reported in room 4. According to psychics, this spirit is nervous about the anticipated arrival of a man who may have been abusive.

It is fascinating to note that this mansion sits adjacent to the derelict Flavel House.

AIRPLANE CRASH SITE

398 North Marion Street
Gearhart 97138

On August 4, 2008, a horrific tragedy occurred at this address. I do not claim that ghosts remain at the site, but there are indelible imprints of emotions there that were created by brave rescuers who came to the scene, neighbors who watched in profound sadness and shock, family members who suffered great loss, and traumatized survivors. The event and its aftermath are still sensitive issues for residents of the neighborhood, so if you visit this site, do so with appropriate regard for their privacy and emotional wounds.

A little before 6:30 A.M., a single-engine airplane took off from nearby Seaside Municipal Airport with a pilot, Jason Ketcheson, and passenger, Frank Toohey. While Ketcheson flew the regulated departure route of two left turns, something went wrong with the engine and caused the plane to plummet to the earth, slamming into the house at 398 North Marion Street.

The impact killed both passengers and filled the house with flames. Residents Ruth Johnson-Reimann and her two children were rescued and transported to the Oregon Burn Center in Portland. Later the bodies of three other children were discovered in the charred ruins of the house. The children's parents, Dr. Frederick Masoudi and his wife, Dr. Marie Johnson-Masoudi, were taking an early-morning walk a few blocks away when the crash occurred. After rushing to the scene of the plane crash, they encountered an unspeakable horror.

Within weeks, all remnants of the house were cleared away and plans for the construction of an identical home were drawn up. Psychics who visit the neighborhood easily detect imprints of painful emotions. Neighbor Connie Hutson noted, "The energy here now, you can just feel the horrible sadness, grief, and sadness beyond words."

As a pilot, I am always moved by crash sites to a careful introspection of rough landings I have made and a few close calls I have had while flying at night. As a psychic paranormal investigator, I find this place deeply touching. The only solace is to pray that the victims truly rest in peace.

PHANTOM SHIP OF SILETZ BAY

Vantage Point: Mo's Restaurant
860 SW 51st Street
Lincoln City 97367
541-996-2535
www.moschowder.com

Phantom ships always fascinate me. They offer us a glimpse of life as it was many years ago and affirm our belief that all things have energy that can persist long after the physical object has ceased to exist.

Many people use terms such as "ghost ship," "ghost bridge," or "ghost car" to describe the paranormal experience of seeing the image of an inanimate object that ceased to exist years earlier. This is not the correct use of the word "ghost," however. A ghost is the consciousness of a dead person. When we see an inanimate object, such as a ship or bridge, we are seeing a "phantom." Phantoms are the visual perceptions of residual energy left on our physical plane. Most phantoms are partial and translucent. I have many reports of phantoms, however, in which the object was perceived as being solid, with great detail, and an exact replica of the original. Most reports of encounters with the phantom ship of Siletz Bay describe it as a solid white object, as if it were a cloud shaped like a ship. A few witnesses have seen it as a completely real vessel that revealed fine details such as knots in ropes and seaweed hanging from the anchor.

This phantom is a residual image of a ship that sank in Siletz Bay between 1860 and 1880 not far from the foot of SW 51st Street. Records of sinkings are unclear, not only because of the obscure dates, but also because many vessels ran aground in the bay and were declared a total loss, only to be refloated and renamed. It is clear that the phantom ship ran aground, because its remains could be seen protruding from the sand as recently as the 1980s.

The phantom ship often appears gliding over the surface of the bay for several seconds before disappearing. Sightings are usually brief, less than 30 seconds. One witness reported seeing the ship on land. As she gazed out her living-room window, she spotted the ship heading straight at her.

The best vantage point for glimpsing this phantom is the pier that extends from Mo's Restaurant over the beach. It is a great place to enjoy snacks and drinks and await the appearance of the phantom ship. The beach east of Mo's Restaurant is a good location to conduct a sweep with dowsing rods to locate remains of the ship.

TAFT PIONEER CEMETERY

SE 39th Street at Highway 101
Lincoln City 97367

Opened in 1904, this cemetery sits on a bluff that offers a spectacular view of the ocean. The graves are surrounded by tall trees and scattered over a broad field that is often windswept. There are no spooky shadows or tall monuments here as you will find at the Eugene Pioneer Cemetery, but many people have had paranormal experiences in this graveyard. Using audio recorders or dowsing rods, you may detect imprints at several graves. Only a few graves seem to have ghosts attached. These are the graves with deeply weathered inscriptions or signs of vandalism. In block 99, I captured an EVP that said, "This is mine!"

If you anticipate a nighttime investigation at this cemetery, it is wise to visit during daylight to become familiar with the graves and the general layout, including the best place to park. You might also identify graves at which you detect a peculiar vibe or motion of your dowsing rods. Never conduct a nighttime investigation at a secluded place such as this alone. Note also that the place can be windy, reducing the quality of EVP recordings.

APPENDIX A

Sighting Report Form

GENERAL INSTRUCTIONS

Photocopy and enlarge the form on the next page to a standard 8.5 x 11 inch format. This form should be completed right after a sighting. If the ghost hunt is performed by a group, a designated leader should assume the role of reporter. The reporter is responsible for completing this form.

The reporter and each witness should make a statement, either audio or written, describing in full their experience at the site. Date, sign, and label these statements with a reference number identical to the report number on the sighting report form. Attach the statements to the report form.

SIGHTING REPORT

SITE NAME _____ REPORT # _____
LOCATION _____ DATE: _____
                                                     TIME: _____
REPORTER _____ SITE # _____
WITNESSES _____
_____
_____

DESCRIPTION OF APPARITION: _____
_____

temperature change	[] YES	[] NO
auditory phenomena	[] YES	[] NO
telekinesis	[] YES	[] NO
visual phenomena	[] YES	[] NO
other phenomena	[] YES	[] NO

Description: _____
_____

Use the reverse side for diagrams, maps, and drawings.
SPECIFIC LOCATION WITHIN SITE: _____
_____

PREVIOUS SIGHTINGS AT THIS SITE?:   [] YES [] NO
Reference: _____
Summary: _____

RECORDS:
audio   [] YES [] NO Ref. No. _____
video   [] YES [] NO Ref. No. _____
photo   [] YES [] NO Ref. No. _____
Summary of records: _____
Disposition of records: _____

WITNESS STATEMENTS—Summary: _____
audio   [] YES [] NO
written   [] YES [] NO
Disposition of statements: _____
_____

APPENDIX B

Suggested Reading

BOOKS

Allison, Ross, and Joe Temples. *Ghostology 101: Becoming a Ghost Hunter.* Seattle: AuthorHouse, 2005.

Auerbach, Loyd. *ESP, Hauntings, and Poltergeists.* New York: Warner Books, 1986.

———. *Ghost Hunting: How to Investigate the Paranormal.* Oakland: Ronin Publishing, 2004.

———. *A Paranormal Casebook: Ghost Hunting in the New Millennium.* Dallas: Atriad Press, 2005.

Brown, Sylvia. *Adventures of a Psychic.* New York: Penguin Books, 1990.

Cobb, Todd. *Ghosts of Portland.* Atglen, PA: Schiffer Publishing, 2007.

Davis, Jefferson. *Haunted Astoria.* Portland: Norseman Ventures, 2006.

Dwyer, Jeff. *The Art and Science of Paranormal Investigation.* CreateSpace, 2012.

———. *Ghost Hunter's Guide to California's Gold Rush Country.* Gretna, LA: Pelican Publishing, 2009.

———. *Ghost Hunter's Guide to California's Wine Country.* Gretna, LA: Pelican Publishing, 2008.

———. *Ghost Hunter's Guide to Monterey and California's Central Coast.* Gretna, LA: Pelican Publishing, 2010.

———. *Ghost Hunter's Guide to Los Angeles.* Gretna, LA: Pelican Publishing, 2007.

———. *Ghost Hunter's Guide to New Orleans.* Gretna, LA: Pelican Publishing, 2007.

———. *Ghost Hunter's Guide to Seattle and Puget Sound.* Gretna, LA: Pelican Publishing, 2008.

———. *Ghost Hunter's Guide to the San Francisco Bay Area: Revised Edition.* Gretna, LA: Pelican Publishing, 2011.

———. *Psychic: Use Your Psychic Power to Experience Ghosts.* CreateSpace, 2013.

Eufrasio, Al, and Jeff Davis. *Weird Oregon*. New York: Sterling Publishing, 2010.
Hauck, Dennis William. *Haunted Places: The National Directory*. New York: Penguin Group, 2002.
Hawes, Jason, Grant Wilson, and Michael Jan Friedman. *Ghost Hunting: True Stories of Unexplained Phenomena from the Atlantic Paranormal Society*. New York: Pocket Publishers, 2007.
Holzer, Hans. *Ghosts I've Met*. Chicago: Barnes and Noble Books, 2005.
———. *True Ghost Stories*. Chicago: Barnes and Noble Books, 2001.
Ramsland, Katherine. *Ghost: Investigating the Other Side*. New York: St. Martin's Press, 2001.
Schlosser, S. E., and Paul G. Hoffman. *Spooky Oregon: Tales of Hauntings, Strange Happenings, and Other Local Lore*. Guilford, CT: Globe Pequot, 2009.
Smitten, Susan. *Ghost Stories of Oregon*. Auburn, WA: Lone Pine Publishing, 2002.
Southall, R. H. *How to Be a Ghost Hunter*. Woodbury, MN: Llewellyn Publications, 2003.
Steiger, Brad. *Real Ghosts, Restless Spirits, and Haunted Places*. Detroit: Visible Ink Press, 2003
Sweet, Lenore. *How to Photograph the Paranormal*. Charlottesville, VA: Hampton Roads Publishing, 2004.
Taylor, Troy. *Ghost Hunter's Guidebook*. Alton, IL: White Chapel Productions Press, 1999.
———. *Ghost Hunter's Guidebook: The Essential Guide to Investigating Ghosts and Hauntings*. Alton, IL: White Chapel Productions, 2007.
———, Robert Wlodarski, and Anne Wlodarski. *Talking with the Dead*. Alton, IL: White Chapel Productions, 2009.
Van Praagh, James. *Ghosts Among Us: Uncovering the Truth about the Other Side*. New York: HarperOne, 2008.
Zwicker, Roxie. *Haunted Portland: From Pirates to Ghost Brides*. Charleston, SC: The History Press, 2007.

ARTICLES

Adams, Anne. "Halloween Haunt Spots." *Portland Monthly Magazine*, 29 October 2010.
Anderson, Jennifer. "Stumptown Stumper." *Portland Tribune*, 30 October 2009.
Associated Press. "Ghost Buster: Ohio Woman inspires CBS' Supernatural Series." *Boston Herald*, 4 July 2005.
Baird, K. "Haunted Eugene." *Eugene Daily News*, 4 December 2013.
Barrett, Greg. "Can the Living Talk to the Dead? Psychics Say They Connect with the Other World, but Skeptics Respond: 'Prove It.'" *USA Today*, 20 June 2001.
Bella, Rick. "Clackamas Town Center Shooter Carried 145 Rounds, Fired 17 Shots." *Oregonian*, 1 May 2013.
Boryczka, Elena. "A Haunted House." *Beaverton Valley Times*, 26 October 2006.
Cadden, Mary. "Get Spooked on a Walking Tour." *USA Today*, 17 October 2003.
Clark, Jayne. "10 Great Places to Get Spooked by Your Surroundings." *USA Today*, 26 October 2007.
Dremann, Sue. "A Haunting Experience." *Mountain View Voice*, 31 October 2003.
Fox, Carol. "Ghostbuster to Tell Secrets of the Hunt." *Los Angeles Times*, 28 October 1989.
Giovannetti, Joe. "Crossing Over: Ghost Hunter Knows Things that Go Bump in the Night." *Fairfield (CA) Daily Republic*, 18 October 2007.
Hannah, James. "Who Ya Gonna Call for the Paranormal?" *San Francisco Chronicle*, 8 June 2008.
Harger, Steve. "Seeking Spirits." *New York Times*, 30 October 2009.
Hill, Angela. "Paranormal Experts Say It's Not All Funny." *Oakland (CA) Tribune*, 18 October, 2002.
Irwin, Richard. "Jeff Dwyer's Ghost Stories Aren't Just for Halloween." *Long Beach Press Telegram*, 17 June 2007.
Jenkins, Chris, and Colin Fly. "Haunted Hotel Has Baseball Players Walking." *San Francisco Chronicle*, 26 July 2009.
Jensen, Evan. "Is There a Ghost in Estacada?" *Estacada News*, 1 October 2008.

King, Tim. "Ghosts and Haunted Places in Oregon and Beyond." *Salem News*, 29 October 2007.
Kirby, Carrie. "Ghost Hunters Utilize Latest in Technology." *San Francisco Chronicle*, 31 October 2005.
Kovner, Guy. "Apparitions Don't Spook Couple: Departed Loved Ones Haunt Home." *Santa Rosa Press Democrat*, 31 October 1995.
Kurhi, Eric. "Investigating the Eerie Historic Hayward Mansions." *Oakland Tribune*, 13 December 2009.
McConahey, Meg. "Local Haunts: Believe It or Not Ghosts, Some Old Homes Can't Seem to Escape the Past." *Santa Rosa Press Democrat*, 29 October 2005.
Massingill, T. "Business of Ghost Busting." *Contra Costa Times*, 8 October 2000.
Mirk, Sarah. "The Ghosts of Lone Fir Cemetery." *Portland Mercury*, 29 October 2009.
Moran, Gwen. "Real-Life Ghost Busters." *USA Weekend*, 31 October 2004.
Newell, Cliff. "Spooky Times for Ghost Hunters." *Portland Tribune*, 30 October 2008.
Pierleoni, Allen. "'Ghost Whisperer' Consultant Speaks Out." *Sacramento Bee*, 2 January 2008.
Ridgeway, Suzie. "Portland Haunted Tour." *Portland Tribune*, 27 October 2006.
Schoolmeester, Ron. "10 Great Places to Go on a Haunted Hike." *USA Today*, 28 July 2006.
Sichelman, Lew. "Plenty of Spooky Sites around the Nation." *San Francisco Chronicle*, 28 October 2007.
———. "Spirits, Specters and Strange Sightings Abound at America's Most Haunted Hotels." *Los Angeles Times*, 15 October 2003.
Thompson, Ian. "Tracking Things that Go Bump in the Night." *Fairfield (CA) Daily Republic*, 29 October 2000.
Wach, Bonnie. "The Dead Zone." *San Francisco Chronicle*, 31 October 2004.

APPENDIX C
Films, DVDs, and Videos

Fictional films may provide you with information that will assist you in preparing for a ghost hunt. This assistance ranges from putting you in the proper mood for ghost hunting to useful techniques for exploring haunted places. Some films, especially documentaries, provide information about the nature of ghostly activity.

An American Haunting (2006). Directed by Courtney Solomon, starring Donald Sutherland and Sissy Spacek.
The Conjuring (2013). Directed by James Wan, starring Vera Farmiga, Patrick Wilson, and Lili Taylor.
Dragonfly (2002). Directed by Tom Shadyac, starring Kevin Costner and Kathy Bates.
The Fog (2005). Directed by Rupert Wainwright, starring Tom Welling and Maggie Grace.
1408 (2007). Directed by Mikael Hafstrom, starring John Cusack and Samuel L. Jackson.
Ghost of Flight 409 (1987, made for TV). Directed by Steven Hilliard Stern, starring Ernest Borgnine and Kim Basinger.
Ghost Story (1981). Directed by John Irvin, starring Fred Astaire and Melvyn Douglas.
Haunted (1995). Directed by Lewis Gilbert, starring Aidan Quinn and Kate Beckinsale.
Haunting Across America (2001). Documentary hosted by Michael Dorn.
Haunting in Connecticut (2009). Directed by Peter Cornwell, starring Virginia Madsen and Martin Donovan.
The Haunting of Seacliff Inn (1995). Directed by Walter Klenhard, starring Ally Sheedy and William R. Moses.
Hereafter (2010). Directed by Clint Eastwood, starring Matt Damon.
Insidious (2010). Directed by James Wan, starring Patrick Wilson and Rose Byrne.
Living With the Dead (2000). Directed by Stephen Gyllenhaal, starring Ted Danson and Mary Steenburgen.

The Others (2001). Directed by Alejandro Amenabar, starring Nicole Kidman.
Paranormal Activity (2009). Directed by Oren Peli, starring Katie Featherston.
Paranormal Activity 2 (2010). Directed by Tod Williams, starring Katie Featherston.
Paranormal Activity: The Marked Ones (2014). Directed by Christopher Landon, starring Andrew Jacobs and Jorge Diaz.
The Rite (2011). Directed by Mikael Hafstrom, starring Anthony Hopkins and Colin O'Donoghue.
Sightings: Heartland Ghost (2002). Directed by Brian Trenchard-Smith, starring Randy Birch and Beau Bridges.
The Sixth Sense (1999). Directed by M. Night Shyamalan, starring Bruce Willis and Haley Joel Osment.
Stir of Echoes (1999). Directed by David Koepp, starring Kevin Bacon.
Thir13en Ghosts (2001). Directed by Steve Beck, starring Tony Shalhoub.
White Noise (2005). Directed by Geoffrey Sax, starring Michael Keaton.

The following movies are not about ghosts, but they are worth watching before visiting Portland and the Oregon coast. They provide a sneak preview of some of the scenery and a bit of local culture.

Antitrust (2001). Filmed in central Portland.
Are We There Yet? (2005). Filmed in the Pearl District, the Max Tunnel, and parts of central Portland.
Cold Weather (2011). A former forensic-science student investigates the mysterious disappearance of his ex-girlfriend.
Gone (2012). Filmed in the metropolitan Portland area.
Goonies (1985). Filmed on the Oregon coast, with many scenes shot in Astoria.
The Hunter (2003). Many scenes were filmed in downtown Portland.
Kindergarten Cop (1990). Many exterior scenes were filmed in Astoria.
Men of Honor (2000). Scenes at a restaurant and other exterior shots were filmed in Portland.
Untraceable (2008). Set in Portland.

APPENDIX D

Internet Resources

www.bridgetownparanormal.com. Bridgetown Paranormal is located in the Portland, Oregon metropolitan area. The goal of this organization is to document claims of ghost sightings under the most similar conditions in which they have been reported. They research and investigate residential, commercial, private, and public locations of historical interest that have been reported to be haunted.

www.darknessradio.com. This Internet radio interview program streams every Sunday from 10:00 P.M. to midnight. Guests range from ghost hunters to trance channels. Host David Schrader adds announcements about meetings for paranormal enthusiasts.

www.ghosthunter.com. Web site of ghost hunter and lecturer Patti Starr.

www.ghosthuntersnorthwest.weebly.com. Ghost Hunters Northwest was established in 2011 as a nonprofit paranormal investigation team that tries to find natural explanations to paranormal claims.

www.ghostresearch.com. Web site for information about ghost hunting methods and equipment and ongoing investigations.

www.ghostresearch.org. Ghost Research Society was established in 1971 as a clearinghouse for reports of paranormal activity. Members research homes and businesses and analyze photographs and audio and video recordings to establish authenticity. This society is headed by well-known ghost researcher Dale Kaczmarek.

www.Ghosts101.com. A ghost information Web site that displays reports, photographs, eyewitness accounts, location information, and information about ghost hunting techniques.

www.ghosttowns.com. Informative Web site that gives detailed information about ghost towns in the U.S. and Canada.

www.ghostweb.com. International Ghost Hunters Society, headed by Drs. Sharon Gill and Dave Oester, researches spirits to produce evidence of life after death. The society offers a home-study certification for paranormal investigators. Membership exceeds 15,000.

www.History.com. Official Web site of the History Channel.

www.hpiparanormal.net. Haunted and Paranormal Investigations is a highly active group of ghost hunters who have considerable experience with spirits in northern California and the Pacific Northwest. E-mail: ghost@snmproductionsco.com.

www.ISPR.net. Web site for the International Society for Paranormal Research.

www.jeffdwyer.com. Web site of author, paranormal investigator, researcher, ghost hunter, and TV and radio personality Jeff Dwyer.

www.mindreader.com. Office of Paranormal Investigations. Directed by internationally known author and researcher Loyd Auerbach, the office investigates a variety of paranormal activity for a fee.

www.northwestparanormal.com. Northwest Paranormal Investigations members investigate private homes, businesses, cemeteries, mansions, historical sites, and any place that may be a source of paranormal activity. Some team members have investigated the Shanghai Tunnels in Portland and the Oregon Country Settlement.

www.olympicpeninsulaparanormalsociety.com. Olympic Peninsula Paranormal Society uses audio, photo, and video methods to find scientific evidence of haunting or explanation for what is going bump in the night. They also offer some guided ghost investigations in order to share their extensive knowledge of the paranormal.

www.oregonparanormal.com. Based in Clackamas County, Oregon Paranormal investigates haunted places throughout Oregon and Washington.

www.oregonparanormalinvestigations.com. OPI offers their investigative services to individuals and other paranormal groups.

www.Paranormal.com. This Web site has a live chat room and links to news articles about paranormal activities.

www.phantombookshop.com. Richard Senate is a well-known author, lecturer, and ghost investigator who focuses mainly on Southern California locations.

www.PNPRS.com. The Pacific Northwest Paranormal Research Society is a group of professional, experienced investigators.

www.prairieghosts.com/ghost.hunt.html. Official Web site of the American Ghost Society, founded by ghost researchers Troy and Amy Taylor. This site provides information about ghost research, paranormal investigations, and books written by Troy Taylor.

www.psioforegon.com. Psi of Oregon is an eclectic group of highly dedicated paranormal investigators. They have an office in Coos Bay from which they stage their investigations. Members of Psi of Oregon can be reached by phone at 541-294-6442.

www.technica.com. This is a catalog of electronic detectors and recorders that may be used in ghost hunting.

www.the-atlantic-paranormal-society.com. Official Web site of the Atlantic Paranormal Society (TAPS). This group of ghost investigators gained fame through the Syfy Channel's *Ghost Hunters*. The organization has more than 50 groups spread through the U.S. and has demonstrated excellence and discretion in its investigations of the paranormal.

www.theshadowlands.net/ghost. Directory of reports of unsubstantiated hauntings and other paranormal events organized by state. This is a good Web site for findings places that might be hotspots for ghostly activity.

www.warrens.net/. The New England Society for Psychic Research, the official Web site for famed researchers and demonologists Ed and Lorraine Warren.

REGIONAL NEWSPAPERS

Access these archives to search for articles about haunted places and local ghost hunters and to learn about special events and tours.

The Bee, www.thebeenews.com
Northwest Examiner, www.nwexaminer.com
The Portland Mercury, www.theportlandmercury.com
Portland Tribune, www.portlandtrubune.com
Statesman Journal (Salem), www.statesmanjournal.com

APPENDIX E

Special Tours and Events

Beyond Bizarre Ghost Tour: At the start of the tour, guides hand out real ghost-hunting equipment before heading to two known ghostly places for a behind-the-scenes look into what hauntings are all about. A highlight is venturing below Old Town Pizza in search of Nina, a former "working girl" who is known to haunt the 1888 Merchant Hotel. Adults $19, 5-10 years $5. April through November: Thursdays, Fridays, and Saturdays at 7:00 P.M. Over-18 only on Thursdays, Fridays, and Saturdays at 10:00 P.M. December through March: check the Web site for the schedule. Meet outside Old Town Pizza at 226 NW Davis Street (between Second and Third avenues) in Old Town. 503-774-4522. www.portlandwalkingtours.com.

Lantern Tour of Fort Vancouver: Each participant will receive a lantern to carry throughout this tour of the fascinating, historic Fort Vancouver. A park ranger will open the fur store, counting house, and bake house to participants who want to search for the ghosts at this haunted place. Tour is 90 minutes. Adults $10, 15 years and under $7. Reservations required; 360-816-6230.

Lost in the Roses Neighborhood Tour: Walk through Portland's wonderful Southeast neighborhood on quiet, mazelike streets that include Ladds Addition, Portland's oldest planned community. Four rose gardens and a unique collection of architectural styles make this tour special. Tour is less than two and a half hours. $19 per person. Meet at St. Philip Neri Church, 2449 SE Tamarack (SE 18th at Division). 503-774-4522. www.portlandwalkingtours.com.

Oregon Ghost Conference: Held annually in Oregon City, usually in March or early April, this conference draws ghost hunters from all over the Pacific Coast who are eager to learn about local haunts. Free. www.oregonghostconference.com.

Pendleton Underground Tours: In 90 minutes, participants tour the historic Pendleton red-light district and learn of ghostly activity that occurs often in many of the area's older buildings. $10 per person. Offered year round, and throughout the day, starting at 9:30 A.M. Reservations recommended; 1-800-226-6398.

The Shanghai Tunnel Ethnic History Tour: The tour provides useful insights into the histories of the Chinese, the Japanese, and the Gypsies and how their experiences relate to those infamous activities in the "Portland Underground." This fascinating tour dispels a lot of myths and attempts to give a correct and concise history of people who once lived or worked in the tunnels. By appointment; 503-622-4798. www.shanghaitunnels.info.

Shanghai Tunnels Heritage Tour: Northwest Paranormal Investigations claims that the Shanghai Tunnels system is the most haunted place in Oregon. Offered by the Cascade Geographic Society, this tour focuses on the history of shanghaiing in old Portland. A knowledgeable guide leads participants through the infamous Portland Underground to see remnants of a shocking maritime history including unique architecture, holding cells, a "deadfall" trapdoor, and unearthed artifacts of this heinous practice of kidnapping sailors. Tour is 90 minutes. Adults $13, 8 years and under $8. Meet at Hobo's Restaurant, 120 NW Third Avenue. Reservations required; 503-622-4798. www.shanghaitunnels.info.

Underground Portland: On this walk, participants will hear of Portland's subterranean culture. Guides tell stories of crime, scandal, and bizarre characters who carried on sordid businesses beneath streets trod upon by the city's proper citizens. This tour is rated PG-13 and not for the faint of heart or those easily offended by tales of bawdy behavior. Tour is less than two and a half hours. Adults $19, 5-10 years $5. April through November: daily at 2:00 P.M. December through March: Fridays, Saturdays, and Sundays at 2:00 P.M. Meet outside Old Town Pizza at 226 NW Davis Street (between Second and Third avenues) in Old Town. 503-774-4522. www.portlandwalkingtours.com.

Walk Through Time Neighborhood Tour: This walking tour includes Portland's Chinatown, the world-famous Chinese Classical Garden, and some of the city's oldest buildings. Tour is less than two and a half hours. $19 person. Starting location is arranged upon booking the tour. 503-774-4522. www.portlandwalkingtours.com.

Walk with the Spirits—Downtown Oregon City Tour: Tour the central 20 blocks of Oregon City while you hear stories of ghosts and other paranormal events. Tour is two hours. Adults $12, under 13 years $10. Friday and Saturday evenings. Starts at the base of the Oregon City elevator on Railroad Avenue. Reservations required; 503-679-4464. www.nwghosttours.com.

Walk with the Spirits—McLoughlin Neighborhood: Tour the McLoughlin neighborhood and visit some of Oregon City's most spirited places while you listen to fascinating ghost stories told by your guide. Tour is two hours. Adults $12, under 13 years $10. July and September: Friday and Saturday evenings. Starts outside Ermantinger House at the corner of Sixth and John Adams Street. Reservations required; 503-679-4464. www.nwghosttours.com.

Walk with the Spirits in Oregon City: The Trail's End Paranormal Society conducts a tour by motor coach that takes participants through the historic McLoughlin neighborhood and Mountain View Cemetery. Covering 20 blocks in the span on one hour, this tour offers a way to travel a lot of ground quickly while hearing spooky tales of bizarre happenings. $12 per person. Late October: tours start at 20-minute intervals beginning at 6:00 P.M. Reservations required; 503-655-7141.

APPENDIX F

History Museums and Historical Societies

Historical societies and museums are good places to discover information about places that figure prominently in local history. They often contain records in the form of old newspapers, diaries, and photographs about tragic events, such as fires, hangings, train wrecks, and earthquakes, that led to the loss of life. Old photographs and maps that are not on display for public viewing may be available to serious researchers.

Clackamas County Historical Society
 and Oregon Territory Museum
211 Tumwater Drive
Oregon City, OR 97045
503-655-5574
www.historicoregoncity.org

Clatsop County Historical Society
P.O. Box 88
714 Exchange Street
Astoria, OR 97103-0088
503-325-2203
www.cumtux.org

Columbia River Maritime Museum
1792 Marine Drive
Astoria, OR 97103
503-325-2323
www.crmm.org

Coos Historical and Maritime
 Museum
1210 N Front Street
Coos Bay, OR 97420
541-756-6320
www.cooshistory.org

Genealogical Forum of Oregon
1505 SE Gideon Street
Portland, OR 97242
503-963-1932
www.gfo.org

Lane County Historical Society and
 Museum
740 W 130th Avenue
Eugene, OR 97402
541-682-4242
www.lanecountyhistoricalsociety.org

Lincoln County Historical Society
 Museum
545 SW Ninth Street
Newport, OR 97365
541-265-7509

Linn County Historical Museum
101 Park Avenue
Brownsville, OR 97327
541-466-3390

Oregon Historical Society
1200 SW Park Avenue
Portland, OR 97205
503-222-1741
www.ohs.com

Oregon Nikkei Legacy Center
Japanese American History Museum
121 NW Second Avenue
Portland, OR 97209
503-224-1458
www.oregonnikkei.org

Seaside Historical Society Museum
570 Necanicum Drive
Seaside, OR 97138
www.seasidemuseum.org

Tillamook County Pioneer Museum
2106 Second Street
Tillamook, OR 97141
503-842-4553
www.tcpm.org

Washington County Museum
120 E Main Street
Hillsboro, OR 97123
503-645-5353
www.washingtoncountymuseum.org

Index

Academy, The, Vancouver, Washington, 138
Adams, Asa, 160
AGHOST (Advanced Ghost Hunters of Seattle-Tacoma), 223
Allan, Amy, 21, 138
American Association of EVP, 49
Anderson, Heidi, 119-20
apparitions, 32
Artillery Barracks, Vancouver, Washington, 149
Ash Street Saloon, 85
Associated Press survey, 21

Bagdad Theater, 114-17
Baker, George, 98, 116
Bandage Man, Cannon Beach, 64, 219
Barclay, Forbes, 34, 165, 170, 172
Barclay House, Oregon City, 170-72
Barrell, Colburn, 111, 113
Battery Russell, Hammond, 229-30
Benson, Simon, 79
Benson Bubblers, 37, 79
Benson Hotel, 78-79, 81-82
Bijou Art Cinemas, Eugene, 216-17
Bijou Theater, Lincoln City, 236-37
Black Rabbit Bar, 124
bouncer ghost, 108
Browne, Sylvia, 56, 63

Brudos, Jerry, 16
Buchanan, Marlowe James, 209
Bundy, Ted, 209
Bush House, Salem, 186-87
Bush, Asahel, II, 185-87

Camp Adair, Monmouth, 204
Camp Vancouver, 144
Cathedral Park, 155-57
CBS News poll, 20
cemeteries, 12, 16, 36-38
Chapel Pub, 102
Chinatown, 13, 15, 34
Clackamas Town Center mall, 203
clairaudience, 31, 59
clairsentience, 31, 59
clairvoyance, 31, 60
Clatsop County Historical Society, 226
Cole, Ian, 135
Columbian Cemetery, 36, 158
Comedy Sportz, 99
Commodore Grocery, 34, 89-90
Condit, Phillip, 195
Crawford, Elizabeth Stevens, 174
Crawford, Mary E., 34
Crow Bar, 34, 104-5
Crystal Ballroom, 87-89

Dark Park, Vancouver, Washington, 131
David Douglas Park, Vancouver, Washington, 131-32
Davis, Jeff, 137, 155, 225
Dead Files, 21
Depoe Bay, Oregon, 239-40
DiSchiavi, Steve, 21, 138
Dobbins, Crawford, 114
Dodd, Westley Allan, 132
Douglas, David, 131
Douglas Cemetery, 36

Earp, Virgil, 37
electromagnetic field detectors, 54
electronic audio phenomena, 32, 49
electronic voice phenomena, 32, 49
Elliott, Jeremiah, 223-24
Elliott, John L., 223-25
Elliott, Margaret, 223-24
Elsinore Theater, Salem, 191-92, 194
empathic, 31
Ermantinger, Catherine, 172
Ermantinger House, Oregon City, 34, 172
Esther Short Park, 138
Eugene Pioneer Cemetery, 215
extrasensory perception, 56

Fairview Hospital and Training Center, Salem, 178, 180-82
Federal Aviation Administration, 13
First United Methodist Church, Salem, 205

Flavel, George, 225-27, 229
Flavel, George, Jr., 226-27
Flavel, Harry M., 227
Flavel, Harry Sherman, 227-29
Flavel, Mary, 226
Flavel, Mary Louise, 227-29
Flavel, Nellie, 226
Flavel House, Astoria, 225-26
FLIR imaging device, 53-54
Forsyth, Steven, 203
Fort Stevens State Park, Hammond, 34, 219, 229-32
Fort Vancouver, 12-13, 17, 33-34, 36-37, 43, 129, 131, 133, 142-44, 148, 153, 161-62, 165-66, 170, 173, 177
Fox Hollow Elementary School, Eugene, 210
Frank, Sigmund, 83-84
Franklin Street Station B and B, Astoria, 224

Gable, Clark, 83
Gallup poll, 20
gang activity, 14
Ganiy, Jackie, 49
Gazelle (steamship), 111
General O. O. Howard House, 35
George C. Marshall House, 35, 150
Georgian Room Restaurant, 84
German spies, 96
Ghost Adventures, 21
ghost definition, 23
Girtle's Restaurant, Seaside, 247
Goodman, Kent, 212
Grand Army of the Republic Cemetery, 36
Grankey, Robert Turnbull, 212
Grant, Ulysses S., 144, 153
Grant House, Vancouver, Washington, 153-54
Gray Lady (Yachats ghost), 245
Great Portland Fire (1878), 83
Gresham Pioneer Cemetery, 12, 36
Guthrie, George B., 192-93

Haine, Arthur, 134
Hale, Kay, 83
Halloween, 28, 44
Hammond, Oregon, 229, 232
Handsome Paul, Astoria, 222-23
Harris poll, 20
Hawthorne, James C., 113-14
Heathman Hotel, 77-78
Heceta Head Lighthouse State Park, Yachats, 244-45
Hendrix, Jimi, 81
Higgins, Henry, 243-44
Hillside Farm, 122
Hoodoo Antiques, 99
Hotel Elliott, Astoria, 223-25
Howard, Oliver Otis, 147-48
Howard House, Vancouver, Washington, 147-48
Hudson's Bay Company, 129, 133, 142, 167, 170, 173
HuffPost/YouGov Poll, 21
Hunsaker, Josephine, 175-76
imprints, 24, 30-32, 35
infrared film, 47
infrared thermometers, 53

Japanese submarine I-25, 230
Jason Lee House, Salem, 196
Jitterbug dancers, 88
John D. Boon House, Salem, 197
Johnson, Curtis, 214
Johnson, Daniel Troy, 120-21
Johnson, Eva, 214

Kaiser Central Clinic, 103
Keller Auditorium, 98
Kells Irish Restaurant, 85
Knepper, Hazel Agnes, 120-21
Knepper, Paul Lawrence, 120-21
KWJJ radio station, 95

Lane Community College, Eugene, 210
Laurelhurst Park, 117-20
Lazukin, Nikolay, 177-78
Leland, Morris, 156-57
Leslie, David, 185-86
Lewis and Clark expedition, 12, 18
Liberty Theater, Astoria, 220-21, 223
light anomalies, 48-49
Lincoln City, 219, 250-51
Little Chapel of the Chimes, 102
Lone Fir Cemetery, 16, 36-37, 110-13
Lotus Cardroom and Café, 84-85
Lovejoy, Asa, 11, 114, 165

Lovejoy, Esther, 114
Lytle, Robert, 127

McCoy, Patrick, 233
McCune family tomb, Oregon City, 176
McDonald's restaurant, Vancouver, Washington, 129-31
McLoughlin, Eloisa, 169
McLoughlin, John, 34, 129, 143, 165, 166-70, 173, 175
McLoughlin House, Oregon City, 34, 165-66, 169-70, 172
McMenamin brothers, 88
McMenamins Edgefield, 121-22, 124-25
McMurphey daughters, 213
Marple, Anna, 206-7
Marple, Richard, 206
Marshall, George C., 144, 151
Masonic Cemetery, Lafayette, 206
Matilda (Lincoln City ghost), 238
meditation, 58
Meier, Aaron, 83
Meier and Frank Building, 82
Mentzer, Wayne, 200
Merchant Hotel, 74-75
Methodist Parsonage, Salem, 197
Mill Creek, Salem, 202-3
Miss Delta restaurant, 105
Mitchell, Mitch, 81
Moberly-Jourdain incident, 60
Morrison, Anastasia, 161-62
Mo's Restaurant, Lincoln City, 250-51

Mount Calvary Cemetery, 37
Mountain View Cemetery, Oregon City, 175
Multnomah County Poor Farm Cemetery, 36
Murder Bridge, Salem, 199

Neer, Billy, 132
Neer, Cole, 132
Nehalem Bay Winery, 233-34
Nelson, Paul, 162
Nelson Residence, Fort Vancouver, 162
New Age movement, 22
night vision goggles, 53
Nina (ghost), 74-76
Nines Hotel, 82
North Portland Library, 101-2
Northwest Paranormal Investigations, 38

Officer's Row, Vancouver Barracks, 143-44
Old City Cemetery, Vancouver, Washington, 37, 133-34
Old Glory Antiques Mall, Vancouver, Washington, 160
Old Town Pizza, 74, 76
Old Wheeler Hotel, 234-36
orbs, 26, 48
Oregon City, 225
Oregon coast, 219
Oregon Coast Paranormal Investigators, 38
Oregon State University, 208
Oregon Territory, 129, 143
Oregon Trail, 133, 143, 165
Oregonian newspaper, 92

Pacific Paranormal Research Society, 38
pallbearer ghosts, Vancouver, Washington, 138
paranormal phenomenon, 24
Parks, Roberta Kathleen, 209
Patton, Frank S., 248
Pearl District, 34
Pearson Air Museum, Vancouver, Washington, 33, 161
Pearson Field, Vancouver, Washington, 144
Peter Iredale, wreck of the, 17, 232-33
Pettygrove, Francis, 11, 67, 165
phantom definition, 30
Phoenix House, Astoria, 248
photography, spirit, 26
Pickett, George, 144
Pittock, Georgiana, 91-93, 95
Pittock, Henry, 92-93, 95
Pittock, Robert, 114
Pittock Mansion, 33, 67, 91, 93, 95
Pleasant Grove Church, Salem, 195
Pollock, Hollie, 181
poltergeists, 24, 77
Power Station Pub, 124
Private Paul (ghost), 105
Prohibition, 78-79, 85, 87-88
Providence Academy building, 36-37
Psychic Method of ghost hunting, 56
psychics, 15, 22, 30-32, 56

psychometry, 60

Queen Mary, 29

Reed, Cyrus A., 189
Reed Opera House, Salem, 189
Reilly, Joseph, 162
retrocognition, 32, 60
Rinehart, Harvey, 235-36
River View Cemetery, 37
Roberts, Jacob Tyler, 16, 203-4
Rose (ghost), 109
Rosebriar B and B, Astoria, 248
Rowdy Ralph, Depoe Bay, 239-40
Rue (Yachats ghost), 245

Sackett Hall, Corvallis, 208-9
Salem Pioneer Cemetery, 184-85, 197
Sasquatch, 220
Schmidt, Andreas, 159
Scooter McQuade's Restaurant and Bar, 85-86
Seaside, 219, 247
Seaside Aquarium, 246
shanghai industry, 11, 15, 18, 23, 86
Shanghai Tunnels, 43, 64, 67-69, 73, 85, 98
Shaull, Daniel, 13
Shelton, Thomas, 213
Shelton-McMurphey-Johnson House, Eugene, 213
Short, Amos, 138
Short, Esther, 138
Siletz Bay, 64
Slocum, Charles, 136, 138

Slocum, Laura, 136-37
Slocum House Theatre, Vancouver, Washington, 136, 138
South Eugene High School, 212
Soviet spies, 96
Spanish flu epidemic (1918), 12, 98, 145, 150
Spouting Horn Restaurant, Depoe Bay, 239-40
St. Johns Bridge, 67, 155-56
Stephens, Emmor, 111
Stephens, James and Elizabeth, 111
Stevens-Crawford House, Oregon City, 34, 174
Stumptown, 67
Sullivan, David Barton, 130
Sully, Alfred, 154-55
Svidersky, Anna Esther, 129-31
Syfy channel, 21

Taft Pioneer Cemetery, Lincoln City, 251
Taylor, Thelma, 155-57
Taylor, Troy, 49
Technical Method of ghost hunting, 46
Thomas Kay Woolen Mill, 195, 200
Thompson, Fred, 183
Thompson Brewery and Public House, Salem, 182
Tillamook, 64
Tillamook Burn (1933 fire), 235
Travel Channel, 21
Travenard, Muriel, 241-43
Troutdale, 121-22
Twisted Fish Steakhouse,

Seaside, 247

Uncle Sandy (ghost), Oregon City, 170-72
United Airlines crash (1978), 14, 173, 126
USS *Hornet*, 49

Vancouver Barracks, 37, 129, 140, 142-44
Vancouver Barracks Hospital, 145
Vanport City neighborhood, 18
Vanport Flood, 67, 163
Venue 126, 97-98
video recording, 52
Voodoo Doughnut, 101

Warineth, Alla, 118-20
Warrick, Sam, 109
Weird Oregon, 242
Wheeler, Oregon, 220
White Eagle Saloon and Rock 'n' Roll Hotel, 34, 64, 105, 107-9
White House, 33, 127
Wilcox, Theodore Burney, 95-97
Wilcox Mansion, 95
Wildflower Grill, Lincoln City, 238
Willamette Heritage Park, Salem, 194-95, 197
Willamette River, 101
Woodfield, Randall, 16
Wyckoff, Nancy, 209

Yaquina Bay Lighthouse, Newport, 240-43
Yaquina Head Lighthouse, Newport, 243
Yuille, Cindy, 203